BLANDA
ALIVE AND KICKING

The Exclusive, Authorized Biography
by Wells Twombly
NASH PUBLISHING, LOS ANGELES

Library of Congress Catalog Card Number: 75-186893
Standard Book Number: 8402-1260-7

Published simultaneously in the United States and
Canada by Nash Publishing Corporation,
9255 Sunset Boulevard, Los Angeles, California 90069.

Printed in the United States of America.

Third Printing

Dedication

To the memory of Albert F. Twombly—who brought the Sporting News *home every Monday night, who knew all there was to know about the infield fly rule, the buck lateral series and the two-handed push-shot, and who died one awful night in 1953, erroneously thinking he was a failure,*

and . . .

to the memory of Michael Blanda—who worked down deep in the mines, who came home filthy black on weekends, who raised eleven children, never letting them know they were poor, and who died only thirteen days after he escaped into retirement,

and . . .

to every other victim of the Great Depression who taught a son how to compete . . .

Contents

FIRST PERIOD

The Wolf in Winter

(Being a description in minute detail of how George Blanda, after only twenty years in professional football, became an overnight sensation.)

EPISODE 1

In the entire universe, there is no more sorely misunderstood creature than canis lupus—the fluorescent-eyed, gray-muzzled wolf. He is the victim, not altogether innocent, of an exceedingly imaginative press. He does not, for instance, roam the snow-glutted hills in a snarling, disorganized pack. He does not attack for the sheer pleasure of splattering blood on the landscape. He is rarely guilty of reckless adventures, although his courage is well documented.

Rather, he is a part of a highly disciplined unit which follows a single leader, an animal which naturalists call the Alpha Male. There is no challenging the Alpha Male's authority. The pack follows him with a singular obedience, because he is the only sensible alternative to starvation. Always, the Alpha Male will find a way to survive, to secure food for his subordinates, to keep the pack together as a warlike group.

It is in winter that the leader's instincts grow keener and his skills become more apparent. There is a curious altruism in the Alpha Male's character, however. Despite his own strong urge for self-protection and his desire to dominate his peers, he is conscious of the common cause. Thus, he trains a younger wolf—called the Beta Male—to take his place someday. It is a pain to his pride, but it is necessary.

It is not in the Alpha Male's makeup to give way gracefully. He will hold on jealously. Only when it becomes absolutely obvious that he can no longer lead the hunt or supervise the denning period—when cubs are whelped—does he retire. Always he departs with sadness. Either the pack deserts him and follows the Beta Male, now moved up in rank, or he slinks away into the night and the cold.

In all of professional athletics there is no occupation quite so stimulating as playing quarterback. It swells the ego and ennobles the soul. Consider the atmosphere: The concrete decks of the stadium are clogged with humanity.

Television cameras peer over a man's shoulder while he stands in the middle of a huddle, telling ten other, larger men how they may grow in grace. He is absolute monarch on the field.

In an era when police are ridiculed and college presidents are evicted from their own offices, the professional football quarterback is the last living authoritarian. The nation is watching it, live and in color: The quarterback matches his massive intellect, his strong right arm, his semi-nimble feet against the monsters on the opposite side of the scrimmage line, men who would remove his helmet with his head still inside.

There he stands behind the center, counting cadence in a burly baritone. There he stands, the Alpha Male. The defenders are jumping around, performing some pitiful little ballet steps, designed to disturb, frustrate or confuse the quarterback. But he remains calm. He cannot panic. By experience he knows that the team—the pack—cannot survive, cannot win, cannot exist as an entity if he shows the slightest sliver of fear.

Now the ball is inserted firmly into his hands. Somewhere in that mass of noise and color and confusion a pass receiver is streaking along a prescribed route. Back goes the quarterback's arm. Now the ball is in the air. Now it settles softly in the flanker's eager little paws. First down!

Ah, the ecstasy of it! Ah, the agony! The crowd loses all its senses, save the power to make inane noise. Emotion spills over every seating tier, until it fairly floods the playing field. Now the quarterback leaps up off his pancreas and marches down to where the new scrimmage line is forming. Here is the Alpha Male strutting forward, to command again and again until age withers and custom stales his infinite variety. And on the sidelines, a field-to-press-box telephone set strapped across his scalp, stands the Beta Male—the back-up quarterback—waiting for all those autumns to pile up, waiting for the Alpha Male to slink out of the stadium and into retirement.

There can be only one first-line quarterback, only one Alpha Male. Is it any wonder that a quarterback in the National Football League is a seething mass of egotism? If he isn't he either goes home and sells insurance or he goes north to Canada, where standards are lower. A quarterback is asked to do the impossible every Sunday, in front of people who have paid seven dollars each for their seats and who think that professional football is some kind of scientific exercise. They ask him to perform miracles and if he falls somewhat short, the customers start braiding ropes and calling for an immediate lynching.

Only a person with a sizeable amount of confidence would volunteer for the job in the first place. Only an Alpha Male.

It is early in the morning of October 25, 1970 and destiny is waiting for George Frederick Blanda, the coal miner's kid, to open his gleaming lobo eyes. George doesn't stir. Why should he?

For slightly more than 20 seasons, Blanda has been waiting for destiny to find him. To hell with destiny! Where was it when he needed it, all those agonizing years with the Chicago Bears when George Halas, his fellow Slav, was attempting to bury him alive? Where was it when George Blanda was kicking all those field goals, gaining all those yards, throwing all those touchdown passes and never getting to call himself the Bears' number one quarterback for more than a few pitiful months?

Was destiny trying to catch up to him those first three years in Houston when he won two American Football League championships and just missed a third? Why, chances are destiny didn't even know where George Frederick Blanda had gone to. It probably didn't even recognize the new league.

Where, pray tell, was destiny when the crowds at Rice Stadium wouldn't let the public address announcer get much past "and playing quarterback for the Houston Oilers . . . No. 16 . . . George Bl . . ." before the boos would drown out the rest of George's surname?

What was destiny doing on the morning when Houston's psychedelic new general manager, Don Klosterman, called the newspapers to report, with a note of boredom in his throat, that five players had been given their outright releases? Let's see . . . uh . . . center John Frongillo, tackle Rich Michael, fullback John Henry Johnson, cornerback Bernie Parrish and . . . uh . . . quarterback George Blanda. And when a *Houston Chronicle* columnist who had always sort of admired George's swagger suggested that the ball club ought to retire his number, was destiny out to lunch when Klosterman called the paper to say such an honor would be an "impossibility"?

And why hadn't destiny permitted the nation to know that George Blanda was sneaking up on some incredible records— Most points scored in a lifetime, Most field goals kicked, Most extra points? And how many people were aware that of all the quarterbacks who ever sweated and bled, only Baltimore's sainted John Unitas had ever thrown more completed passes into the enemy's end zone?

Club owners and sports writers and coaches had spent the better part of two decades trying to push George Frederick Blanda into a corner and forget him. His accomplishments were ignored. His sins magnified. They never talked about all those points he placed on the scoreboard, only about the inter-ceptions he'd thrown.

So the bloody hell with destiny! Let it go find some slick, lanky quarterback just graduating from college and anxious to make $300,000 in quick bonus payments. At age 43, how much does a man still hunger after fame? Better to take the money and let somebody else's wife worry about scrapbooks.

Ah, but this was destiny's day, a moment right out of Bill Stern's book of fables. Remember how it was back in the 1940s? The whole family—or at least those Blanda brothers and sisters who happened to be living at home at the time—would tune in the Colgate Shave Cream Man every Saturday night at the white house on South Third Street in Youngwood, Pa. How did Bill Stern used to say it? Oh, yes . . . "Portrait of Destiny Catching Up with the Quarterback Nobody Loved."

So, on the murky gray morning of October 25, 1970, with wild geese honking in the air above his apartment located on a lagoon near the western shore of Alameda Island, George Frederick Blanda staggers to his feet and starts his rendezvous with destiny by going to the toilet.

Breakfast is bubbling in the other room. The routine never varies on the morning of an Oakland Raider home game. In fact, it never varies during the week before. It is always the same. George Blanda is not a superstitious man. He makes that perfectly clear. He just doesn't change his routine. He eats at the Grotto in Jack London Square every Thursday night. He attends the race meeting at Bay Meadows across San Francisco Bay in San Mateo every Friday afternoon. He eats the same dry cereal, drinks the same juice (orange!), consumes the same amount of toast, has the exact and proper number of cups of coffee on the morning before a game.

There is no change this morning, even though destiny is only a yard behind him and closing fast. Inside of eight hours he will, after only twenty years and four months in the game, be on his way to becoming an overnight sensation. Publicity will overwhelm him. George Frederick Blanda, whose national fame has heretofore been predicated upon two minor stories in the Sporting News, one in 1956 when he was with the Bears and another in 1964 when he was with the Oilers, will become the most sought-after interview in the entire commercial sweat industry. Magazine writers will call at incredible hours, begging two or three days of his time. Television commentators like

Walter Cronkite and Heywood Hale Broun will come trailing after him, microphones flopping in the dust. His fee for speaking will double and then triple. Everyone will want him to say that he smokes their cigarette or drinks their beer or splashes his jutting jaw with their cologne.

He will endorse only two products, the breakfast food he eats every Sunday morning and is eating right this moment on October 25, 1970, and the after-shave lotion he has just got through using. He will tell everyone else that he cannot accept money to say he likes something he has never used.

Because of his age, he will become the towering hero of the Support Hose Set. One columnist, nationally syndicated, will describe how her husband kicked his tonic bottle 32 feet after a George Blanda field goal. Another will scold him for taking the alibi of age away from every man over 40. And yet another will say that he has become a bigger sex symbol to the middle-aged man than the 63-year-old company president who gets his teenage secretary pregnant.

Through it all, George Blanda will behave with his own brand of spectacular ambivalence. On the one hand, he will talk like the brass-plated old football hero that he knew of and read about as a small boy in western Pennsylvania. He will say that what he has done was exactly what he was paid to do, no more and no less. And on the other hand, he will shimmer in the golden glory that has avoided him for so long. He will enjoy every opportunity to speak to a reporter from a national publication. He will give away so much of his spare time that the Oakland Raiders' publicity director, Tommy Grimes, will be amazed.

But ever faithful to his image as the last of the old-style quarterbacks, who spit out teeth and drew plays in the dirt and who responded to serious injuries by suggesting that the best cure for a broken arm was to strap a ham sandwich on it, he will turn to Arnold Hano of *Sport* magazine and say, as if Arnold were destiny itself, "Where the hell were you when I needed you twenty years ago?"

And Hano will echo, "Yes, indeed, where was I twenty years ago?"

It is October 25, 1970, early in the morning and the Raiders are about to play the Pittsburgh Steelers at the Oakland-Alameda County Coliseum, just across the water. This will be the beginning of the most amazing season any football player ever had. George Frederick Blanda, whose father worked all week in the mines and drank too much on weekends, will make miracles for the entire nation to see. He will kick field goals from awesome distances with seconds left to play. He will throw touchdown passes. He will move the Oakland offense . . . move it magically, majestically.

"When George is on the field, the rest of us listen pretty good," guard Gene Upshaw will say. "It's like listening to your father. I mean, George speaks from experience, so much experience you hate to argue with him over the slightest little thing. Some of the guys on the team weren't born when he was a senior in college. He played against people like Steve Van Buren and he played with Sid Luckman. Those are names out of the distant past to most of us."

It has been raining for several days, first a sleazy drizzle, then a lashing, drenching purgatory of a storm. Now the water is all in the ground. The clouds are swirling off toward the Pacific Ocean, which lies crouched behind the San Francisco peninsula only eight miles away. Quarterbacks worry about the weather. It is part of their instinct. Sometimes wet turf means poor footing, so passes must be thrown short and flat, ball carriers must pound straight ahead on quick, secure handoffs. Deep mud would favor the Steelers, under ordinary thinking, because the Raiders worship the extravagant play—the long forward pass, the breakaway run. It is a reflection of the style of their number one quarterback, Daryle Lamonica, whom the literary set refers to, snidely, as the Mad Bomber.

With waterfowl still flapping in the dank atmosphere, Blanda backs his leased car out of the carport and leaves the parking lot at the Coral Reef Motel. He turns right on Doolittle Avenue and spins along in silence. Music on the car radio is for other, more frivolous times.

"I still like this game," he tells a newsman riding with him. "I love the routine. People say that football meetings and game films are boring. Hell, I love both of them. I like getting up for the 'big one.' I like doing calisthenics. I like the action on the sidelines. I like being with other football players. I don't want to coach when I'm through with the game, but I don't know how I could get away from this. It would be hell leaving the routine. Coaching would be a way of staying in the game, wouldn't it?"

The car turns left on High Street and rumbles across a low, flat bridge. The neat 1930-style bungalows of Alameda give way to warehouses and oil tanks, boat yards and rubble-pitted heaps of Bay fill. It is still too early for the Nimitz Freeway—that merciful stretch of highway that takes a motorist right through Oakland without ever getting him dirty—to be clotted with traffic. It is almost serene, if a freeway can ever be described just that way. The Coliseum is less than two miles from the apartment Blanda rents during the season for himself, his wife of 22 years and their 15-year-old daughter, Leslie. Alameda is comfortable, white, middle class and conservative. It is culturally distinct from Oakland proper with its hard hats, its housing developments, its Hell's Angels and its burgeoning black population.

Life is not peaceful for the Oakland Raiders. They are 2-2-1 and this is not to be tolerated. Defeat is sinful because the Raiders are an Organization (always with a capital letter). They stress, according to their management, "pride and poise." The words are stenciled everywhere. There are only two commandments with the Oakland football club. Thou shalt have Pride and thou shalt have Poise. Thou shalt also make damn sure thou win, too.

Other teams approach professional football from other angles. The Raiders are a paramilitary organization, about as frivolous as the Gestapo, about as lighthearted as the CIA. They are commanded by Al Davis, who believes that other people are watching. He may be right. Security is strict with the Oakland club. Nobody gets near practice without proper clearance. Squad cuts are never announced to the press. Reporters simply have to hang around and see who's missing. Player deals are Byzantine in nature. Taxi squads—the ready reserve units of the National Football League—are limited to seven athletes, but the legend is that Al Davis has 20 men hid out in the hills. Bartenders at the Orinda Country Club all weigh 285. Either that or they can get to your table in 4.7 seconds, even if it is located 40 yards away.

As a means of expressing their determination, their unyielding focus on victory, they dress in black and silver. No blues, no reds, no golds or greens. Just black and silver, convict colors, elite guard colors, men-living-together-in-an-insulated-group colors.

"I like The Organization," says George Blanda, who looks like country singer Eddie Arnold, who speaks with a voice that sounds like John Wayne, only in a slightly higher register. "Some players knock it. But they're part of the new breed. They don't want to work for a thing. They want it all passed out to them. I could have quit a dozen times. I damn near did. Betty, my wife, has been wanting me to get out since 1959, the year the Bears decided they didn't want me playing pro football anymore.

"But the Raiders are a strong organization. They don't panic. They don't yank you out of the starting line-up. They give you a job and even if you have a bad day and have to come out, you know you'll be back in the next week. They don't panic. So the ball club doesn't panic. Maybe that sounds corny, but it's true."

For this reason, George Frederick Blanda cannot hope to start in this, his 261st professional football game. Lamonica is the Oakland quarterback, the number one man. Blanda will kick extra points and field goals. But he will not start. He is a natural freak, a man who has lived as a Beta Male, become an Alpha Male, only to lose and regain the status. Now he exists in a special category, neither one nor the other. He is a wolf alone, a solitary figure—an Alpha Male in winter. He should be dead, but he isn't. He is alive in a game designed for young legs, young backs, young muscles.

"My wife says that my career is 'Death and Resurrection' over and over again," says Blanda, chuckling at his wife's intellectualism. He much admires his wife. She paints seriously. She majored in the dance and has taught classes in the subject. She reads heavy books. She thinks swiftly and cleverly.

Indeed, there is truth in Betty Blanda's observation. She starts a new scrapbook every generation, she says, and the pages are littered with clippings from the *Chicago Tribune*, the *Chicago American*, the *Houston Press*, the *Houston Chronicle*, the *Oakland Tribune*, the *San Francisco Examiner*. The headlines rise and fall with the movement of the planets in and out of George Blanda's astrological chart.

"Blanda Benched! Bratkowski New Bears Quarterback!" shouts one. Two crinkled yellow pages later there is another story that says, "Halas Says Blanda Is Best Quarterback in Professional Football." The Houston years are similar. "As They Say in the West, Blanda's Back in the Saddle Again," says the *Post*. A month later, the *Chronicle* reports: "George Through as No. 1 Quarterback. Trull in Charge from Here on Out."

So it goes. Blanda has outlasted every single one of them. They are all either retired or hiding in Canada—John Lujack, Steve Romanik, Ed Brown, Ron Knox, Tommy O'Connell, Bob Williams, Jacky Lee, Charlie Milstead, Don Trull, Bobby Layne, Glyn Griffing, Randy Kerbow and, Good God, is that all? They brought them in by the planeload, in Chicago and in Houston. Old George survived. (Do you know they were calling him "old" in 1960 with the Oilers when he was a mere lad of 31?)

The parking lot is circular. It lies in a bomb-crater depression between the 54,000-seat Coliseum and the 16,500-seat Sports Arena. Neither is fancy, just grim concrete. The place where the athletes leave their cars is heavily guarded, lest some espionage agent from the New York Jets sneak in and bug somebody's dashboard.

The younger Raiders are not sure how to take George Frederick Blanda. He is a figure out of the romantic past. He is fully nine years older than their head coach, John Madden, who at least has the decency to be the youngest coach in the NFL.

The children walk around George cautiously. He is too old to be a player and, almost, too old to be a coach. Besides, he has an ego-shattering presence about him. His face is hard, but handsome. He walks with a strut. His eyes are demoralizing. They are singularly lupine. They wither, accuse and challenge, all at the same time. On occasion—not often—those gray-green eyes have transfixed defensive players, rooting them to a spot, while a pass whistles over their helmets. The gaze is so disturbing that Blanda's sweaty, uncomfortable enemies have described him as "evil" and "sinister" and "manipulative."

"That's a lot of bullshit," Blanda says in that John Wayne-in-*Rio-Bravo* voice. "I'm a pretty simple, straightforward person. I'm independent. I like to compete. I say exactly what I think and I guess that threatens some people."

On the way to the dressing room, several rookies, dressed in jump suits and floppy hats, bow respectfully to the senior citizen. They look like curates caught suddenly in the presence of the archbishop. Blanda smirks. The man has an eloquent smirk, straight out of the Bowery Boys movies of the 1940s. He enjoys the reverence they show. No one will ever tell those rookies what a bold-faced young varlet George Frederick Blanda was when he was new to the Chicago Bears, way back in 1949 when Harry Truman was president and Milton Berle's television show cleaned out saloons every Tuesday night.

Blanda wears mildly modish clothes now. His slacks are flared. His shirts are reasonably fashionable. His sideburns extend far below his ear lobes. But they are neat and trimmed. His face looks like nature meant it to wear a duck's ass hairdo. His pants should be pegged and shoes should be white bucks. Still, he assimilates well. He has been around so long that the

snapshot of him taken outside Wrigley Field in 1950 wearing a
wide-lapel suit and a fat tie looks stylish. His clothes were out
so long that they are suddenly in again. George Blanda has
transcended something so artificial as fashion.

Some of the athletes are nervous. They have pregame jitters.
They are hiding them by wearing what cliché experts call "game
faces." In other words, they are nervous as hell, so nervous they
cannot work up a decent look of terror. Blanda is gray, both at
the muzzle and at the ears. Standing in the corner, near where
the other quarterbacks, Daryle Lamonica and Ken (Snake)
Stabler hang their clothes, he is placid, imperturbable. It is
nearly noon on October 25, 1970 and Blanda is about to
become a national hero.

The sky is starting to clear outside. Pittsburgh coach Chuck
Noll is concerned. If the sun shines, the Raiders can throw deep
and run wide, and that ain't good.

"The bomb," he says, "is always on their mind. Oakland
wants to go for that big one. Basically, they're a long-striking
team. You have to worry about Lamonica all the time."

But not today. The game starts splendidly for Oakland and
Daryle does get off a picturesque scoring pass to tight end
Raymond Chester, a young man of real talent. The play covers
37 yards and soon afterwards Lamonica, who suffers physical
torments that would impress Job, pinches a nerve in his back
and retires. Now destiny, after all these years, has thrown a
sweaty arm around Blanda's shoulders.

Where have you been, old boy?

Madden has two choices: (a) He can go with Ken Stabler,
young, left-handed and impressionable or (b) he can use old
George, elderly, right-handed and a born adventurer who could
have saved a lot of interceptions over the years if he weren't so
damned determined to throw the ball into the end zone.

In a situation so tense there is only one intelligent move for a
coach to make: forget all the technical nonsense. A man has to
go with experience. And who has more experience than George
Blanda? Once again the Alpha Male, George stomps out onto
the grubby field. The customers are dubious. Here is an ancient

gent who has been primarily a place kicker. He had some
interesting moments as a relief passer, but he has thrown the
ball only 138 times for Oakland over a period of four years.

On his first play from scrimmage, he throws 29 yards to
Chester. Touchdown! The crowd of 54,423 gets hyperactive.
Whoops! Somebody has been holding. Pittsburgh gets the ball
and scores to tie the game. Now the Steelers get a brilliant idea.
What is the best way to detach a quarterback from his intellect?
Simple. Just blitz him until he cannot think anymore. The blitz
is a murderous device. The defensive unit forgets finesse and
just sends kamikaze pilots roaring through the line. The idea is
to kill the quarterback before he can get the ball in the air.

There is a tactical risk. In order to free men for the blitz, it is
necessary to give up all pretensions of double coverage of pass
receivers. It is strictly: one man—one ball catcher. Period!

"They don't know how much we love to have the other team
blitz," Blanda says afterwards. "I got two touchdowns against
that damned blitz and they decided to quit it."

Quarterbacks take a physical smashing, no matter how they
enjoy throwing against the blitz. As soon as the ball leaves their
palm—wham! bam! thank you, m'am!—somebody splatters
them all over the turf.

"Do I give a damn about that?" Blanda asks. "I've been hurt
only once in an athletic event. That was in 1954 when I got a
shoulder separation that just about finished me as the Bears'
number one quarterback. Don Colo came up on one side of me
and Len Ford on the other. I don't even remember who won
our last four games of the year that season. Other than that, I've
never been hurt."

So Blanda stands in there against the fearsome charge. As the
second period ends, he finds Warren Wells—a troubled lad, but a
brilliant pass receiver—streaking for the horizon. The touchdown play covers 44 yards and George is all hyped up. Seems
like old times, he says later, humming the words to a long-dead
popular tune.

Back he comes with a 27-yard field goal and a 19-yard
scoring pass to Chester again, just before the half. Now the

stands are overreacting. Now it is October 25, 1970 and destiny
is getting just a little bit ahead of George Frederick Blanda.
When it is all over, the statistics are impressive. Blanda has
thrown a dozen times, completes seven passes for 148 yards.
Three of his passes have gone for touchdowns.

The next afternoon's *Examiner* will refer to this game as if it
had been something transitory. "Blanda's Day of Glory—Indian
Summer in Oakland." Indeed, George has turned the winter of
his discontent into glorious Indian summer. But his career is just
starting to get good. What an incredible thought! Babe Parilli
was a freshman at the University of Kentucky when George was
a senior. Poor Parilli lasted only until he was 39. Now he is an
assistant coach and Blanda is on the verge of becoming famous.

Afterwards, Blanda sits naked in front of his dressing stall,
flashing those lobo eyes at wandering reporters. This is when he
is at his snappish best. He has competed in a football game. He
has done what they pay him to do. He stands above and a bit to
the right of the rest of the world, waiting to reenter. He has
competed. He has dominated. Now he cannot stop competing.
This is something about the man that reporters have never come
to understand. The game has just ended. Blanda's glands are still
pumping. His jaws are still wet with saliva. How in the hell can
he calm down and say nice, polite things to people who insist
on asking the dumbest questions?

It is still mano-a-mano as far as George is concerned. Those
writers, they bring up those insipid questions and they expect
him to cool down and be calm, tactful, reserved—even chatty.

"Do you have any trouble reading modern defenses?" asks a
writer from a suburban newspaper. The kid is young, not more
than four years older than Blanda's son, Rick, age 19. It is an
insulting, condescending question. Maybe it isn't meant to be.
But it is. So George competes. He has been challenged. Now he
responds. The answer is something of a put-on. After all, on the
sidelines, before Lamonica's injury, he had noticed that
Pittsburgh cornerback Mel Blount could be had. On the long
pass play involving Wells, he faked a running play and then
watched with animal delight as Blount took a couple of fatal

steps back toward the scrimmage line. By that time Warren Wells was off and running. By the time the pass reached Wells, it was apparent to Blount that he had been conned.

"Of course I don't read defenses," Blanda tells the insolent young writer. "If I watched them, I wouldn't be able to see my receivers."

Nearby, looking tall and serious as a Baptist deacon, is Hamilton P. B. (Tex) Maule, author, critic and retired trapeze artist. He takes it down, word for word, as if George is serious. It appears just that way in *Sports Illustrated*, the weekly magazine that makes sweat smell so sweet.

Now it is time to shower and leave. Nobody spends so much time in the bathhouse as George Blanda. Since writers rarely roll up their slacks, take off their shoes and walk through the rain drops, George takes long showers.

When it comes to newspapermen, Blanda is selective. He likes to talk to journalists whom he thinks make sense. He will spend hours talking to the *San Francisco Examiner*'s Bucky Walter, who looks, sounds and writes like W. C. Fields. He considers Bill Feist, a kindly acting man from the *San Jose Mercury-News*, to be a personal friend. He tolerates the *San Francisco Chronicle*'s bearded poet, Glenn Dickey, not because he likes him, but because Dickey says what he thinks and George admires that quality. He will speak to no one on the *Oakland Tribune* staff but Ed Schoenfeld, the paper's myopic, hard-working golf writer.

Blanda has his list and he sticks to it religiously. One flagrant violation is enough for dismissal. People rarely get second chances with George Frederick Blanda. Experience—starting very early when he was a small boy playing snooker in Buckley's pool hall in Youngwood—has taught him that as soon as a man shows his unreliability, it is best to leave him alone.

What is right is right, George thinks, and what isn't right is best avoided. So Blanda divides the world in half, a regular Papal Line of Demarcation—good guys over here, bad guys over there. John Wayne would be proud. In future weeks he will work miracles far more spectacular than the one he has per-

formed on this day—October 25, 1970—against the Pittsburgh
Steelers. He will amaze millions of people and justify the
expectations of those good, solid, beer-swigging lads back there
at the VFW Hall in Youngwood.

No matter where George Blanda goes, no matter what he
does, he is not far away, spiritually, from Youngwood. He
remains a tough, competitive Slavic boy struggling—always
struggling—to avoid the choking horror of the mines.

Now he is about to be recognized as a genuine, walking,
talking, bright-eyed football immortal. In future years, jock
historians won't bother to recall how close George Frederick
Blanda came to quitting before the miracle season of 1970 ever
got started. But it is true. You could look it up. Right here in
this book, in fact.

EPISODE 2

The summer sun hangs high and hot, scorching the piebald
hills of Sonoma County and making birds sweat. All morning
long the professional football heroes have been thumping and
bumping in the awesome heat. A training camp is supposed to
be a miserable experience. Adversity, so the theory goes,
tightens the muscles, strengthens the spirit and refocuses the
attention. It also makes the athletes work harder so they can get
back to civilization, where the beer is chilled and the airline
stews are willing.

Since the Oakland Raiders are an army brigade rather than an
athletic team, they go to intricate lengths to convince their
employees that this is no vacation resort. Security at the
practice field is agonizingly strict. Reporters covering the club
must stop every morning to have their press cards checked at
the entrance to a compound that is surrounded by a board
fence so tall that Kareem Jabbar could not look over it. It
makes no difference if a newsman has passed through the gate a
hundred times. He is still checked. One never knows when a spy
from the New York Jets will arrive disguised as George Ross,
sports editor of the *Oakland Tribune*.

Meals are simple and bland. They are served in a temporary

mess hall, carved out of a conference room at El Rancho-Tropicana Motel. Under ordinary circumstances, humor is frowned upon. These weeks in Santa Rosa, way up in the wine country of Northern California, are for the solemn contemplation of football. A small exception is being made today, however. After looking dreadful in two straight exhibition games, the Raiders had snapped out of their trance and defeated the San Francisco 49ers—the haughty 49ers, upon whom Al Davis takes out much of his frustrations.

The score had been 31-17. Very convincing and very satisfying. Al Davis is happy . . . well, as happy as he ever gets during the football season. So the inmates of The Organization's summer labor camp are still chuckling three days later, on September 9, 1970, a day that will live in infamy, at least as far as George Blanda is concerned. Tackle Tom Keating, a lumpy imp, has his tape recorder going. Everybody is sitting around a mess table singing, with glorious incongruity, "Santa Claus Is Coming to Town." No matter how hot it is in those hills, let it snow, let it snow, let it snow. And screw the 49ers. The merger between the two leagues is complete. The Oakland Raiders are members in good standing of the National Football League and almost as socially acceptable as their neighbors across the Bay. So, let it snow, let it snow, let it snow. Santa Claus is coming to town.

Near the pool, which the players are not permitted to use, a reporter is talking with Ken Stabler, whose hair is long and mod, and whose passes are thrown left-handed. This was going to be a big summer for the Snake. He looked brilliant in a couple of the early exhibition games. But then his father dropped dead of a heart attack. Only 46 was Leroy Stabler of Birmingham, Alabama, when he died, only three years older than George Blanda, whose health is excellent.

Stabler is just back from the funeral. Talking about football helps get his mind refocused, he says. It's all right. He doesn't mind talking.

Al Davis has said that Stabler reminds him of "those clever left-handed pitchers, control artists like Preacher Roe and

Whitey Ford." This praise from the Most High. You can
consider those words written in concrete by a fiery hand—
namely, Al Davis's. Having been thus anointed, Stabler all but
glows. He is free to pass wisdom on to the press.

"Everyone is always saying how complicated the Raider
system is," he says in the most deliberate of drawls. "It's not
complex to me. Now, ah'm not boasting. Ah'm just talking
about the beauty of the system. It's very flexible. The Organization doesn't give you more than you can use. There's a lot a
quarterback can do with the Raider system."

Professionally, Snake Stabler is a direct descendant of George
Blanda. It is staggering to consider, but it is true. They both
played quarterback for Paul (Bear) Bryant—George at Kentucky
and the Snake at Alabama. Once 19 years separated them. Now
they are teammates.

"George is an amazing man, as amazing as coach Bryant in
many ways," says Stabler. "At first I was tempted to call him
'Mr. Blanda' or even 'coach.' I've learned a whole lot just being
around him. Mostly I've learned when to do something and
when not to. Don't think that isn't important.

"In one way, it's kind of too bad George's career has lasted as
long as it has. I think he'd have made a fine coach. Maybe it's
too late for him to start. What do you think? Why, he's liable to
play until he's 50."

In another part of the El Rancho-Tropicana, in a suite where
nobody goes without the highest security clearance, they are
placing George Blanda's name on revocable waivers. Anybody
who wants his elderly hide can have him for the clearance sale
price of $100. It is right after lunch on September 9, 1970 and
all somebody has to do to destroy George Blanda's rendezvous
with destiny later in the year is to claim him off the waiver list.
They have exactly 24 hours to ruin his miracle season. If he
does not pass waivers, he probably will not report to another
team.

All morning long, Al Davis has been scheming and plotting.
He has a number of younger players that he wants to save. If he
can get them through this mandatory cut-down date, he can

probably sneak them past waivers once the regular season
begins. Therefore he decides to ask waivers on three older
players, hoping that nobody will file a claim for them because
of their age. It is a gamble, but Al Davis enjoys the intrigue.

No journalist has ever captured Davis properly. None ever
will, because he will not permit it. Here is a man from an
Irish-Jewish neighborhood in Brooklyn who enjoys his silky
reputation as a rogue and a schemer. He purposely portrays
himself as an intellect so strong that no one can overwhelm him
in the market place.

There is everything about the man physically to make the
public think he is as sinister as he pretends to be. His deep-
freeze eyes seem to be entities in themselves, wholly separate
from one of the most agile minds in professional football. They
float for awhile as if they are searching for some mystical
kingdom in the clouds. Then those eyes dart and swoop,
attempting to record every detail within their range. Every now
and then, they feign innocence. It is a superb act, worthy of
some kind of dramatic award.

Then there is Al Davis's face. Sometimes it is hawkish.
Sometimes it is furtive. Occasionally it is impish. The posture is
so overdone that it cannot be totally real. It is not. It is part
pretense. However, it is not advisable to go into a business
transaction with the managing general partner of the Oakland
Raiders with only a few hours sleep. There is an hypnotic tone
in his voice, one he has carefully cultivated. The accent is not
native to any region. It has been assembled: a touch of
Brooklynese for toughness, a strong dash of courtly Virginian
(picked up in one year at The Citadel) for flavor and gentility,
and a broad base of Western drawl for body. The overall effect
is like the sound of honey being poured over velvet.

Sometimes Al Davis seems too shrewd to be the commander
in chief of something as prosaic as a football club, even one that
dotes on discipline and secrecy with the fanaticism of the
Raiders. He ought to be the boss of a powerful political
machine in a city like Boston or Newark or Akron. It requires
no mental exercise to see him, in a black homburg and white

scarf, being driven to city hall in a long limousine with a whisky-nosed flunky at the wheel. Honest Al Davis is straight out of James Michael Curley and Boss Prendergast, with strong overtones of Richard Daley. He missed his true calling, but he tries hard to make up for it.

Authors have been picking at him for better than a decade since he rose out of an obscure position as an assistant coach at the University of Southern California. Everyone has failed. Honest Al treasures his mystery. It forces other teams to worry a little bit more. Davis likes any edge he can get. Besides, magazine writers give him hives. In some cases he leaves himself vulnerable to ridicule. Like most men with vast pride, ridicule wounds him deepest.

A couple of years ago, Leonard Schecter, the fastest man with a typewriter or a hand axe this side of movie critic Rex Reed, spent a half-hour at the Raiders' summer camp. He came away with a story so slanted against Davis that even Al's old tribal enemy, Sidney Gillman of San Diego, felt sorry. It openly suggested that Davis had lied about his athletic career, which was modest at best. (A minor letter in football for playing five games for Syracuse.)

It was also hinted that Davis was so sensitive about his own slender physique that he made a special point of hiding his hands. It was a cute, cunning piece of literature. It implied far more than it revealed, which is what Schecter is famous for. Honest Al Davis was utterly disgusted. He was wounded. He never forgot. So he waited and waited.

One morning about three years later, he received a telephone call from Paul Brown, head coach and supreme leader of the Cincinnati Bengals. Brown had been alerted that Schecter was bearing down on him. What would Davis advise? Well, said Honest Al, the best thing to do would be to confront him in the midst of his peer group and then turn the rascal out. Which is exactly what Brown did, informing Schecter that he, Paul Brown, had witnessed the journalistic mayhem that had been committed upon Vince Lombardi, Pete Rozelle and Al Davis.

Rising magnificently to the occasion, Brown described all of

Schecter's victims as being saintly men, pillars of professional football's holy church. He, Paul Brown, would not be treated in a like manner. Out! Out! Out! Naturally, the Dayton-Cincinnati press corps recorded everything. The next day, Al Davis had his revenge. It does no good to cross Al Davis. It does no good to cross George Blanda. And on this September 9, 1970, Davis was preparing to hurt Blanda's feelings. It was necessary to the survival of The Organization. There is a great deal of Alpha Male in Honest Al.

He sent somebody to find George, to knock on his door and let the last of the old-style, blood-sipping football professionals know that the managing general partner wanted him present at the blockhouse.

"I understood it when he called me into that office of his at Santa Rosa and told me what he had done," said George long after the incident, long after the miracle games had come and gone. "I personally didn't like it. I was called in the day before it was going to appear in the papers. I knew exactly what was happening when the kid knocked on the door. I'd seen it happen to many, many people before. I got sick down in the middle of my guts.

"At least he had the decency not to have the kid say, 'Bring your playbook with you.' That's the kiss of death. Afterwards I went up there and talked to Al and I knew I'd be around. But it was embarrassing for me. Hell, I'm a mass of pride. If I wasn't I wouldn't have stayed in this game as long as I have.

"It wasn't as embarrassing for me to be put on waivers as it was for me not to be claimed. He told me he was protecting the young players for a couple of weeks. I accepted that. It hurt, but I accepted it. He put two other veterans on at the same time—Wayne Hawkins, who passed, and Al Dotson, who passed. He put me on. I passed. Damn, but that was painful. Of the three, I'm the only one still playing football.

"When I left Al's room I wasn't the happiest guy in the world. It isn't true that I walked out without bothering to open the door. Here I had to get up in the morning and go out to practice and it was going to be in the paper that George was released. It was a very embarrassing situation. I always figured that when I quit football it would be under my own power. I didn't want someone telling me, 'George, you're not good enough.' Hell, I've got to be smart enough to figure that out myself.

"I knew the end wasn't at hand. At least that's what Al had told me. I told him that I probably would quit . . . go home . . . just quit. He told me to think about it. I didn't sleep at all that night. I called Betty and asked her what she thought I ought to do. She said, 'Quit, you don't need the money. You don't need the grief.' Of course, she's been after me to quit since God knows when. In fact, she's wanted me to quit so often, I can't count the times. I guess I knew what she'd say. So I flopped around my bed like a fool. And I got mad at everybody.

"Then the next morning, I got up and went to practice. Al didn't say a thing to me. I guess he knew exactly what I'd do. I like Al. I'm funny, I like people other people don't like. I like Al Davis. I like Howard Cosell. I like Tex Maule, too. I guess maybe it's because I'm the kind of person other people don't like. I don't know. Hell, I respect Al Davis. I don't give a damn what some folks say about him, he's a man of his word.

"The turning point of my career was when I came with the Raiders. I had some good years before. Probably I had some excellent years, too. Imagine that! The turning point of my career came at age 39. That sounds funny as hell, doesn't it? But that's what happened. I always admired Al's style. Think of the things he's done. He was a great coach. I don't mean a good coach. I mean a great one. As commissioner he got the two leagues together—pronto! He ended all that stupid spending for college talent, just like that. He does things directly, like I do.

"He said to himself, 'How can I end this war?' And right away, he got the answer back. Let's see the National Football League play without any quarterbacks. Now that's good, hard thinking. He has a manner I like. I look up to a person like that—even if he is younger than I am. I looked up to George Halas of the Bears, too. I know I knock him. Hell, I hate Halas and I love him. I guess everybody had that attitude toward him. What's wrong with being a hardnosed son of a bitch?

"Al's a brilliant man, like Halas. He's responsible for building The Organization. He understands men, he understands football, he understands talent. Halas was the same, only I think pro football passed him by—about 1954, I'd say.

"So I went on Al Davis's word and he didn't let me down. He put me back on the regular roster in time for the opening game. I still didn't like it. I'd never been on the cab squad before. That's no place for a 43-year-old athlete. I think maybe the main difference between Halas and Davis is that Al keeps his word. Halas would give me his word and then he'd shaft me.

"There was one funny thing that happened the day I was cut. I come stomping out of that door and here's some poor guy from *Life* magazine and he comes up and says, 'Aren't you George Blanda?' And I said, 'Used to be!' And he says, 'I'm doing a story on Daryle Lamonica!' I blink.

"He says, 'Can you give me a few comments on Daryle Lamonica?' And I said, 'Daryle's a fine fellow and everything, but if I said anything about him at this point you couldn't write it.' Hell, I was upset. If I hadn't been upset what kind of a competitor would I be? So he goes off and writes this damned story about how surly I am and how I don't want to say anything nice about Daryle. Well, it's the same old crap—being quoted out of context again.

"My pride was hurt. If I didn't have that pride I'd be back home in Youngwood, working for the railroad or mining coal or working at the Robertshaw thermostat company. That's all anybody in Youngwood does. I wasn't trying to put Daryle down. I just wanted to get rid of this guy from *Life*, who doesn't know what's happening.

"That night in the mess hall, I see John Madden the head coach, and he says, kind of offhand, 'You seem upset.' Isn't that a big surprise? I mean, what does he expect? I said, 'Hell yes, John, I'm upset.' I couldn't sleep for a couple of days. I didn't want to leave football. I got up and got a sandwich at

2 A.M. the first night and Davis sees me and says, 'It'll only hurt for a little while.' Then he told me I'd passed waivers. He said he was surprised it had happened. I guess I started to get over it then.

"It's a good thing I didn't quit. They wouldn't be writing about Blanda's miracles, they'd be saying, 'Whatever happened to George Blanda?' I tell you one thing, I played better after that waiver thing happened. I got a second wind . . . well, maybe, considering how long I've played, it was my 123rd wind. I wouldn't say it made a better ballplayer out of me. It just made me more determined. Damn, I was going to prove that one of those other 25 teams should have claimed me.

"But you know, when you look back at those miracle games, I really wasn't that much better an athlete than I was in Houston. I played better at Houston. I just happened to get into some situations . . . the team got into some situations . . . and I happened to be in at the end of some important games. The time we got 38 points against Kansas City for the Oilers in 1965 was bigger than that miracle stuff.

"Everybody talks about all the damn pressure that was supposed to be on me during the miracle games. I've never had any pressure in football. As a factor in the game, pressure is overrated or overplayed by the press, maybe. John Brodie of the San Francisco 49ers always says there's no such thing as pressure where a professional is concerned. Pressure is something you make yourself. I go out there in practice and kick 17 out of 20 field goals from the 37-yard line. And I can kick three-out-of-three from the 47-yard line. When I get back there and try a 52-yard field goal, I know I can make it. Hell, I've made them from 55 yards out. If there's any pressure it comes from within. Pressure happens when you don't have faith in your ability. I think positive. I don't build up any pressure.

"Hell, I've been in all those so-called 'miracle situations' before. I know I can kick long field goals. I know I can take a team and move it for a touchdown. The pressure is all up there in the stands. I've got a great football team around me, so it's easy to do things that look impossible. I don't ever remember having pressure on a football team. When I go in, as far as I'm concerned the score is 0-0. I just go out there and 'think win.' That's all.''

Ah, how sublimely simple it all sounds, doesn't it, sports fans? There you were during the last half of the 1970 season, all crumpled up like used pieces of toilet paper, in front of your television sets, thinking that you were watching the impossible. And all it was was a combination of crazy circumstance and one elderly quarterback's infinite understanding of the nature of the game he plays.

EPISODE 3

Somehow it always seems to come down to Kansas City and Oakland, as if God only follows those two football teams. It wasn't always so. In the early years of the American Football League, when most people came to the stadium disguised as empty seats, the Chiefs were the Dallas Texans and they were more preoccupied with beating the Houston Oilers and George Blanda. But there wasn't room enough in Dallas for two clubs. And so, in a scene filched from a Johnny Mack Brown movie (circa 1939) the two antagonists met in a showdown.

There was Tex Schramm, the Rhineland baron who runs the Dallas Cowboys of the National League, meeting eyeball-to-eyeball with Lamar Hunt of the Texans. Perhaps both men would have preferred to go for their guns, there being a war on and all, but they flipped a coin instead. Lamar Hunt lost. If he had won there would be a team known as the Kansas City Cowboys now.

About the time the old Texans were getting used to life in Missouri—Hunt wanted to call them the Kansas City Texans, but somebody talked him out of it—the Oakland Raiders decided to stop being the baggy pants comedians of the American Football League. They brought Honest Al Davis in from San Diego, where he had been taking scheming lessons at the knee of his master, Sidney Gillman. Once in charge of a whole franchise, there was no stopping that boy. He built The

Organization and designed it to last a thousand years, if necessary.

At first he gathered all the problem children of football together, the tired, the poor, the wretched refuse of everybody else's teeming shores. He brought in the homeless, the tempest-tossed. In other words, if you had a talented athlete who complained a lot, who loafed when your coach felt he should be sprinting or who stirred up "trouble" in the clubhouse, Al Davis was willing to take him off your hands, no questions asked.

It was a successful system, because he really didn't give a damn about a man's past as long as the athlete behaved himself in the present. It was a means of getting the Raiders respectable while Davis searched through the college draft lists, looking for "Oakland types," players who physically and mentally suited The Organization. By the time George Frederick Blanda was through in Houston, the Raiders were consistently challenging the Chiefs in the American League's Western Division. In fact, Kansas City went to the first Super Bowl and Oakland went to the second.

And on November 1, 1970, with the merger complete and the American League dead as a separate entity, the blood rivalry continues. The Raiders are on board a bus rumbling across the crumbling backwater of Kansas City. The driver is looking for Municipal Stadium, an old bush league baseball park that was rebuilt and repainted for the Philadelphia Athletics who moved there in 1954. It is bright, cheerful, well tended. It is like an ancient company house whose sagging clapboards have been covered with aluminum siding.

Its dressing rooms are built for occupancy by 25 slender baseball players, not 40 overgrown football players. The press box was built with midgets in mind. And the crowd sits too close to make visiting players comfortable. There are other, more subtle hazards. Several years ago there was a young photographer who hovered very close to the visitors' bench. He listened very carefully, never took pictures and always seemed to be rushing over to tell Kansas City coach Hank Stram something. The Snoopy Snapper, he was called, and when he was exposed, the Kansas City management broke the old record for disclaiming knowledge of a spy, set by the Eisenhower administration in the Gary Francis Powers U-2 flight incident.

Winter is swooping down on Kansas City. The sky is cloudless and full of sunshine . . . brittle, distant sunshine. There is no parking around Municipal Stadium, so the streets are already busy. Rather than take a chance on missing the first period, the people are willing to get up early and beat the team buses to the stadium. It is a matter of survival.

George Blanda sits back in the bus alone, aloof, lost in thought. He has ridden to the stadium 261 times, not counting exhibitions and playoffs and super bowls. This is no new thrill. A writer leans forward and makes conversation. It isn't an interview, just conversation.

"How much of a help is it, really, for the Chiefs to have Billy Cannon on their roster? I mean, other than the fact that he's a good football player. Can he help their game strategy?"

Blanda sucks in his breath. Sometimes he reacts warmly to a writer. Sometimes he snarls. This is his morning to be warm. Destiny has him by the eyeballs, remember? By the time the day ends and television sets are turned off, he will be on his way to becoming a national folk hero.

"Well, Billy has got to know our system," says George. "After all he played for the Raiders for seven years."

The Oakland club has been busily substituting younger players for older ones. Defensive end Ike Lassiter has been peddled to the Patriots and replaced by Tony Cline. And Cannon is no longer the Raiders' tight end. A supple young giant named Raymond Chester plays the position. Now Cannon is with the Chiefs, getting one more year on his pension plan credit before he retires permanently. Billy and George know each other well. They are not close personal friends exactly. They have been through much together. Cannon was a Heisman Trophy winner at LSU. He signed with Houston for $100,000, a sum that left the public breathless back in 1960, before Joe Namath got $424,000 and Donnie Anderson got $600,000.

Cannon was Blanda's halfback with the Oilers. Then he was his tight end in Oakland. They have fought many wars.

"That sort of stuff is overrated," says Blanda. "What can Billy tell them that they don't already know about us? He knows all about the character and personality of the Raiders and we know all about him. But these two teams have been at each other's throats too long. We know what they are likely to do and they know the same about us. I can say this honestly—no bullshit—I've always preferred to have Billy playing with me, rather than against me."

Something about the Chiefs seems to irritate George. He is at his angry best against them. Once, in Houston back in 1965, management told him to go sit down. They had this genuine Texas quarterback from Baylor, a snaggly-toothed young man named Don Trull, they wanted to try. Besides, the public had been threatening to lynch George.

Since they had roughly $300,000 invested in the kid, they gave him the ball and told him to make his first official start against the meanest team in the league, like some bubble-eyed rookie matador taking his *alternativa* against the largest bull in the province. It was too overwhelming. By the end of the second period, Trull was running all over the landscape. The state of Texas was barely big enough to contain him and Kansas City had a 17-0 lead. The Oilers' coach-of-the-year for that year, Hugh (Bones) Taylor, had to personally beg Blanda to start the second half. With a fine, smoking rage, Blanda took Houston to five touchdowns and a field goal, good for a 38-36 victory. Those were the days when George's miracles weren't remembered much past Monday afternoon's newspaper.

Again in 1968, this time with Oakland, he came on against the Chiefs in the third period after Lamonica had twisted his knee, and he set a club record for accuracy, completing 11 of 14 passes for 129 yards. That accomplishment was largely ignored, too. But now, on November 1, 1970, the cycle has turned. Miracle II, coming right up! Just wait a couple of minutes.

The game turns out to be one of those classic matches that

ought to be recorded on bronze and nailed to the wall at the Hall of Fame in Canton, Ohio. All it lacks is a reenactment of the Sack of Troy with the original cast at halftime. It is typical of others in the series. No one dominates the other. The same characters who have participated in earlier episodes take large parts in this one.

In the second period, Len Dawson, the boy-child quarter-back, barely 36 years of age, throws a 56-yard pass to Otis Taylor, the Kansas City receiver who can be the most devastating pass catcher in the league when the notion strikes him. Later, Taylor is to play a smashing role in the dramatic finish of this sweaty pageant. All he does now is set up the Chiefs' first touchdown, which fullback Wendell Hayes scores on a four-yard run.

"Frankly, it's hell standing over there on the sidelines watching," says Blanda. "Once you've been a first-string quarterback, it is rough watching somebody else do the job. Oh, I have respect for Daryle's skills. But a man wouldn't be a man if he didn't think he could do the job, too. Hell, that's what quarterbacking a football team is all about."

This is one of Lamonica's finer days. Daryle is an excellent counterpoint to Blanda. He is built along modern lines, tall and rangy like a gunfighter. His eyes are cold and serpentine. As a postgame interview he is marvelous, always moderate, always careful of his words, a regular IBM trainee-type. Late in the second quarter he passes three yards to Chester for the touchdown that ties it 7-7. Early in the third quarter he passes eight yards to the same receiver. Now Oakland is up, 14-7. But don't turn that dial, sports fans.

Now the temperature is dropping and the fragile sunlight is turning into a cold pink twilight. The lights come on and Jan Stenerud, a tritely blond Norwegian who kicks with his instep, sends a field goal flopping end-over-end into the net behind the Oakland goal posts. The ball travels 33 yards. Now Kansas City is behind by only four points, 14-10.

After this is all over, George Blanda, eyeballs blazing, will turn to Glenn Dickey of the *San Francisco Chronicle* and say, with exploding sarcasm: "So Jan Stenerud is the greatest field goal kicker who ever lived, is he?"

Matters begin to get hairy. With 5:14 left on the clock in the fourth period, with darkness moving in from all directions, Dawson calls a pass play from the Oakland 14. The ball is to go to Otis Taylor. The man covering him is Kent McCloughan, a cornerback whose love of the game is fading so quickly that this will be his final year in the league. They play bump-and-run defense a lot, these two old American League clubs. Somebody bumps McCloughan and down he goes. It isn't supposed to happen quite that way. The defensive back is supposed to bump the receiver as he comes off the scrimmage line, not the other way around.

"I was shoved," McCloughan yowls afterwards.

"Who is there to complain to now?" asks Honest Al Davis.

So Taylor is untended in the end zone. Len Dawson, far too slender and much too pretty-looking to impersonate the fine quarterback he really is, lays the pass in there and Kansas City is ahead 17-14.

In a sense, Len and George are soul brothers. Several National League clubs looked at Dawson and decided that he would be better suited to modeling sweaters and bathing trunks. He found shelter in the American League and proceeded to become one of its first great heroes. "Isn't that a lot of crap?" asks George Blanda. "They called me a castoff quarterback and they called Len Dawson a castoff quarterback. The NFL gave us both a raw deal, we went to the new league where we did well and they call us castoffs. Hell, Johnny Unitas was released by Pittsburgh before he became what he became with Baltimore. Would anyone have guts enough to call him a castoff? Isn't that what he is? I mean, if we are, isn't he?"

Now there is 1:08 left in the game. It is third down and 11 yards to go on the Oakland 40-yard line. This is not a good situation for Oakland. There is no reason to expect Stenerud to fail to kick a field goal that would put the decision hopelessly out of range. There are still two time-outs left to Dawson as he looks at the Raider defense.

Up in the radio booth, announcer Bill King, a smallish man with mountain goat chin whiskers, is letting his voice idle.

In his heart, he suspects that the game is over, the Raiders have lost and it will be a long, dull plane ride home. Bill King is one of those great undiscovered talents. There are not many men who describe football games better than he does. But he suffers from the fact that Oakland has no image. It is simply something that keeps the other half of the San Francisco Bay Bridge in place. He broadcasts over KNEW, which is neither the most powerful nor the most affluent station in Northern California. In the next few weeks, he will (a) stir hysteria over George Blanda to such a level that hippies in Berkeley coffee houses will be impressed by this ancient football player who sounds like John Wayne and looks like Eddie Arnold and he will (b) gain some national prominence in his own right.

He is just sitting there, like Russ Hodges getting ready to describe Bobby Thomson's home run. Something is going to happen that will alter his career too. His catch phrase, "Holy Toledo," will become as famous as Hodges's "The Giants Win The Pennant . . . The Giants Win The Pennant . . . The Giants Win The Pennant." It will reach the point where the mayor of Toledo, Ohio, will call him and say, "Bill, in our town we usually say, 'Holy Oakland,' or 'Holy George Blanda.' We thought you'd like to know."

King is also having some precognitive flashes. He senses something large is about to happen. He is afraid to say it. So he just idles.

"This is one of those stories, I think, that writers who look for that sort of thing were angling for today. Billy Cannon playing against his old teammates after playing seven years as an Oakland Raider . . . the first pass he caught today was a big one . . . it kept that drive, on a third-down play well back in Kansas City's own territory, and from that time on they marched inexorably down for the score that got the Chiefs in front."

He seems to know that the day will belong to an ex-Houston Oiler. He just selects the wrong one.

On the field, which is illuminated now only by the stadium
lights, the Chiefs line up in what appears to be a sure passing
formation. Gloster Richardson flanks to the left, with Nemiah
Wilson of Oakland covering him. Otis Taylor stations himself on
the right. Dawson takes the snap and Bill King quickly identifies
what is about to happen.

"Here's the bootleg by Dawson running to the right himself,"
he shouts. "He's got a first down! He's down to the 35 . . . he's
brought down on the 29. There's a flag. There's Ben Davidson
being jumped on by one of the Chiefs . . . two more Chiefs
come in . . . there's a big pile-up . . . Taylor and Davidson are
going at it . . . there are at least eight Chiefs . . . here come all
the Raiders . . . Holy Toledo! . . . it's a free-for-all . . . now
another fight breaks out . . . there are too many of them going
for me to tell you . . . one stops, another breaks out . . ."

Tripped up, Dawson had sprawled in the frost, face down. He
was happily contemplating his success, when Ben Davidson's
right knee struck up a nodding acquaintance with the small of
his neck. This is the sort of thing that Gentle Ben, the Raiders'
malevolent defensive end, does so beautifully. He is a person-
able lad with a bright red lumberjack's mustache. He has two
real passions in life. He likes to ride his motorcycle through
lonely Mexican mountains. He also enjoys knocking hell out of
people when they least expect it. This time he has been
watched. The air is full of fluttering hankies, thrown by
officials.

That should have finished the Raiders right there. They
should have been penalized. They should have lost. They damn
near did. They should have come away from Kansas City with a
3-3-1 record. But destiny had drawn George Blanda into its
loving arms. Now Otis Taylor is advancing on Gentle Ben. His
eyeballs are communist-flag red. By any standard, Otis is not an
easygoing man, no more than Davidson is. He fairly crackles. He
begins to beat on Ben something fierce. The officials excuse
Taylor for the rest of the afternoon. Then they step off a
penalty to the Oakland 14. They have decided that Davidson is
guilty of piling on, which seems reasonable.

"They make such a big deal out of those miracle games," says Blanda. "But think of this: If Taylor doesn't jump Ben, we're dead. I don't kick any field goal. We lose. Circumstance is what made me a miracle worker. The situations came up and I was there. That's all there is to it."

The officials, led by referee Bob Finley, take the ball down to the Oakland 14 and tell Dawson that he has a first down. Honest Al Davis blows smoke out of his nostrils. He and Finley have this vendetta. Its roots are lost in the distant past. They do not love each other. Now Davis is convinced that the Raiders have been treated unfairly. So is middle linebacker Dan Connors. He marches back and forth between officials.

"Wait a minute," he screams, "wait a minute. If Taylor was thrown out of the game, that's a 15-yard penalty against them for unsportsmanlike conduct. That's offsetting penalties. If you don't penalize them too, I'll walk off the field and take the rest of the Raiders with me. Just how the hell will that look on national television?"

On the bench, George Blanda moves forward, watches the brawl and decides that his time could be better spent warming up. In another era, in another life-style with the Chicago Bears, he would have been one of the first people on the field, swinging his fists. But experience teaches a man many things. One of them is: You can't help your ball club if you've broken your hand swinging on somebody's helmet. Another is: If they throw you out of the game, it is difficult kicking field goals or throwing passes from the locker room.

"I really don't know what's going on here," says King, admitting something few sportscasters would dare reveal. "Connors is walking around out there. He's burning behind the ears. Morris Stroud comes onto the field . . . double tight ends for Kansas City now . . . there's Connors walking across the field to talk to John Madden . . . this has been a confusing sequence of events . . . our producer, Ron Fell, makes a point . . . they're talking to the television people . . . maybe they're going to check the videotape on that controversial play that started the free-for-all."

This turns out to be a fine, fanciful, far-looking thought. They are doing no such thing. Even in an age when electronic machines put millions of dollars into professional football, human judgment is the only acknowledged authority on the field. What they are doing is asking the cameraman where the line of scrimmage is.

"If they move this ball back," muses King, "don't think this place won't come apart. Here they go . . . now the Chiefs are fighting among themselves . . . Dave Hill is getting it pretty good from Jim Tyrer . . . now the ball is being moved back . . . now we've got a declining signal . . . Kansas City caught an unsportsmanlike conduct penalty, which offsets the personal foul . . . so the play will be run over."

One unsuccessful running play later, the Chiefs punt into the end zone and the Raiders take over on their own 20-yard line. There are only 40 seconds left when Lamonica passes to Fred Biletnikoff, who slants in and takes the ball into his hands on the midfield stripe. He staggers three more yards with Chiefs dangling from his chin strap.

"There are 23 seconds left," says King. "The Raiders are 47 yards away, with one time-out left. It's too far for a touchdown, considering the time, and it's too far away for a decent percentage field goal."

This is when professional football grabs the nation, when it ceases to be organized mayhem and turns into chess on a meadow. It is this curiously cerebral quality to the game that gives it its mass appeal. The violence is taken for granted, a fact of living. Now one team is maneuvering. It is no longer a sport, it is a 100-yard war and everyone sitting in front of a television set is either a quarterback or he is George S. Patton.

So Lamonica does what everyone at home would do. He decides to throw two quick passes to receivers who will catch the ball and step out of bounds, thus stopping the clock. He will try to move in 20 yards closer, so Blanda will be closer to a field goal. His first throw is to Chester, who gets hit before he can get out of bounds on the 43.

"The clock is still running," says Blanda. "It's cold and I'm

feeling it. Just when I start to worry about having enough time
to warm up, a Chief gets hurt."

Unaware that he is giving aid and comfort to the enemy,
safety man Jim Kearney is flopping around on the frozen turf.
His injury, which is minor, stops the clock with 12 seconds left.
Blanda, ever the fatalist, cannot help thinking that if a Kansas
City defensive back had not been hurt, there probably wouldn't
have been time enough for Oakland to even get into a huddle.

"An incredible break," says King up there in the booth.

"Still, it would take a miracle kind of play at this moment to
win or tie," says King's color man, Scotty Stirling, who has over
the years served the Raiders as a beat writer for the *Oakland
Tribune*, as a publicity director and as general manager while
Davis was away fighting the war against the infidels as the last
commissioner of the American Football League.

So a miracle play is needed, according to Scotty Stirling,
whose Scottish and Jewish ancestors were pragmatic enough to
believe that no descendant of theirs would ever meddle with
extrasensory perception right there on the radio. On cue,
Warren Wells flanks left and Fred Biletnikoff flanks right in a
double wing formation. Lamonica passes to Chester, who jumps
out of bounds at the 41, a gain of two yards. Now Scotty stops
thinking about miracles, pro tem. So does Bill King. On the
Oakland bench, Madden, who looks like a large red teardrop in
the onrushing midwestern winter, yells for George Blanda.

"George, you have to kick it," says the younger man.

"No problem," says the older man. "We've got it. It's all
over."

This is amazing confidence, considering that in the first game
of the regular season, at San Diego, Blanda had failed to win a
victory. He had missed a field goal from 32 yards out with 1:55.
The score had remained tied and Bob Ortman, columnist for the
San Diego Tribune, had kissed the odd old gentleman goodbye
with the following words, which Ortman later had to chew
without benefit of milk or sugar: "As a kicker, Blanda is fading
away. He appears unsteady at field goal time, like Ben Hogan
hanging over a putt."

That was a predictable response. For the 11,377th time since he went out for the varsity at the University of Kentucky in 1945, George Blanda had been pronounced dead by the press. Shoot, he was just starting to live.

"Just hit it like you always do," says Madden.

"Give it hell, George," says Lamonica, his holder. "I'll give you a good hold. I promise."

Lamonica kneels at the 48-yard line and yells something to center Jim Otto. It makes no difference what he says, not really. Athletes are always screaming brave, incomprehensible words at each other in the heat of battle.

"I looked up and there was Buck Buchanan lined up in the middle," says Blanda later. "This is the same guy who tries to kill me a year later. There he is, all 6-7 of him. He wants me to either kick the ball over him or through him. What he really wants to do is block it, any way he can. Behind him is this Stroud who is 6-10 and ought to be doing something constructive with his life, like playing basketball. This is going to have to be a high kick.

"Now it doesn't have to be the highest kick of my life. Once, when I was with the Chicago Bears, they sent me out to try a field goal against the Los Angeles Rams at the Coliseum in L.A. I line up and there's Big Daddy Lipscomb. He's a 6-8 tackle and standing on his shoulders is Don Burroughs, a defensive back who is only 6-5. I'm supposed to get the ball over 13-1 of defensive players! The next year they outlawed all that."

So George Blanda measures two steps backward and waits. He concentrates on the spot where Lamonica will place the ball, with the laces forward. Jim Otto, the center, snaps the ball. It comes to rest just perfectly. In order to gain the proper altitude, Blanda hits it a little low with his right toes. His form is always the same, it hasn't altered since he joined the Chicago Bears, back when Truman was president and Dagmar was the fiercest thing on the tube and Tommy Henrich was playing right field for the Yankees.

"The ball got up quick and I knew it was going over," he says. "I didn't sweat. It was 48 yards from the right hash mark.

The damn thing was good by a yard. There were three seconds left on the clock and we ran it out on a kickoff. That 17-17 tie turned the season around. Suddenly we were in first place by ourselves."

Up in the booth, King's tonsils are twanging furiously. This was the start of something incredible, something a sportscaster can hear on a special record put out by the station or the network and called: "Bill King Describes George Blanda's Moments of Glory."

"Lamonica will spot at the 48. It's snapped. It's down. It's good. It's good. It is good. George Blanda has kicked a 48-yard field goal. Three seconds are left on the clock. Kansas City will have a chance to run back the kickoff. Holy Toledo! Holy Toledo! One thing I overlooked, Scotty, in this now 17-17 game was 6-10 Morris Stroud, who was under the crossbar, leaping as if he were trying to block a Wilt Chamberlain dunk shot. George's field goal effort cleared the bar—it's difficult to say from here—maybe a yard."

In the visitors' bathhouse, the writers are anxious to hear some heroic words. George disappoints them. When he stands astride his world, he has a tendency to fall back on princely platitudes. This is a rogue, sure enough.

"This was just another kick," he says, with maddening simplicity. "It was just like all the rest. The real heroes were Daryle Lamonica and Tom Keating and Jim Otto. Write about them."

This is a grand gesture, straight out of the purple past. This is something that football folk heroes did when George Blanda was a small boy. It suits George to drag it out now. Let those varmints with the notepads take that cliché and chew it. There are two or three or, even, four George Blandas. Here is a simple man, a complex man, a compound man. Here is a man tough-as-hell who won't get caught in your coal mines. No sir!

The air is desperately cold. The sky is dark. George Blanda showers long, shaves his beard which has been growing since Thursday because of his devotion to routine, and walks outside. Some children rush up. He signs their scorecards. He glares at an adult who asks for the same thing. He will not fly back with the team. Betty is waiting outside. There is a postgame party.

He thinks that this is just another football game, one that will fade and be forgotten with the rest. He is wrong, dead wrong. The immortal stars now favor him. Nothing he will do for the next few months will go wrong. After only 20 seasons in professional football, George Blanda is an overnight sensation. The nation has been watching. Telegrams are pouring in.

"On behalf of the senile wrecks of America, we salute you!" wired an Over-40 Club from Los Angeles. "After watching last two Sundays we have thrown away our Geritol bottles."

Big deal. Where were these people when George Blanda needed them in 1960 or 1961? That's when it really hurt, when folks kept calling him the champion quarterback of the Mickey Mouse League. That was when George was 31 and 32 and pride hadn't been stretched as far as it could go. Screw those well wishers. He and Betty, blonde and still brilliantly bright, are going to a party.

EPISODE 4

Cocktail glasses are clinking and invited guests and sundry dignitaries are making less-than-memorable remarks to each other. The 17-17 tie between Oakland and Kansas City is a fact of life. Tom Kole, trucking genius and expatriated Pole who has shortened his name, has invited the Blandas to a social event. This is the man who has set George Frederick Blanda up in business, who has even got the quarterback into the horse-breeding business.

Tom Kole is a smart man, barely 42, who moves from trucking firm to trucking firm, taking his best employees with him. George likes him and trusts him. They are both mid-western Slavs on the make. Soul brothers.

There is cold shrimp with red sauce. There is liquor. There are small, tasteless sandwiches set out on silver trays. There are elderly black waiters who never heard of Willie Lanier or Buck Buchanan and still shuffle through force of habit. They blend with the woodwork. Athletes are present at this function, along with businessmen, friends, fans.

Out of the darkened crowd steps Billy Cannon. His face is so overpoweringly familiar that it is difficult to think of him as anything but a teammate, a colleague.

"George," he says, "when you came out on that field, I turned to somebody—I forget who it was—and I said, 'This is a tie ball game. I know there's no way old George is going to miss this one.' Damn, that's how it turned out."

Blanda grins appreciatively. The best kind of compliment is the one that comes from a man you've played with and against. Now the miracles will come so fast, it will be difficult remembering them all.

EPISODE 5

There was a time when Ron Fell was considered the boy wonder of Oakland radio, which is very much similar to being thought of as the theatrical genius of Hamtramack, Michigan. Nevertheless, the lad has a flare. He was still a junior in college when KNEW hired him. He was their first-round draft choice. Now he is producer of Oakland Raider football broadcasts. an item which permits the staff and management of KNEW to continue living in their splendid suite of offices above Jack London Square.

Now Fell is in one of the spare studios, playing with records, sound effects and bits of tape. He is creating. He is helping the George Blanda miracle streak get some of the national publicity it so richly deserves. He is putting together a "promo," which is radio-talk for a house ad. Fell grins wickedly while he works. Several hours later, he steps out of the studio, crooks his finger toward a disc jockey and asks him to listen to the result.

The thunderous, sound-of-doomsday music from *2001: A Space Odyssey* comes on first. It is followed by someone imitating Arch Obler, the old radio suspense king. The voice is straight out of "Inner Sanctum," which was popular when Blanda was in college.

"Welcome," says the fraudulent Obler, "to The Perils of George Blan-DAH!"

Now there is a flashback to Bill King describing the madness at Kansas City. The words are sharp and even more exciting now that everyone knows how the game came out.

The "Inner Sactum" voice returns, along with the music from *2001*.

"Can George do it again? Tune in, same time, same station, for another episode in The Perils of George Blanda. See if George can do it again."

Fell is still grinning. As the weeks go by reality will come to mirror his art. No matter how gaudy his promos sound, George Blanda will discover a way to make them appear mundane in comparison. The streak is on.

EPISODE 6

"Age is not all decay; it is the ripening, the swelling, of the fresh life within. . . ."   —George MacDonald

"If wrinkles must be written upon our brows, let them not be written upon the heart. The spirit should not grow old."
                                                   —James A. Garfield

"It is always in season for old men to learn."   —Aeschylus

"Few persons know how to be old."   —La Rochefoucauld

"As long as you can play the game of football, nobody should ask you for a birth certificate."   —Erich Barnes

"When I was 28 and George Blanda was 36, I thought he was an old quarterback. Now I'm a 36-year-old sports writer and I get offended when somebody refers to John Brodie as an 'old quarterback' just because he's 36."   —Wells Twombly

"That George Blanda must be crazy as hell, running around a football field at his age. One good whack from a defensive lineman and he could be crippled."   —Alex Karras

"You can't hurt a Polack."   —George Blanda

EPISODE 7

After all these years, the nation is just now starting to learn that there is a football player named George Blanda. Where have you been hiding, old fellow? Reporters are crawling all over the place. Could it really be true that George is 43, going on 44? And what in the hell is he doing on a football field?

On the other side of the Nimitz Freeway, directly across from the Oakland-Alameda County Coliseum Complex is a silver-and-black office building. Parked outside is a silver-and-black Cadillac. At the top of the stairs is a huge room with a silver-and-black desk in it. Seated behind it is Al Davis, wearing black slacks, a black Banlon shirt and a silver sweater. He identifies very closely with his football team.

"So ... ah ... you ... ah ... want to know about George Blanda?" he says to a reporter. "Well ... ah ... he works for our little football team. He's ... ah ... a place kicker and a quarterback and ... ah ... they tell me he's about 43 years old, going on 40. He's ... ah ... two years older than I am and I really look up to him."

The Davis voice is sweeter than usual, because he is in a mood to put somebody on. He considers himself a genius at the art. No one has the heart to tell him that when he is putting somebody on, he gives himself away by spacing his words with "ah."

"Well, George is with our club because he gets the job done. We're not interested in keeping him because he's some kind of freak. You could have a whole team of guys in their mid-40s, only they wouldn't be physically able to do the job.

"I think in some respects, George is bitter. I don't blame him. He got a very raw deal in the National Football League. He has a perfect right to be bitter about the way the Chicago Bears treated him. With the exception of Johnny Unitas, I think he was as good a quarterback as anyone when he was in his prime. He never got a chance to show it in Chicago. They always had somebody else they were anxious to use.

"At Houston he was a fantastic quarterback. He was practically a one-man offense. Look at some of the things he did in the early years of the American Football League. They said that our pass defenses weren't good. Maybe they weren't but George did some fantastic things. He passed for seven touchdowns in one game.

"When I was an assistant coach with the Chargers, we had an

outstanding defensive line, as good as a lot of them around today. Well, George beat us for the championship two years in a row. Another thing about George is that he is practically a walking history of pro football's modern era—you know, the years since World War II. He's played in both leagues and he's the only man whose career has spanned four decades."

The silver-and-black telephone rings. Some general manager from another club is on the line. Al Davis turns away. His voice gets even sweeter—honey being poured over velvet. He and George Blanda go well together. Football is life, bread, mother and father to both of them.

But the times, they are a'changing. Younger men take the game less seriously. They have less pride and less poise. Why, do you know, says George Blanda, that one of Oakland's defensive tackles, Art Thoms, showed up for the New York trip dressed in overalls and wearing a railroad engineer's cap and carrying a Snoopy lunch bucket? What kind of crap is that?

EPISODE 8

All week long the promo with the Arch Obler voice spins along on KNEW. Everyone laughs and thinks it's funny. At practice, tackle Tom Keating imitates it until some of the Raiders suspect he did the original.

The next opponent on the Oakland schedule is Cleveland and this rouses another of the old furies that sleep in George Blanda's soul. When he was with the Chicago Bears, he had this traumatic experience with the Browns. The All-America Conference, the first postwar attempt at starting a new football league, had just collapsed in a smoking pile of unpaid bills. Three of the survivors were taken into the National Football League. The other five clubs were mercifully destroyed.

The All-America Conference perished because one club had simply been too strong. The Cleveland Browns had strangled competition. They had Otto Graham, Mac Speedie, Marion Motley, Dante Lavelli, Dub Jones, Lou Rymkus—Lord, you name them.

"But our great coach, George Halas, didn't believe the

Browns were that good. The first time we played them, he spent the whole week before getting us psyched down by telling us how bad they were. 'Champions of a Mickey Mouse League,' he'd say. Hell, we wouldn't have been surprised if they had come out wearing skirts," Blanda recalls. "Well, they just rip our guts out. They beat us 42-21 and, as they say, the score didn't indicate how bad we played. We get them on our schedule two years later and here's Halas saying the same thing. Damned if they don't whip us 39-10 this time."

Never in his life, not once in 21 seasons, has George Blanda played on a football team that has beaten the Cleveland Browns. This is a point of pride. And those little points sometimes burn holes in George's brain.

Watching Blanda's passion for vengeance on the Browns utterly amazes Keating. Younger players tend to be blasé about such things. George says he is, but he isn't.

"George is the damndest person I've ever met," Keating admits. "He's so mature on one level, but on another he's as enthusiastic as a kid. God, in training camp, he's like a rookie. Most of the veterans privately think camp is a drag. But George and the rookies are bouncing around. I really think Blanda thinks it's fun. For him, I guess it is.

"Physically and mentally, he's like a 25-year-old. He firmly believes that he could take a good team and quarterback it all the way to the Super Bowl, even at his age. Watching him I'm beginning to suspect that age is mental condition and nothing more.

"In the huddle the guy can be fierce. There are times when I'm glad I'm a defensive lineman. If you miss a block, you hear about it. He really likes Gene Upshaw, but if Gene blows one, he gets it like everyone else. It's really something when George goes into a rage. It's more than temper, it's solid fury. Sometimes you wonder what it must have been like to have broken in when George did, back in the late 1940s. God, did everybody act like that? Maybe all modern players are soft and they don't know it.

"But there's another side too . . . you're always finding sides

to George you never knew existed before . . . anyway, there's
this other side to him. Most guys his age wouldn't go to the
team parties because of the difference in ages and all. But
there's George having a hell of a time. He's a very witty man.
But there's a competitive side to his humor, too. Try needling
him and he'll cut you down to two inches tall with a remark.
He's also a great mimic. He does an imitation of . . . well, never
mind.

"The young players, especially the rookies, call him Mr.
Blanda. Some of them are afraid to talk to him, I think. You
know it's hard for me to think of George as being that much
older than me, but he was a big name with the Bears when I was
just starting grammar school in Chicago. Oh, sure, I told him he
was my boyhood idol.

"He's going to have to be told to retire. He won't quit on his
own. He's always talking about 'this time I was going to quit' or
'that time when I almost retired.' But that's just him talking.
He'll play until he's 55. I hope he doesn't quit before I do."

He won't. Nothing to worry about, Tom.

EPISODE 9

In the entire span of human history, no city has ever suffered
so sorely from comparison to a neighboring community. It is
the roughest sort of geographic break. If only that other town,
the one with the golden image, were located on the other side
of the world. If only that accursed bay were a few hundred
miles wider, there might be some hope for Oakland.

But across the water, in all its picture-postcard prettiness,
with all its quaint little cable cars and shimmering lights, its
magnificent bridges and nude cocktail waitresses, lies San Francisco—the modern Xanadu. It is the Pearl of the Occident, the
most cried over, sung about, devoutly worshiped town in the
world. It evokes uncontrollable emotions.

Ancient Baghdad would have had trouble competing if it had
been situated just eight miles away from San Francisco, on the
wrong side of a bridge that seems to have only one socially
acceptable end. What chance has Oakland ever had?

The situation is almost laughable. San Francisco is a painted beauty, cooing and beckoning seductively. Oakland is a blue-collar worker with stubble on its chin, beer on its breath and a hard hat on its head. San Francisco has art and drama. Oakland is the international headquarters of Hell's Angels motorcycle gang. San Francisco is Fisherman's Wharf and Telegraph Hill and Golden Gate Park. Oakland is housing developments and oil storage tanks and rusty freighters. San Francisco is Victorian mansions and pastel shades. Oakland is warehouses and gritty, gray tones.

When major league sports came to Northern California, the franchises were plopped down in San Francisco. No one ever even vaguely considered settling in Oakland. Want to see a game? Come across the Bay Bridge. The 49ers had been in business 15 years when the American Football League was created. Don't get the idea that there was any prodding desire to place a team in Oakland. The eighth AFL club was going to Minneapolis-St. Paul.

But somebody got to the Minnesota syndicate and slipped them a National Football League franchise. Oakland wasn't even the second choice. Atlanta was. But Barron Hilton was the owner of the Los Angeles Chargers and he said he'd be damned if he was going to have the only club on the West Coast. How about Seattle? Too far from Los Angeles. Well, then would Oakland be acceptable? Why not? That was fine, except there wasn't any place to play there.

The owners of this orphaned franchise tried to rent the University of California's stadium in Berkeley. The board of regents all but gagged at the thought of having people who took money openly to play football polluting their fine amateur atmosphere. So the Raiders dragged themselves reluctantly across the Bay to Kezar Stadium, which they were able to use on weekends when the 49ers were out of town. They expected that 40,000 people would watch their first match, against Houston. After all, the Oilers had some recognizable names— Billy Cannon, George Blanda, John Carson. Only 12,703 showed up.

The next season they slithered down the peninsula to Candle-stick Park; attendance got worse and so did the Raiders. They became the source of unrelenting sarcasm. On the Captain Satellite television show, a seven-year-old girl informed the host that she had a joke she wanted to tell.

Okay, said Captain Satellite, hoping it was something clean, let us hear what you have to say, dear.

"What has 22 legs and lives in the cellar?" she asked.

"I don't know," said Captain Satellite.

"The Oakland Raiders," she yelled, snorting at the punch line.

It was about this time that the majority stockholders, Wayne Valley and Ed McGah, decided that something drastic would have to be done.

Somebody finally explained to them that you couldn't give sex away in San Francisco if the word Oakland was somehow associated with it. Better a temporary stadium on the eastern side of the Bay than all the playing fields of San Francisco combined. So they erected a plain pipe rack of a stadium called Frank Youell Field. The place had a tendency to quiver dangerously when the crowd stomped its feet, begging for a rally, but there were two undeniable charms: (1) there was a crowd present to stomp its feet and (2) Frank Youell Field was situated in the proper town.

Then Valley, a former Oregon fullback who looks like he could catch bullets with his teeth, went after Davis and promised him time and money enough to do something about the ratty condition of the playing roster.

"Somebody told me that when Al was recruiting in college he was so clever at picking regional accents and voice inflections he could convince a prospect that he was from their part of the nation," Valley said. "They say he could just about convince a black kid that he had grown up in the ghetto. Man like that is a genius."

And "the Genius" Davis remains to this very day. Valley cannot go more than five minutes without using the term to describe his partner. There is no evidence that the two men love

one another. But love is not an essential emotion in The
Organization. Pride and poise are.

The Organization gave Oakland a consistent winner. Because
of a consistent winner Oakland and Alameda County gave the
Raiders a Coliseum—nothing frilly, just a huge concrete soup
tureen, really. And finally, on November 8, 1970, on a wet and
clammy afternoon, Oakland finally got what it had lacked so
long, a tourist attraction: George Frederick Blanda.

EPISODE 10

In the dressing room before game time, Blanda is thinking
about another old wound. Scars form but those wounds never
heal. Once, with the Bears, he had finally become the first-string
quarterback. Halas was saying such pretty things about him.
Then a couple of Browns gave him his only serious football
injury in 21 seasons, a shoulder separation. He never really got
his job back.

On another occasion . . . ah, let George tell it: "Here comes
that Lou Rymkus . . . he was my first coach in Houston, but as
a player he was a sneaky son of a bitch who was always looking
to blindside you . . . I catch him coming up out of the corner of
my eye and I figure, it's just him versus me . . . Polack against
Polack . . . I figured I'd get him in his bad knee . . . I hit him as
hard as I ever hit anyone and I knocked him ass-over-shoulder.

"Now Cleveland's so damn mad at me they send two guys
down field the next time I kick off and their only assignment is
take old George apart. They came pretty close, too. It was one
hell of a fistfight. I never did like those damn Browns. You got
to respect them as a football team, but I could never get very
fond of them."

Nobody realizes it when the two teams take the field, but
Blanda's field goal in Miracle II at Kansas City the week before
has turned the whole season around for Oakland. Now the
Raiders lead the Western Division of the American Football
Conference. What George Blanda will do today, in Miracle III,
will give them "momentum," to steal an important phrase from
the *Coaches' Book of Standard Clichés* (revised).

Early in the afternoon it appears that there will be no need
for any further witchcraft by elderly athletes. As they so often
do, the Raiders bounce out in front but then . . . well . . . they
sort of lose interest until the fourth quarter.

"Our club plays best under pressure, so we kind of like to let
the pressure build," Blanda is fond of saying.

Everything starts to fade for Oakland until, suddenly, the
Raiders look up early in the fourth period and discover that
their 13-0 lead is now a 17-13 deficit. Pressure enough? Well, it
will only get worse. Lamonica drops back to pass. The football
just barely departs from his delicate fingers when an enemy
agent, Ron Snidow, attacks from the blind side. It is perfectly
legal. The resulting collision puts undue stress on the bones and
ligaments in Daryle's left shoulder. Pain goes rattling through
his nerve endings and then ebbs. He barely notices that the pass
has fallen on the ground, incomplete. The crowd of 54,463,
which is either the 18th or the 19th or the 20th straight sellout
crowd at the Coliseum (where have you gone, Kezar Stadium?)
moans loudly enough for the noise to reach San Francisco.

Blessed numbness is spreading through the damaged tissues
when Lamonica comes trotting off the field, straight into the
anxious arms of a team physician. Only when the pain returns
will either of them have a clearer idea of whether Lamonica has
suffered a shoulder separation. As Daryle slumps backwards on
the bench, his eyes turn upward toward the Coliseum scoreboard.

Clearly this is a poor time to get bruised. There is only 10:05
left in the final period of a very important football match.

Madden turns and yells: "George!"

If it were fiction, the author would be unemployed. But this
is stark reality. On comes Blanda, who was throwing passes at
Kentucky when Madden was struggling with seventh-grade
math. Other people age. Only George Blanda, Hoyt Wilhelm and
Dorian Gray are exempt. And everybody knows Dorian
cheated.

Lamonica sits there, flexing and unflexing his left hand,
thankful that he hadn't been struck on the other side of his

body, the side he throws with. He is not permitted private pain. The television camera crew zooms in for a close-up. Photographers turn their lenses toward his face, gathering around him in a ghoulish pack. Cheerleaders and reporters, waiting for the game to end so they can get to the dressing room rapidly, move in for a better look. Lamonica draws a coat over his shoulder and looks hurt and disturbed, like a spaniel who has been grazed by a bus. Injured, he is no longer the Alpha Male, only a disabled athlete.

The Raiders punt. They get the ball back when Nemiah Wilson steals a pass in the end zone. There is 8:17 of working time left. Zip! Zip! Zip! Blanda completes three passes. Then it happens again—the curse of his career. He throws an interception. There is muttering and moaning in the press box. It grows louder and more vile when Cleveland moves in and kicks a field goal. Poor Lamonica is shattered. His fault! But how could he have avoided a blind-side charge?

"Here's another place where the miracle streak could have ended," Blanda says later. "If they hadn't blindsided Daryle, I wouldn't have even got in the game. Who the hell says Lamonica wouldn't have pulled the game out, too?"

Well, any astrologer can tell you 1970 was a big year for Virgos—George Frederick Blanda, born September 17, 1927 at Youngwood, Pennsylvania—and not so hot for Leos—Daryle Patrick Lamonica, born July 17, 1941 at Fresno, California. The stars were right, possibly for the first time in George's career.

Now there is 4:11 left and Blanda raises himself up for another glorious adventure—Miracle III. After the Kansas City game, what could he do for an encore? Ah, glad you asked.

The doctor was talking with Lamonica again as Blanda pitched a strike down the center of the field to Warren Wells from the Oakland 31. The play covers 31 yards, ten of which the Raiders give back on the next play when George gets pounded into the muck for a ten-yard loss.

Nothing to do but call 99-in-Y-in, Blanda's favorite pass play. The ball is supposed to go to Raymond Chester, who has defenders dangling from his wishbone. The rush is on, so George unloads to Fred Biletnikoff, throwing off balance as Cleveland linebackers bring him to earth.

Now age creeps up subtly on George Blanda. He is calling plays rapidly to keep the clock from killing him. He calls time out and walks over to the sidelines. He breathes hard. The humidity is stealing his breath. He slumps down, kneeling on one knee. Madden wants him to run. He wants to throw. Madden says okay.

"Hell, I've got the best set of pass receivers in professional football out there . . . Raymond Chester, Warren Wells and Fred Biletnikoff . . . what do I want to run the ball for? I tell Warren the ball is coming at him. It's going to be low and it's going to come fast, because I don't want any more interceptions. It's going to be 99-in-Y-in again and if Chester goes down the middle, the strong safety will try and nail him. That would leave Wells one-on-one on the cornerback. One-on-one, he's got to be tough."

The rush is murderous. The pass comes in low and fast, just as Blanda said it would. Wells, who has been playing in spurts all afternoon because of a deep shoulder bruise picked up in the Kansas City skirmish, clutches the ball up against his navel as he falls in the end zone for the tying touchdown. The outside back has been badly barbecued. A linebacker comes rushing up. Too late! The score is 20-20. There is 1:39 left. This was the 228th touchdown pass of George's career.

Now Lamonica's interest in football has returned. He stands up, almost knocking off the ice pack the doctor has been rubbing his shoulder with. Kent McCloughan snatches the ball away from a Cleveland receiver and Lamonica cannot feel even a sliver of pain. But Blanda's glands are pumping. No time-outs are left. So George throws incomplete passes, letting the pressure build, letting Miracle III seem even more incredible. He doesn't plan it that way, it just happens.

It is third down on Cleveland's 49. There are 16 seconds left when Jack Gregory assaults Blanda from behind. This was taken as singularly crude behavior. By way of response, George takes a

swing at Gregory. Now there are 12 seconds left. The pass goes
to fullback Hewritt Dixon, who crashes out of bounds on the
46. It is time now for the impossible.

Back Blanda marches until he is 52 yards away from the goal
posts. Between the touchdown and this field goal attempt,
George has been sucking air on the bench. He looks as old as
gnarled wood when somebody hands him an oxygen inhalator.
Only a few minutes later, he's back on the field, the Alpha Male
again. Seven seconds remain. Holding is Snake Stabler. The
regular man is Lamonica. But he is through for the day.

"I knew I was going to kick it," Blanda says. "I'm thinking,
just do it like you always do. When I go out onto the field, I
don't hear the crowd. I don't hear other players shouting at me.
I'm in a bubble. I'm going over the fundamentals of place
kicking my mind. Hell, I know I've got this field goal. I know
I've finally got the Cleveland Browns right where I want them.
The minute I hit the ball with my toe I knew it was good. I
didn't worry about the distance. I knew it was good."

Short of getting a gun and shooting straight, there is no
earthly means of restraining Bill King. He has a death grip on
the microphone. His eyeballs are blood red. His knuckles are
awash with sweat. His tonsils are twanging furiously.

"Waiting for the snap . . . fourth down . . . here it is . . . snap!
spotted down! It's kicked. That's got a *chance!* That is—good!
It's good! Holy Toledo! Holy Toledo! This place has gone wild.
Wheeee-U! I don't believe it! I do not believe it! There are three
seconds left in the game. If you can hear me, this place has gone
wild . . . the Oakland—gasp!—Raiders, 23! . . . the Cleveland
Browns—gasp!—20.

"George Blanda has just been elected king of the world! I
don't believe it! Holy Toledo! It went 53 . . . no . . . 52 yards!
George Blanda has just been elected king of the world!"

The latter remark is a trifle excessive. Kings rarely get elected
and there are at least 750 million mainland Chinese who not
only don't know George, but have no clear idea that Americans
play armored rugby and call it football. What the hell! King is
delirious and it sounds like a classy thing to say. So he says it.

This is the 251st field goal of Blanda's career and it touches off utter hysteria. In the stands people are kissing strangers and throwing things and making animal sounds. Madden keeps hugging players as they come off the field until he gets to George, who plops down on the bench. Somebody hands him a blob of ice. Instead of sucking on it, he rubs it across the back of his neck and grins wistfully like a heavyweight boxer who has just dropped a much younger opponent with 11 seconds to go in the final round.

"You know, John," he says. "That wasn't my longest field goal. I got a 55-yarder once in Houston."

It is an incredibly cool thing to say. Chances are Madden doesn't even hear. He is bouncing up and down, his red hair flapping, his red face crackling, his red belly jiggling. Now the Cleveland kickoff return man is flattened on his own 36 and the gun goes off. The two teams leave the field—the Browns stagger; the Raiders sprint. Near the dressing room door, Blanda sees a San Francisco newspaperman who has covered his adventures for years, first in Houston, now in Oakland. He pauses.

"Thank you for a wonderful column," he says. "I really appreciated what you said about me. Wonderful!"

This is the same George Blanda who goes inside and spends so much time in the shower avoiding the press that nearly all of the other Raiders will have left when he finally appears, innocently toweling himself off.

"Oh," says the maker of Miracle III, "you guys want to see me?"

He knows damn well they do. His lips move backwards into a tight, hard grin, followed by a throaty chuckle. George Blanda is dominating again.

Naturally the press is bubbling with enthusiasm, almost as if this latest piece of witchcraft had been performed by somebody with a typewriter. Blanda finds this mildly offensive. Do these same people ever come over after a poor performance and say something civil? Some newsmen, George suspects, are pleasant to athletes only when they want something. So he handles their vicarious sense of victory with astounding nonchalance. It is a superb performance, one that causes a veteran Blanda-watcher to want to applaud openly. The rogue in George is in full command.

"I don't get nervous about anything in football anymore," he says. "I've done everything. I kicked field goals. I've missed field goals. I've thrown touchdown passes that won games. I've had passes intercepted that lost games. What is there left to get excited over? That's why I'm so calm."

The rest of the nation is not. After ignoring him shamefully for better than two decades, the people of America are about to go stark, screaming mad over George. It has finally happened. He has outlasted just about everybody who ever said an unkind word about him or ever tried to bury him alive. Now he was rising above the herd, becoming—pardon the unavoidable cliché—a living, breathing legend.

EPISODE 11

Football players are having a party in Oakland. Newspaper-men are slamming away at their keyboards, making beautiful music. The customers are just now pulling off the freeways and, in varying states of sobriety, heading for their homes. Meanwhile back at the studio, high above Jack London Square, on the waterfront, Ron Fell is at it again. He is creating another masterwork out of tape and records and shoes and ships and sealing wax.

He emerges several hours later. There's that evil smirk again.

This week's KNEW promo is better than the week before. The Hallelujah Chorus comes on first, driving hard and loud. Now here's Bill King describing with that awful urgency of his "The Miracle at Kansas City." More Hallelujahs follow. "That was Sunday before last," says the narrator's voice. The Chorus builds to a smashing finish with King shouting, "It's Good! It's Good!"

"That was last Sunday," the narrator continues, "before the final three seconds." The Chorus is almost deafening now.

"This is George Blanda," says George Blanda's recorded voice. "I'll be here and I hope you will, too."

"We're sure George will be here," says the narrator, "but tune in Sunday to see if Bill King is. Can Bill come back after the past two Sundays or will he do this Sunday's game in Braille? Be here on KNEW when the Raiders and Broncos tangle direct from Denver."

Hallelujah! Hallelujah!

"Tune in to find out if George Blanda can kick one over the Rockies and through the goal posts."

Hal-lay-LU-yah! Beautiful!

Fell starts playing it immediately.

EPISODE 12

Now every man over 40 in the nation is young again. Now every man in his late 30s who was dreading his 40th birthday is looking forward eagerly to the real ripening of his years. Now the telephone is ringing insanely in the silver-and-black office building. Publicity director Tommy Grimes and his assistant Ken Bishop cannot handle all of the requests. The networks are sending crews over to make film clips. Will George cooperate?

Sports Illustrated has already placed Hamilton P. B. (Tex) Maule on board an airplane with instructions on how to get from the San Francisco airport to the Oakland Coliseum without being tempted by San Francisco's boiling flesh pots. John Peterson of the *National Observer* is begging for time. Both *Time* and *Newsweek* are interested. Good God, now the editor of *Slovak v Amerike* has discovered that George isn't really Polish, as he says he is in his more whimsical moments. Blanda is a fine old Slovak name and Mrs. Mary Blanda, the 75-year-old mother of the folk hero, was born in Prague.

Every columnist on every major paper in the nation gets on the horn and dials the Raiders' number. It's Pete Waldmeir calling from the *Detroit News* and Edwin Pope from the *Miami Herald* and Bill Gleason from the *Chicago Sun-Times* and Arthur Daily from the *New York Times* and . . . well, just about everyone except Jack Gallagher of the *Houston Post*.

Arnold Hano, a small, intense hornet of a man, free-lances for *Sport* magazine. He lives in Southern California and he is on

board a Hughes Air West flight, convinced that all he has to do
is call Blanda up and the old quarterback will gladly donate two
or three days of his time. It will not necessarily work out that
way.

"Do you know," says George, revealing yet another old
wound, "that in 21 years I have had only two national stories
written on me, both in the *Sporting News*, that weekly newspaper out of St. Louis. No magazine has ever done a piece on
me. Isn't that something?"

It turns out that Blanda's attitude toward publicity is similar
to the classic example of the spinster who is not so much sorry
that she never got married, only that she was never asked.

Hano arrives, introduces himself and asks to spend some time
with George. Just that day, Blanda has heard from *Sports
Illustrated*. They are sending out one of their agents to do a
three-part series for which they will pay plenty. So George
looks at Hano and says: "Where were you twenty years ago
when I needed you? I don't need you now. I've got this deal for
a three-part story for another magazine. I can't talk to you."

For a long while, Hano considers what George has told him.
Then he decides that Blanda is probably right. He sits down at
his typewriter and moralizes. It is probably the first time any
writer has really had some flash of insight into Blanda's
complex personality, which is like a piece of Oriental sculpture,
full of swirls and curlicues and inlays. He hates injustice and
stupidity, real or imagined. Sometimes he reacts openly. On
other occasions he can be extraordinarily subtle. The object is
to make the punishment fit the crime. If George is complex, he
is also simple: strive and succeed; adversity strengthens the soul;
never forget a friend, never forget an enemy; don't let the
bastards get you down.

"I am not here to bury George Blanda, but to praise him,"
Hano writes. "I am here to hammer out a likeness, hero-sized so
someday others will copy it in bronze and put it on the wall at
the Hall of Fame in Canton, Ohio. Bronze! Hell, pure gold
would be better.

"And I am here, mainly, to apologize for being so late. He's

right. Where was I twenty years ago, or at least ten? Where were
we all? We should not have needed twilight to recognize George
Blanda. He stood tall enough and splendidly bright at noon."

Those are fine, high-sounding words. George accepts the
apology and temporarily suspends Hano from his list of writers
who are not to be trusted. However there is an asterisk next to
the name.

"I don't know about this paragraph," he says, pointing
toward something very early in Hano's story, just before the
apology.

It tells of a small boy who comes up to Blanda in the dressing
room, begging an autograph, and is told, "Can't you let me get
dressed!" Hano thinks George should have been less grumpy.

"Those children shouldn't be in the dressing room anyway,"
says George. "They have no business being in there. The talk is
pretty gamey. Everyone is trying to get down after being up for
a football game. Why do parents bring their children anyway?
And how do they get in?"

And the magazine writer does not see George walking down
the long tunnel leading from the Oakland dressing room to the
players' parking lot. Hano does not see him moving slowly,
signing autographs, asking children from Oakland ghettos what
their names are, talking in a stagy, football hero's voice. He does
not see George come to a complete stop beneath the walkway
that leads between the Coliseum and the Sports Arena and let
the kids swarm all over him. Other Raiders are hustling through,
anxious to meet their wives and girl friends and get the party
started.

George Blanda stands there. It is something he likes. It is part
of being a professional football player. Some athletes hate it,
just like they hate watching films, hate going to meetings, hate
going to training camp. But Blanda enjoys. Hell, maybe he'll
play forever. Wouldn't that drive the writers nuts?

EPISODE 13

It is Thursday morning and the last geese of autumn are
flapping along in the heavy air over the Bay. The rainy season,

that smothering monsoon that passes for winter in Northern California, is moving closer with each ponderously dull gray day. In keeping with The Routine, which is just as important to George Blanda as The Organization is to Al Davis, the family will eat at the Grotto that evening. To dine somewhere else would be tempting nature. This is not a superstition, just The Routine.

Blanda is scheduled to have breakfast with a columnist at Alameda Joe's. (There is a Joe's of some sort in every Northern California community.) It is located next door to the Coral Reef, where the Blanda apartment is. The waitress has been listening to the Hallelujah Chorus promo all morning. She recognizes Blanda immediately.

"You'll do it," she says confidently.

"What?" says George, cocking one lupine eye.

"Kick the ball over the Rockies," she says. "You know, like in the ad on KNEW."

"If that is what it takes to win," Blanda muses, utterly amazed at what turns some people on.

This talk about his feuds with sports writers genuinely puzzles George. Someone has stated, in print, that win or lose, Blanda's disposition remains the same—bad.

"They're always talking about my dislike for writers," he says. "Well, it's not *all* writers, per se, it's *some* writers. One of them was Jack Gallagher of the *Houston Post*. He really had it in for me. Some of the things he wrote about me, I personally thought were libelous. If you put his game story up next to the one that appeared in the *Houston Chronicle*, you would have thought we had played two different games.

"Gallagher wouldn't even talk to me directly. He'd ask everybody else about me and then write something so slanted I couldn't believe it was me he was talking about. Gallagher was a good friend of the Oilers' publicity man, Jack Scott. Now there was a dandy, too. He hated athletes . . . called them 'dumb jocks' and laughed at them. He was supposed to be our public relations man. Well, he wanted to be general manager of the Oilers and he was always trying to boost Jacky Lee, our second-string quarterback in Houston, at my expense, and he fed this Gallagher stories.

"The other Houston writers were good to me . . . Bob Rule, Hal Lundgren, Harry Gage, Dick Peebles and old Frank Godsoe . . . of course, Frank smoked all the time and he'd lean way over and damn near burn a hole in your shirt while he talked to you. But at least he was an honest writer.

"But let me say this about writers . . . if a guy comes up and asks me something, I tell him, and I always had a good relationship with most writers. The only thing that really teed me off was, I'd know a writer and when things were going good it was 'Hi, George old buddy.' And when things were going bad, the writer wouldn't talk to you for five or six weeks at a time.

"Then, all of a sudden you do something and here's the writer back, yelling, 'George, old buddy,' again. I don't understand that. One of the best friends I have out here is Bill Feist of the San Jose papers. I can talk to him any time, whether things are going good or they're going bad. Now you take Glenn Dickey of the *San Francisco Chronicle*. He'll come around for a story one day and for the next six weeks he'll walk right by you and not even say hello.

"I'm a truthful person. I don't hem-haw around. Somebody asks me a question, I'll give them a straightforward answer. If I think somebody stinks, I'll tell them. Why can't these writers be as straightforward? So after a while you learn you can't be honest with some writers. You have to be a politician with them or they'll stiff you good.

"I either like a person or I don't. You can figure out, without too much trouble, who's going to stiff you and who isn't. Bill Gleason, the *Chicago Sun-Times* columnist, is another great guy. I tell him anything and he's out trying to inform and entertain his readers. He's not trying to ruin some football player's career by printing something out of context and trying to make it sound sensational. There are a lot of guys who respect the fact that I've got a public image and that I'm telling them something privately, friend-to-friend.

"I never really had a bad time with a writer until I got to Houston. Here was this Gallagher and he was always tearing down the Oilers and calling the American Football League 'Mickey Mouse.' I honestly think he would have liked to have run the Oilers out of town so the National Football League could come in. Here's a writer in our town, running down our league. Jack taught me to be on the alert for guys who are ready to cut and stab.

"There was another guy on the *Houston Post* who was a cutter, too, Steve Perkins. I think those writers helped give me a reputation for being against the press, because of my reaction to what they did to me. You'd be surprised how few of the stories in the *Post* ever quoted me directly. It was all hearsay and I caught hell for it."

As it so often happens, destiny gave Blanda a chance to strike back. Don't think he wasn't aware of the deadline schedule difference between morning and afternoon newspapers. Some athletes never give it a thought. But George knew that morning journalists have only a few minutes after the game to get downstairs to the locker room, get some fast quotes and get back to the press box to send their reports over Western Union wires. Newsman employed by afternoon papers work—if that is the word you care to use—at a more fashionable pace. Their copy doesn't have to be in their offices until something like 4 A.M. So they putter around the dressing room longer. They head out for a meal and either work at home or at their desks at the paper.

So, on the afternoon when he worked his 1965 Miracle, running up 38 points against the Kansas City Chiefs in the second half at Rice Stadium, he decided he'd go for a grand slam. He had shown the Oiler management that it had made a horrible error replacing him with Don Trull. Now he bore down on the *Houston Post*.

After the game, the Houston writers surrounded Blanda in the dressing room. There was the villain from the *Post* who had beaten and flayed him. Standing next to the villain was the guy in the white cowboy hat who worked for the *Chronicle* and who had tried to be fair about this latest quarterbacking crisis.

"No comment!" roared Blanda.

"Does that mean me, too?" asked the *Chronicle* representative.

"It means everybody!" said George.

So the writers shrugged and left. Just another grumpy day for grumpy George. The man from the *Post* went back and pounded out something for the morning paper to the effect that Blanda had insulted the press by refusing to talk after one of his finest performances. The *Chronicle* man went to his home in Spring Branch, way out in the Houston suburbs, to do his work. He had barely walked in the front door when the telephone rang.

"Hello," said Blanda's voice, very pleasantly. "Sorry about that scene in the dressing room. If I talked to you that son of a bitch from the *Post* would have heard and I wasn't going to give him anything. Now . . . what does the *Houston Chronicle* want to know about the game?"

The reliable writer got his story. The unreliable writer was vanquished and in his own media, too. The morning paper carried an embarrassing headline condemning Blanda's surly silence. The evening paper had a quote-littered news piece about George's triumph, which ran right next to a column that had Blanda chatting cheerily after the game.

Five years have passed and the same writer, once with the *Houston Chronicle* and now with the *San Francisco Examiner*, is having breakfast with Blanda in Alameda, right next to the Bay. And he is curious.

"George, you planned that in advance, probably in the shower," he says. "Did you realize how bad that would make the *Post* look?"

"You're damned right I did," Blanda says, bringing his lips together as tightly as he can draw them.

His eyes are the eyes of a wolf in winter, savoring old victories. He no longer needs sports writers. Despite the impressive records he set, kicking and passing, they never did a thing for him in Chicago, in Houston or prior to this time in Oakland. They couldn't take the time to interview him directly. Nobody ever did a national magazine piece on George Blanda in 21 years . . . only two stories in the *Sporting News.* To hell with the press. Television is making Blanda an American folk hero. Right now!

EPISODE 14

The water beyond the restaurant window is as black as a football game official's heart. Up the cut between Alameda and Jack London Square, the hills and towers of San Francisco literally shimmer in golden fantasy tones, blocked out every now and then by a passing freighter. Every Thursday night, George and Betty Blanda, accompanied by their daughter Leslie, sit at the same table, in the same seating arrangement. This evening, Hamilton P. B. (Tex) Maule has joined them.

He is living handsomely on a *Sports Illustrated* expense account. He is a former college roommate, at the University of Texas, of Blanda's two least-liked sports writers, Jack Gallagher and Steve Perkins. It makes no difference. Blanda likes Maule. It is part of the ambivalence in George's nature. Besides, he undoubtedly thinks that Maule has learned something since college—better taste in friends, perhaps.

Hamilton P. B. (Tex) Maule is a self-confessed genius, opinionated and ruthlessly stubborn. Once he assumes a stance, he will not flex a single sinew. He should be a smashing bore. It should be easy to dislike him. Instead, it is almost impossible to be anything but his friend. There is a certain baroque charm to his unyielding nature. Gaunt and mustang-faced, Maule is an archbishop among his fellow football writers, heavy with dogma and ready to defend the one true faith (his own!) until either 2 A.M. or until the free liquor runs out, whichever comes first.

Maule sits there watching George Blanda at play, bouncing around like a teenager, smiling and joking. *Drugstore cowboy* they used to call kids like that in Youngwood, Pa. back in the early 1940s.

"I'm ordering the turbot and salad," George says. "I've got to watch my weight. At my age, I gain three pounds walking by a bakery."

Autograph seekers are scurrying over from all corners of the Grotto. Blanda has been a steady customer every Thursday (and sometimes Fridays) since he came over to the Raiders from the Houston Oilers in 1967. But this is different. He's a folk legend now. Television—mighty television—has told the country so. It can't be a mistake.

George signs eagerly. He tells Maule that his biggest fans are middle-aged white businessmen and small black boys. The former identifies with him and he identifies with the latter. They seem to know it. Youngwood wasn't much more than a ghetto. The men were trapped. They either worked for the railroads or the thermostat company or they went away all week and swung a pick in the mines, returning only on the weekends, which was drinking time.

"We had a warm house and we all had serviceable clothes and we had food," says George, "but if my old man made more than $2000 it was one hell of a year. I didn't even know we were poor for a hell of a long time."

At the next table, a lush who has somehow wandered across the Bay Bridge to eat in Oakland, leans over and says, without much grace: "I'm from San Francisco and in a couple of weeks you guys are going to get cleaned out by the 49ers and John Brodie."

Blanda shakes his shaggy gray head and snorts. "John who?" he asks. ("God, I hope nobody tells Brodie I said that. He's a hell of a quarterback. I don't want him coming over here all angry or something," Blanda says later.)

Later on, two other Raiders, tackle Bob Svihus and defensive lineman Tom Keating, come by the Blanda table and sit down. These are two very important colleagues. Keating is a source of good conversation, being witty, inventive and somewhat arty. And Svihus! Ah, Svihus. He is George's lamb. He fancies himself a gin rummy player. He isn't. Blanda loves him.

"I have always wanted to write my autobiography and call it,

'George Blanda—Portrait Of The World's Greatest Gin Rummy Player.' Football is just a sideline. My real sport is gin rummy," Blanda says. Svihus winces.

Eventually, somebody brings up the subject of football. Now George is off and running, discussing what life is like under the blitz. He says he doesn't believe in getting mad if a lineman misses a block and he gets hit. Everybody is bound to get beat sometime.

"That's not so," says Keating. "I remember you yelling like hell once when you were playing quarterback for Houston. I got through and sacked you good once at Rice Stadium. You got up on your feet and you had the ball in your hand. There was a look in your eye like you wanted to throw that football right through my skull. Then I noticed it was Bob Talamini, your right guard, who was ducking."

Blanda reaches way back in his memory. There are so many games to sort through. Oh, yes!

"I remember. I wasn't mad at Tally for missing the block on you. I had a receiver open, and if he had just slowed you up another second, we would have had six points on the scoreboard. Tally knew I wouldn't throw the ball, because my temper never gets the better of me on the football field," he says.

It is a pardonable lie. Once when he was with the Chicago Bears, a fine fullback for the New York Giants named Ed Price did something—George forgets—to anger him. On one running play, Price went crashing out of bounds near the Chicago bench. Immediately, Blanda went over and slammed Price as hard as he could with his helmet. Why?

"Damned if I remember, but it certainly must have been important at the time. Poor Price! Nobody caught me, either."

Then there was that memorably murderous afternoon at old Jeppesen Stadium, the moldly old urine-reeking high school ballpark they fixed up in Houston and passed off as a major league facility the first few years the Oilers operated. Denver was in town and their middle linebacker was a playful lad named Jerry Hopkins, whom Houston had once cut. George had never cared much for Hopkins. It was strictly a personal thing. He was pleased when Hopkins was placed on waivers. On this particular day, Hopkins was slamming through the Houston line with more regularity than his talent called for. Blanda was in a white rage.

"All right, playing as hard as you can is part of the game, right?" asks George. The other two athletes nod. What else?

"Well, this dizzy s.o.b. comes charging through for about the tenth time and throws old George down hard, That's all right, too. I look over at him and he's laughing as hard as he can."

So George Blanda stands up, pivots neatly and, with a punting style he hasn't been permitted to use since he was at the University of Kentucky, aims his toe straight at Hopkins' rectum. Bam! Right on target. The crowd gasps, then applauds. This is machismo, Slovak-style.

EPISODE 15

As horse parlors go, Bay Meadows is a high-classification minor league. It is for animals that can't quite make the big time—places like Santa Anita or Hollywood Park or, even, Del Mar. The grandstands are neat, if not gaudy. The crowds are enthusiastic, although they are rarely larger than 10,000 in size. The track is located in San Mateo—on the fairgrounds, in fact. To get there from Alameda Island, you simply wheel your car, which you have leased for the football season, onto the Nimitz Freeway and keep going until the signs indicate the San Mateo Bridge is coming up quickly. The approach to the western side of the bridge leads through Foster City, a Los Angeles-style suburb built on Bay fill that may or may not slide into the water during the first good earthquake.

The road crosses over the Bayshore Freeway. At this point you are only a mile and a furlong from the action.

These instructions are very important if you do not happen to be George Frederick Blanda and the day does not happen to be Friday. If you are Blanda and it is Friday, you simply slide behind the wheel and say, "Take me to Bay Meadows, car!" The car is that well trained.

Whirling across the bridge, which seems to go on toward the jagged edge of eternity with no opposite shore visible in the midday fog, Blanda explains how The Routine works. It is all a matter of discipline. It conditions the mind. It gentles the nervous system. It also gives you something to look forward to. This is important, because George Blanda hates surprises. Roughly nine-tenths of all surprises are unfriendly ones.

"On Mondays I take a steam bath and get a rubdown at the Executive Club in Oakland. Then I either play golf or I make a public appearance. Booster clubs and stuff like that. Tuesday morning there's the game films of the last game.

"On Wednesday, they concentrate on defense, so I hang around and do some field goal kicking. Afterwards, I get another steam bath and have a rubdown. I usually eat alone at Francesco's in Oakland because the quarterback meeting is at night and there's no sense going back and bothering Betty about dinner. On Thursday we all go to the Grotto. Afterwards, I go back and play cribbage with Leslie. She's tougher than hell."

Indeed, she is. This is a pretty, spirited, determined teenage girl who looks and acts like her father. Here is the great irony of George's life. George Blanda, the toughest competitor of our era, has a son. Nice boy. Very artistic. Takes after his music-appreciating, landscape-painting, book-loving, modern-dancing mother. For a while, he had his own rock group in La Grange Park, Rick Blanda and The Jackson County Transfer. The boy never went out for football, but made the swimming team. Oh, God!

("There was some friction at first between father and son," says Betty Blanda. "I think it has been resolved. I really think it has.")

As the leased car pulls into the parking lot at Bay Meadows, George Blanda reveals something special. He has gone every Friday and hasn't had a losing day yet. This is very important to him. Winning is the name of the game—right? Oh, right, George, right!

This is Friday the thirteenth. Only a fool would go to the track on Friday the thirteenth, says George Blanda, who stresses the fact, once again, that he is not superstitious. Horse racing has been a passion with him since he was a student at the University of Kentucky, which is located in the bluegrass country, which has a lot of horses. He owned, in partnership with his boss, Tom Kole, a mare named Sturdy Gurdy. The Blandas now have a brood mare which is in foal to My Dad George.

Blanda buys a copy of the *Racing Form* at the gate, proving he's serious about all this. His passion for small-time gambling— card games, press bets and $10 windows—has already gotten George Blanda into trouble. Twice when he was with the Oilers there were rumors that he was engaged in some sort of sinister business with gamblers, shaving points, throwing games and other wild activities so absolutely foreign to Blanda's basic character that people who knew him well were aware the stories were utter fabrications. Twice he was investigated—once by American Football League commissioner Joe Foss, himself, and again by the Houston vice squad.

Both times it was discovered that his only crime was winning too consistently in nickle-a-point rummy games on airplanes going to Oiler road dates.

"I wonder if people really thought I'd take a chance on getting suspended from football for life?" he asks. "I'd be a hell of a hypocrite."

Sitting in a corner of the clubhouse, Blanda bets on every race, shredding losing tickets consistently. Up comes something named Rosie George. Blanda decides to bet on it because, by sheer dint of superior handicapping, it is the best horse in the race.

"It isn't a hunch bet?" a writer asks.

"Hell, no."

Regardless, Rosie George lopes home by better than two lengths and pays $4.80 on a two-dollar win ticket. Big deal. Driving back across the bridge, Blanda explains how he happened to have his first losing Friday of the season. Too many long shots came in. Little old ladies are sitting all over the place, sticking hat pins in the program. How can a superior handicapper fight that kind of nonsense? What he needs is Bill King describing the action.

EPISODE 16

To the innocent layman who has no concept of what it's like to sweat and bleed every weekend from early summer to mid-winter, it seems like an exotic way to live. Everybody pampers the football pros. It is a well documented fact. They fly off to distant cities on chartered jets. The ball club's management insists that they feed on the choicest steaks and rest their expensive physiques in the finest hotels. Starlets—or girls who look like they ought to be in the movies—constantly surround them.

It is a living, breathing, blue-eyed racket; a regular bird's nest on the ground. So much for romantic fiction, so much for lies that people tell each other around neighborhood bars. A road trip is nine-tenths boredom and one-tenth serious combat, with a dash of agony just to keep you alert. The ritual is always the same, varying only when you make a longer trip, because you get up earlier and twist uncomfortably on the plane a few hours more. Airline seats were constructed with small children and malnutritioned females in mind. There is usually a movie on board, something so bad no neighborhood theater would dare show it. The Oakland Raiders seem singularly cursed by the flicks the airlines select for them.

They tell great stories about the exploits some athletes have on the road. The reason they tell stories is because there is so little action that when something does happen, no one forgets about it. Hey, remember that quarterback that used to put on the damndest sex shows? What a broad old Charlie had in Miami. The stories get riper every year with each retelling. Some of them are even true.

If you enjoy a trip, you probably fall into one of two categories, either a rookie eager for a fresh experience, or a bleached-out veteran savoring for the last time the things you once took for granted. The initial indignity is a small one, but it galls just the same—the coach has been thoughtful enough to schedule an early flight, so that there will be plenty of time to work out before going to the hotel. What do they have player associations for, someone asks.

Once it was possible to at least share a hotel room with the best friend you had on the ball club, but no more. That was a real blessing. You could either share a few hours of compatible conversation or restful silence, whichever the two of you preferred. Now the teams insist that you stay with another guy who plays the same position you do, on the wobbly theory that you will spend your time in serious discussions of football technology. Personal camaraderie is not supposed to be a factor in your relationship.

The people who meet you at the hotel are rarely love-starved ladies. Before you get your room key—in a mob scene that resembles the beach at Dunkirk—your mailbox is stuffed with messages. Relatives want tickets. Old teammates from college want tickets. Guys you never heard of want tickets. If a female calls, chances are strong she doesn't want passionate companionship. She wants two on the 50-yard line for her and her fiance. At home your wife worries needlessly. She's read Joe Willie Namath's book. She's read all the exposés, in fact. There are groupies who follow the club, but they're strictly for rookies and the normal assortment of freaks among the players.

Most of the players go to dinner in groups of four or five. Football games attract people from out of town. They fill up hotels and jam restaurants. You have roughly four hours to eat dinner, if you can make reservations on such short notice and if you feel you can afford to eat on the $8 in meal money the team gives you for your Saturday night meal. You have to be back in bed, dreaming of football, naturally, before the 11 P.M. bedcheck. (And when, dear wife, is it that you think I cheat on you during road trips?)

In most cases you end up eating at a second-class joint because the best ones are so crowded you can't get seated until 10 P.M. and that's cutting it too close. When you do fall back into the sack, you discover that the hallways are overflowing with people doing what everybody is sure you're doing on the road, drinking, chasing broads and having a party. They run out of fuel at 3 A.M. Then you go to sleep. The telephone rings early. The pregame meal, steak and everything, is waiting for you. So is the trainer who wants to tape your lovely, shaven ankles. The bus will be going to the stadium in just two hours. Big deal! Big damned deal! It's a *wheeeee* weekend all around.

When the game is over, everybody dresses, jumps on board another bus and rumbles out toward the airport. Everybody staggers up the stairs to the airplane. The night air is even colder and your wounds begin to ache. In the morning you'll bleed from a million pores. For the moment, you enjoy your utter lack of feeling. Someone has left a sandwich and two cans of beer in every seat. They don't look even mildly sinful. You drink them quickly and crumple the cans in your hands like the college boy you once were. Does Joe Namath really have all that fun?

Early in his career, George Blanda decided to ease the boredom of long airplane flights to exotic towns like Denver by muffling the roar of jet engines with the flutter of playing cards. The stewardess has barely bolted the cabin door shut when he stretches a blanket over a board and starts to shuffle. On every club he has ever played for, he has had a flock of sheep which he has sheared with agonizing regularity.

The Raiders' charter has barely lifted off the runway at Oakland's jackrabbit-infested airport when the first card hits the blanket. The sound invigorates George.

"Ah, the National Anthem!" he says, stealing a line from Dick Barnett, the New York Knickerbocker guard.

"George, I don't think you are really a gambler in the truest sense of the word," says Keating. "A gambler is someone who takes chances. You don't take any chances at all. You know you're going to win."

Blanda grins that grin-of-fiendish-pleasure, which is a cross between John Wayne's controlled smirk and Burt Lancaster's full-set-of-teeth sardonic smile. He is in his element and he is happy. He cannot resist explaining strategy. In card games he is not the Alpha Male. He is a lone wolf, distant from the pack and dangerous.

"Now . . . in poker," he is saying, "when I run a bluff on a guy and chase him, I make a point of showing him my cards so he'll know what I did to him. It doesn't hurt to get him a little angry. Then he comes after you. And the next time I may not be bluffing."

At Houston, his lamb fold contained a genuine general manager, Carroll Martin, who seemed to have a death wish when it came to gin rummy and George. The players would file on board the decrepit old propeller-driven DC-7B the Oilers used, always being careful to leave a seat open opposite the quarter-back. Martin would be the last man on, checking to make sure everyone was present and accounted for. When he was through, his eyes would turn to George, who would be crooking one finger seductively toward the general manager.

"I think George was always playing cards for next year's salary," says Jim Norton, a free safety with the Oilers for nine years and now a Houston sportscaster.

There are other heroic stories about Blanda's card playing. Once, when no one would play with him on a flight, he went up and down the aisles trying to draft somebody.

"How about you?" he said, ruffling the cards in linebacker Bill Laskey's ears. "You aren't doing anything, are you, Bill?"

Laskey turned over sleepily. "Sorry, George, all I have is 43 cents. That's not very big stakes."

"Well, that's about as much as I take off my daughter Leslie at cribbage on Thursday night," George decided. "Tell you what, I'll bet you 5 dollars I can get your 43 cents between here and New York."

It took the entire five-hour flight, but by the time the charter dropped out of the cloud covering and found JFK airport, Laskey was totally without change.

Now the plane is soaring over the Rockies, bringing Blanda closer to Sunday, November 15, 1970 and Miracle IV, and George is raking in the cards and explaining the competitive urge.

"It comes from my childhood. Hell, first thing you wanted to do was escape the mines and that image of being a drunken, stupid, dirty Polack miner. So you'd compete hard as you could so you could grow up and do something different. Then there was the size of the old Blanda family. I had six brothers and four sisters. Not all of us lived at home at the same time, but there was enough people to give you a sense of compete or starve. You got all those hands reaching for the eggs at breakfast. If you're slow you don't eat. Besides, if you lost at anything in my family, everybody teased you so badly you wished you were dead."

At the Denver airport, a television camera crew is waiting. And another and another. Are the electronic whiz-bangs of the airwaves getting ready to greet an arriving chief of state? The President of France? The Emperor of Ethiopia? The Sultan of Mysore? No, they are there to film in-depth, 30-second interviews with America's freshly minted football folk hero. George Blanda has been coming to Denver every year since 1960 to play against the Broncos. No one ever said a word to him. This time it's different.

"What's the script for this week, George?" says Big Daddy Deepthroat from Channel Something-or-Other.

"George Blanda! Are we going to see yet another miracle out there on Sunday at Mile High Stadium?" asks Percy Dovetonsils of Channel Umpteen.

When confronted with absurdity and placed in a position where he must be charming when it would be more sensible to snarl, George reverts to a courtly Kentucky accent. Only a few hardened Blanda-watchers realize what he is up to.

"We just come here to try 'n' win this ball game," he says. "And ah'm sure that's what we're gonna do."

End of interview. Lots of smiles. A big wave. Walk away grinning.

EPISODE 17

The retreating sun is turning the snow-covered peaks of the Rockies a delicate pink and up in the radio booth Bill King is telling Scotty Stirling that it cannot possibly happen again. All afternoon, the Broncos' defensive line has been massaging the Raiders violently. The charge is being led by end Rich Jackson, an Oakland expatriate. The trade is one of the few personnel mistakes Al Davis has permitted to occur.

It is the fourth period and disaster is threatening to overhaul the Raiders, once again. They have blown a lead to Pete Liske, the second-line Denver quarterback whose reputation as a passer is somewhat less than intergalactic. He has come on in relief of Steve Tensi, who has tendonitis misery in his right shoulder. Liske has passed ten yards to tight end Jim Whalen for one score to come within 17-12 of the Raiders.

Then Oakland's Alvin Wyatt had lost a punt when specialty team serf, Billy Masters, attempted to remove several of his teeth. Denver had recovered and Liske had taken them in for a touchdown that had given the Broncos the lead, 19-17.

"Well, Scotty, we've gone to the wire in two straight ball games," says King, as Oakland gets ready to receive the kickoff. "And now, with 4:01 to go there is enough time. But how many times can you expect a team to come back so late in the game?"

"That's right, Bill," says the faithful voice of Scotty Stirling, "not to sound pessimistic, but I think it's asking an awful lot to ask Oakland to come back. The Broncos are all fired up after that big break. Wyatt fumbled the ball. Of course, they recovered on the Oakland 35. They had two penalties on that drive, but they took the action to Oakland."

On the sidelines, Madden is picking up thought waves. Who from? Is St. Jude, patron saint of the Impossible, a Raider fan? Is he trying to get through to the coach?

"Don't ask me why or how it happened," Madden explains later. "I look up at the stadium clock. There's 4:01 left to play. I just got this feeling that George ought to finish up the game. Daryle has been having trouble with that sore shoulder he got in the Cleveland game and he couldn't pivot properly with experiencing pain. I was going to send either George or Ken (Stabler) in before Wyatt lost the punt. But as we lined up for the kickoff, I got this feeling about George. Was it ESP? I don't know."

In the press box sits the odd couple. In one chair is Hamilton P. B. Maule. Next to him is Samuel J. Skinner. They deserve each other. Maule is tall, thin, white and opinionated. Skinner is short, round, black and opinionated. Skinner is also ubiquitous, loud, gossipy and hardworking. He is the sportscaster for a San Francisco soul station. He writes magazine stories, does public relations, edits the sports section of a black community paper and will speak at your son's bar mitzvah party for a fee. He and Maule have been attempting to hector each other all afternoon, with no notable success.

"It looks like I arrived just in time for the miracles to run out," says Maule.

"It's your *Sports Illustrated* jinx, Mr. Tex Maule, that's what it is," says Skinner. "You show up and everything falls apart. Who sent for you anyway?"

"Maybe I'd better not give up too soon, Samuel," Maule decides, looking down at the Oakland bench. "Here comes the miracle worker."

Indeed, Blanda has his headgear on, ready to go in. It is a good thing his scalp is protected. It has been snowing and the customers at Mile High Stadium are notorious for their consumption of antifreeze. They are not pleased at the sight of George. They know what he has been up to in recent weeks. They do not want Miracle IV to take place in their town. Somebody unloads with a snowball. Here comes another and another and another. They drink better than they throw in Denver.

"And George Blan-DAH comes on at quarterback!" announces King, trying not to sound too hysterical. After all, he's been getting all that heat about his emotionalism.

On the first play from scrimmage at the Oakland 20, Blanda nearly has the football taken away from him. He sends Hewritt Dixon, his fullback, swinging out of the back to catch a pass. Up steps a Denver linebacker who begins to paddle Hewritt smartly around the wishbone before the big Oakland runner can really bring the ball under control. The linebacker makes a swipe at the ball with one thorny paw and misses. Dixon falls down for a two-yard loss.

For a moment, Blanda pauses on the frozen turf, down on his left knee, thinking. Then he moves slowly back to where the huddle is forming. He goes deep with a pass to Warren Wells, who is streaking along on a fly pattern. Now it is third down and 12 yards to go and even infants in their mothers' arms must be aware that George will have to throw.

In comes Rod Sherman. The crunching sound made by the onrushing Denver defensive line is loud enough to freeze the blood in midvein. Blanda drops back on those short, deliberate steps of his. He's a good seven yards behind the line of scrimmage. The play is George's favorite, Y-In-99-In. He doesn't even bother to look for Sherman. He knows where he'll be.

The fact is that if Sherman isn't where he's supposed to be, he might as well keep running, right through the dressing room door and down the street. The rush is so vigorous that Blanda steps up a yard inside the nice, warm, cozy, temporary pocket his offensive linemen are holding for him. Now Sherman is behind exceedingly loose coverage. Trouble is George has to get the ball over the heads of three defenders who stand between him and the primary receiver. This is not as simple as it looks up there in the stands when you are a half-sloshed customer.

So George trains those eyes of his on the free safety, Paul Martha, and stares him down. Instead of rushing to help the man assigned to covering Sherman, poor Martha just stands there transfixed. Now the ball is in the crisp mountain air. Now Sherman is running free. Now one Dave Costa is attempting to plant Blanda about six inches under the grass of Colorado. Now the ball lands in Sherman's hands and he gains 27 yards.

This whole little drama is played out in exactly 6.5 seconds.

Somewhat apprehensive over the possibility of becoming the innocent victims of Miracle IV, the Broncos only intensify the fury of their charge. Blanda, now with a first down on his own 45 with 2:47 left, spits on his palms and marches up to the scrimmage line. When things are going well, George struts out of the huddle. The closer he gets to the goal line, the brisker his swagger.

At this point, George decides to save time by dropping back only six and a half yards. Later he explains that he had to do this. Why? Well, he's too old to get back any further.

The sun is almost out of sight when Blanda drops back into the pastel-tinted twilight. Oops! He bumps against one of his blockers, Hewritt Dixon, who is being driven back by the frantic Denver charge. The ball goes up and George goes down. On the Bronco 20, Warren Wells, who is doomed to spend all of the next season in jail, sees that the pass will be short. He retreats a couple of yards, makes the catch and scrambles back to the 20.

"I don't know how Blanda could possibly have completed that pass," Stirling tells his listeners. "The ball was thrown to a spot. George couldn't have even seen his receiver. Wells was a little bit surprised to see the ball coming. It was just an amazing play. Blanda never saw the completion, he was surrounded by Broncos. Things are really getting mean in there now."

Now a fourth straight Blanda miracle is certain. With 2:38 left, George has three solid shots at either throwing the ball into the end zone, or failing that, sending one of his ball carriers in for the score. On fourth he can try a field goal and he isn't likely to miss from 27 yards back. Oh, it's wonderful to be old and be a Raider!

The crowd of 50,959 is too frightened to throw snowballs. Most of the drunks in the congregation can feel themselves sobering up fast. The pass play is supposed to go to Biletnikoff, but he's covered. So Blanda wings the ball out of bounds, re-groups his offense and decides to come right back with the same play. On the busted pass, the Raiders' offensive line had gone offsides. Naturally, Denver takes the down rather than the penalty.

On the snap, Blanda back-pedals, no more than six or seven yards. Common sense says that ten yards is the safest place to be when the rush is super-hard, super-fast. But George hangs in there and lifts the ball on a high, soft parabola. This time Bill King seems curiously prepared.

"Touchdown! Raiders!" he screams as if he's trying to reach Oakland listeners without benefit of a radio transmitter. "Biletnikoff took it on the one-yard line ahead of George Garrett and stepped into the end zone. Blanda has driven them [the Raiders] 80 yards for the touchdown, completing four of five passes . . . no, no . . . four of six. The kick is good. The stunned Denver crowd is motionless. They can't believe they've seen 43-year-old George Blanda come off the bench with 4:01 and put his team back in front, 24-19, in less than two minutes against a defense that has contained Oakland well all afternoon."

There are other heroes besides George Blanda, although it seems difficult to recall that there are 39 other players on the roster. One of them, Jimmy Warren, a 31-year-old defensive back, preserves Miracle IV. On first down after the kickoff, Liske throws with the idea of getting the ball to Billy Van Husen on the right side. Instead Warren gets in the way, making his second interception of the day with 1:56 to play. They give him the game ball and, in the Oakland bathhouse, Blanda points at Jimmy and says:

"Hey, give that fellow some newspaper space. That one over there, the fellow with the game ball in his locker."

Percy Dovetonsils wants George on Channel Umpteen. A cameraman is pushing newsmen out of the way to make room for yet another 30-second in-depth interview.

"Winning is nice," he tells the space cadets from the television station, "but we're going to have to start winning these things by more points. You know, I'm old. I can't take this kind of pressure for long."

On the long plane ride home, Ron Fell is creating in his mind the next promotional spectacular for KNEW. This soap opera announcer's voice will come on with the following lead-in: "Welcome to the continuing saga of George Blan-DAH!" Now a few seconds of "America, the Beautiful."

"Oh, beautiful, for spacious skies, for amber waves of grain . . ." (Bill King's voice: "That's good! That's good! I don't believe it! I don't believe it!") ". . . for purple mountain majesties . . ." (King: "Back goes George, he's throwing for Biletnikoff . . . *TOUCHDOWN*, Raiders!" ". . . above thy fruited plains . . ." (Soap opera voice: "What does George do this week? George has done everything. What does he do for an encore?") ". . . America, America! God shed His grace on thee . . ." (Voice imitating Blanda's voice: "Oh, say, this is me and I'm jest forty-three.") ". . . And crown thy good with brotherhood . . ." (Soap opera voice: "Will George sing 'The Star-Spangled Banner'? Will George be on key? Will George master the banner? Will George pull out Old Glory?") ". . . from sea to shining sea . . ." (Soap opera voice: "Find out this weekend when the Raiders play the San Diego Chargers . . . listen on KNEW . . . the station that . . . er . . . let George do it.") ". . . America! America!"

Perfect! Fell's eyes rotate wildly. Blue smoke pours out of his ears and nose. It is soothing to watch real genius at work. It is the same when Wayne Valley drops by the Raiders' offices to watch Al Davis think.

EPISODE 18

Now the nation has gone bonkers. It is necessary to screen all the calls directed at the Blanda apartment. The girl on the switchboard at the Coral Reef looks as if she had been through a war and lost.

One of the Bay Area newspapers, for sale in the racks on the front steps of the motel, has decided that George's miracles are routine news now. "Ho-Hum! Blanda Does it Again!"

The cast and crew from the television show "Mission Impossible" have sent a telegram to George chiding him for stealing their story line. Somebody wants Blanda to be the front man for a franchised chain of health salons. All the promoters, advertising men and general all-around exploiters are on the make at the same time. A recording firm in Hollywood wants him to sing. A movie studio sees him as another . . . well, if not another John Wayne, at least another Johnny Mack Brown. Everybody wants him to speak at their banquets, which are still months away.

Since he has no agent, wants no agent, he is pretty much at the mercy of the dingbats who telephone.

"No! No! No!" he says, straining to get away so he can play a little golf (he has a six-stroke handicap) on his off-day. "I never heard of your product. How the hell can I tell people I like it when I've never heard of it. For crying out loud, you must be joking. No, I don't need the money. I get paid well by the Raiders. I get paid well by REA . . . yeah, well, goodbye."

The telephone receiver goes back in its cradle, rests for a second and yowls again. George shakes his head. This time it's somebody who wants him to come to Honolulu and speak at a charity dinner, no fee, but Betty can come with him and they can stay a week, free of charge. That sounds like a possibility. Blanda says he'll get back with the guy as soon as the season is over.

There is a cartoon in one of the papers, showing a saggy, seedy, bombed-out looking businessman surveying the damage the years have done to him. He is standing in the bathroom, in front of the mirror, horrified. "Am I really the same age as George Blanda?" he is asking his wife. And she is nodding her head. The whole thing amazes George, who never really expected it.

"Betty," he asks, "why would anyone want me to make a recording?"

"Maybe Bing Crosby is playing golf," she suggests.

The whole business is wildly incongruous to Blanda. Why is he being rewarded now simply because he happens to be in the right place at the right time?

"I'm not that much better a football player than when I was in Houston," he says, shaking his head at the incredible furor he's caused. He was sort of an invisible giant in Houston and Chicago. He was there, but he was the only one who knew it. Now he is literally being worshiped and there is a strong indication that people consider him some kind of vague freak. Is he being applauded, finally, for being a great football player? Or is he simply some crazy fad, like a hula hoop, because he is able to play violent games at an age when he ought to be getting fat, bald and winded walking up stairs?

"I honestly played the best football of my life in Houston. Ask Al Davis. He thinks so, too. Just evaluate what's been happening these past four games. The team just keeps getting into situations . . . and I happen to be in on the end of things . . . none of this stuff is any more outstanding than scoring those 38 points in 1965 against Kansas City. Writers laugh when I say that was a bigger deal.

"Hey, one year with the Oilers I had 36 touchdown passes and we won the league championship. Wouldn't you call that a better season than this one? You know how many offers I had that year. None! In all the years I was with Houston, I had one speaking engagement down there. One! Now my wife and I get a week in Hawaii if I speak. How do you figure this?"

Well, there is nothing so sensational as an idea whose time has come. Everyone has a George Blanda remark. Good grief, Daryle Lamonica even shows up to practice on Tuesday with a button that says: George Blanda For Mayor. Somebody gave it to him and he says he plans to keep it in his scrapbook. If Daryle is jealous he is keeping the emotion beautifully secluded. What else can he do?

"Good Lord," says San Francisco television personality Rollin Post. "I'm three years younger than he is and I have trouble getting out of bed in the morning and that old man is out there throwing touchdown passes. I think he ought to have the decency to let his arteries harden with the rest of us."

By now King has become a mini-celebrity himself. A newsman asks him what his reaction to all this is.

"A 43-year-old man has no business doing things on a football field that would make another 43-year-old man jump around like that in the broadcasting booth."

So overwhelmed is San Francisco Chronicle columnist Ron Fimrite that he announces he has come out of retirement at 40 and will pick up his touch football career as soon as he can drag

21 other players out to Golden Gate Park. He discovers that he has made a serious mistake.

"To many of us, the important thing about George Blanda's recent heroics is not what they have done for the Oakland Raiders but what they have done for, or perhaps, *to* us. At a time when he should be perfectly content watching the Raiders play on his living-room screen, old George is actually playing with them. Not only that, for four straight weeks he has been their star. This has given many of his contemporaries heart," Fimrite writes.

"We are all beginning to look at our bodies, swollen as they may be by years of disuse, a hard second look. Perhaps there is a little life left in the old corpse after all. After the initial shock of Blanda's twilight success, the Middle American feels shame, then a renewal of that old urge to self-destruct. Inspired by the Raider quarterback's refusal to surrender to support hose, a number of chaps in my office decided to test their rusting skills on the greensward once more.

"Our game would be flag football, which requires a defender to snatch a flag from the back pocket of the ball carrier before he is considered down. Since the flags—actually old rags purloined from the pantry—come in various sizes and are placed in pockets of varying tightness, snatching one is not as easy as it may sound. As a result, we found ourselves playing something frighteningly close to tackle. The older fellows in our group determined to take on some of the younger studs, who, in tribute to the playing apparel of their captain, chose to call themselves The Big Red.

"The first week, we did well enough, winning, in fact, by 18-0 (one Big Red touchdown was disallowed on a rules infraction). But the following Saturday, the opposition beefed up its ranks with even younger competitors. We were defeated, 12-0, which was bad enough. But consider the Over-40s' injury list: one broken leg, one broken little finger, two cracked ribs, one bruised back, several lacerations of varying severity and several severe muscle pulls.

"Several members of the Over-40 set did not appear for the

rubber match of the series. A more intelligent reaction to Blanda was that of Michael Harris, a reporter for the *Chronicle* who did not appear for the third game.

" 'At first,' he said, 'I thought Blanda was a boon to people my age. But after three weeks of trying to imitate him, I decided he was merely an exception and to try to parody him was a very rapid form of suicide.'

"It might be wise, then, for all of us to simply let George do it," says Fimrite, in conclusion. "I, for one, am now content to retire to Mr. Perry Butler's saloon on Union St. and let liquor and the natural aging process have my worthless carcass."

Under the circumstances, it is the proper choice.

EPISODE 19

Like an automobile designer, nature constructs all great football players along standard lines. Few variations in style are tolerated by the public. All the best linemen have triangular upper torsos. Fullbacks must be built like fighting bulls. Pass receivers must be bursts of living flame. Quarterbacks are lean and deadly like gunfighters.

Image is not only important in professional football, it is pretty nearly everything. To look slightly different is to confuse both the customers and the press. And when those discerning creatures are confused, they tend to get grouchy, which makes George Blanda grouchy.

The trouble with Blanda always has been his physical appearance. His body is a trifle too compact. His shoulders seem to be rounded, although they aren't. His jaw practically rubs against his face mask when he wears a helmet. He walks and runs with an economy of movement, giving people the impression that he is not graceful, another distinct mistake. Chances are nature originally intended him to be a heavyweight boxer. He just never got the message. He is 6-2 and 215 pounds. Once again . . . he seems to be smaller, say 6-0 and 200.

This optical illusion creates many printed errors. A *Time* magazine story, attempting, perhaps, to make the incredible sound impossible, refers to George as "fat and creaky," an observation which deeply distresses Edwin Pope, the noted literary figure from Miami, who springs to his typewriter.

"The *Time* magazine writer obviously had not seen Blanda in the flesh. Maybe on television, he looks that way. The camera lies," Pope writes. "But George's body is as firm as a stiletto, about as creaky as a shock-absorber on a Rolls-Royce."

All right, then, how does he stay that way? How does he continue to exist in this violent universe of his? Surely there must be some exotic system, some mystical explanation. The boxer Archie Moore said that he had received this special weight-reducing formula from an old Maori sheepherder in New Zealand. That sounds more like it. There must be some old Slovakian secret for staying young and strong to the age of 43 or 44, passed on to George's mother at his birth by an old maiden aunt with some gypsy blood. Maybe, like Dorian Gray, there is a portrait in the attic at the Blanda home in La Grange Park that is fat, wheezing, worn and bald while George remains forever virile.

"It's so simple that nobody wants to hear my explanation," Blanda says. "I try to stay in shape. I try to keep my legs young. You know Dutch Van Brocklin retired at 35. He said his arm was good enough so that he could have thrown passes indefinitely. It was his legs that went. Before I come to camp I run two miles every day for six weeks. I play golf as much as I can. I don't mean any of this riding around in a cart. That's not golf. That's motorized shot making.

"I play all the handball I can squeeze in. I do that until the weather clears in Illinois. Then I play golf. I eat the same things my mother used to put on the table back in Youngwood. I go heavy on protein. But I eat potatoes, not as much as I used to. But I eat them. I smoke, but not all the time. I do some drinking. I like good old Kentucky bourbon. I stick mostly to sissy drinks like frozen daiquiris and creme de menthe during the season.

"Those are good because you can drink socially and they're so rich you're not likely to throw them down like water on a hot day. You've got to follow me around pretty close and stick to me for a long time to catch me drunk, though. You can't work a whole lot of alcohol out of your system soon enough to play properly.

"Hell, I'm a professional football player. I do what I have to do to stay in shape. It's part of the discipline. I get sick and tired of people coming up to me and saying, 'Did you get tired out there?' and 'Do you get a lot of mail from people over 40 asking how you stay in shape?' Those are just dumb questions. If I got tired I wouldn't play. And I don't have any secret formula. Just stay in shape. It's so damned simple people can't believe it.

"They get all these pills and reducing schemes and health salons shoved at them, until they think they can stay in shape by pushing some button. I think that's where the American public goes wrong. They think you can solve anything by running it through a computer. You can't knock weight off unless you work and work damned hard. You never get something for nothing. That may be corny but it's true.

"I've had three injuries, only the shoulder separation was a serious one. I had cracked ribs in Houston so bad I could hardly breathe, but I played with them. And I had tennis elbow that kept me from throwing properly the last year with the Oilers, but that's it. I never told anyone but Bobby Brown, the Houston trainer who was my close friend, about the elbow. But nothing bad has ever happened to my legs since I had a knee operation at Kentucky in 1946. My body is my livelihood. During the season I do what everybody else does. I do wind-sprints. Jim Otto says it's embarrassing to run with me, because I don't try to get out of anything because of my age. Why should I? If I'm going to play at 43 or 44 or 45, I can't make any concessions to my age and I don't want anybody else to, either.

"As far as my arm is concerned, it's as strong as it ever was. I can throw as far as I ever could. But I've always been considered a short thrower. Nearly all of your top quarterbacks are really great short passers who take advantage of a long pass situation when the occasion arises.

"I come to camp and I start kicking first. That's because I want to get the soreness in my leg fast. The faster the soreness comes the faster it goes away and it doesn't come back until the next year. As for throwing the ball, well I don't do much of that. I never really did, except when I had to because of requirements in practice sessions. On Tuesdays I throw to the backs for about ten minutes. On Wednesdays I throw to the ends for about ten minutes. That's it. You see, I don't work with the team as much. That's up to Daryle and Kenny.

"I manage to keep my arm in shape. Now I don't warm up on the sidelines much anymore. I usually go in when somebody's hurt. There's no time. Hell, I'm always ready mentally. As a field goal kicker, you're always on call. You have to go in right now. I don't take 19 practice kicks or I don't do any kicking balls behind the bench or any of that crap. I'm ready to play.

"One of the questions that really rips me up is, 'Do you get any stiffness in your arm?' and that is usually followed by, 'Do you think you could play the whole game?' Christ, yes! There's no stiffness. I get hit once or twice in the game, but I never got hit that much anyway.

"Baseball pitchers are always complaining about sore arms. Well, baseball players are the worst prima donnas in sports. They always give out a lot of bull about how much their arms hurt. They're different kind of people than football quarterbacks. They get a damned hangnail, they can't throw the ball. I probably have thrown more footballs in my lifetime than baseball pitchers have ever dreamed of throwing. And footballs are a hell of a lot harder to throw than baseballs. My arm never gets sore, except for that one time. I didn't go crying to the coach or moaning to the press.

"I got that elbow trouble from palming the ball too much. I played. I went out there and I threw the ball long and short and you name it. I don't say I had my best year, but I wasn't running around crying. I think baseball pitchers are always 'thinking sore arm' so they get one. Hell, I never worry about it. Those guys get four days' rest. You throw hard on Sunday and you're right back on the practice field throwing hard on Tuesday with one day's rest. That's all.

"As for my weight, well, I was 180 pounds in college, because coach Bear Bryant used to run our tails off, frankly. He had us running up and down stadium stairs. He had us practicing 11 months of the year. We got Christmas off, sometimes. My last year in high school I was 195. My weight with the Bears was around 205. But I used to be dumb then. I'd eat in the off-season, get my weight way up and count on running it off at training camp. Well, I cut that crap out before I was 30 years old.

"I used to get tired some in Houston. That humidity down there just drains you. The temperature was so high on the floor of Rice Stadium that some of our guys came close to passing out. But I was never so tired I couldn't get to practice and I sure as hell was never so tired I missed the team parties on Sunday night. It was a temporary thing because of the humidity. But that's not a factor here. I could play a whole game, a whole season.

"One of the factors that has kept Old George around so long is the fact that quarterbacks have a different conditioning requirement than a lot of other people who play other positions. Certainly if I had to get out and run pass patterns like Fred Biletnikoff or like Charlie Hennigan used to do . . . I'd die. You can't run 50 yards down the field every time and play to 44 years of age. Quarterbacks expend a lot of energy, spinning and handing off or dropping back to set up. Then you can rest for a little bit. Our movements are all quick . . . little short, choppy steps and then you're all through for a while."

For nearly half an hour, Tom Keating has been listening. He is not the sort who can stay still that long. He has something to say.

"Tell the truth," he says, "only a stumpy Polack body like yours could take all that pressure and that pounding all those years. It's not conditioning, it's just breeding. The hills of Czechoslovakia are filled with 50-year-old quarterbacks. Tell the truth."

So maybe it is a genetic freak, a blip in the Blanda bloodline. George's own explanation doesn't really wash. Other athletes stay in shape. Others run a lot in the off-season. Others play golf and don't use carts. Others haunt handball courts until the whole world begins to flash before their sweat-washed eyeballs. They do all those things and they are through at 34 or 35, just like every other normal human being.

Up close George Blanda doesn't look that old. As Walt Hecox of the Livermore, California, *Independent* says, out-writing and out-reporting *Time* magazine: "Blanda is as an Egyptian pit viper and sinewy as Albert the Gorilla and, if you ask the teams the Raiders play against, they will tell you he is as dangerous as either or both of them. Only a fellow who was out of his mind would not want to look like George at the age of 43 or 44 and a hell of a lot of younger ones would like to borrow one or another of his male virtues. Ken Willard of the San Francisco 49ers, for instance, would probably settle for a handful of hair."

All that is really necessary to put Blanda's age in the proper perspective is to locate some old football brochures. Turn back in time to 1949. George is a rookie with the Bears. Andy Robustelli is a senior in college at a school that no longer exists. The best rookie in the National Football League that year was Chuck Bednarik. They thought he was remarkable because he lasted 15 years. For crying out loud, George Blanda was a contemporary of Bulldog Turner and Sid Luckman and Sammy Baugh and Bosh Pritchard, all of whom were playing football when dinosaurs still roamed downtown Pittsburgh.

Why, the advertising in the program they sold at George's first professional game, against the Philadelphia Eagles, contains sales promotions for Dumont television sets with ten-inch-round screens and for those Studebaker cars that looked like they were going frontwards and backwards at the same time.

EPISODE 20

Nobody knows an athlete better than his trainer, not his wife or his children or his coaches or his teammates. The trainer is mother. The trainer is also the family priest. The training room is both home and confessional box. The trainer may snarl and tell you that you really aren't hurt, to stop being a candyass and get out there and play. But deep in his rotten, yowling little heart, you know that he truly cares about you. So you tell him everything. You tell him things he doesn't even hear. He is there to minister unto you, to slap your craven fanny, to shave your smelly ankles and then tape you. And he knows you . . . ah, how well he knows you. He can always tell when you're faking being injured. Sly, these boo-boo kissers.

For 17 seasons, man and boy, Bobby Brown has been a trainer. He has worked for teams in four leagues—the Buffalo Bills of the All-America Conference, the New York Yankees of the National Football League, the Ottawa Rough Riders and Winnipeg Blue Bombers of the Canadian League and the Houston Oilers of the American Football League. He has seen every injury, including sudden death on the field. He has heard every excuse, every sad story. He has been tinkering with the idea of writing a book. All he has is a title, "My Funny Friends In The Plastic Hats."

He's out of the rackets now. He is the owner of Bobby Brown's Athletic Club, right off the Southwest Freeway in burgeoning, oil-drunk Houston. It is an unbelievably luxurious place to sweat off a ten-martini lunch. In addition to sauna baths, steam rooms, exercise machines and other twentieth-century torture devices, there is a restaurant and a circular bar, just the place for an oilman to take his mistress. ("Where am I dear? Why, I'm down at the health club, getting in shape. Where else?")

Working for Brown is Charlie Tolar, the human cannonball who played fullback with Blanda on those early Oiler championship teams. Tolar wears a T-shirt that looks like it was sprayed on. He is incredibly short for a former professional football player (5-6), but his physical ability never could be measured in altitude.

Brown is still remarkably boyish for a man who cannot be much younger than George Blanda. He very much resembles a rampant chipmunk. He is also a spiritual soul brother to George. In recent weeks Bobby has been watching his former patient on the tube and getting misty. Once a trainer, always a trainer, and

a $250,000 chrome-plated health club doesn't really make up
for the loss of 40 funny friends in plastic hats. The Oilers fired
Bobby, one of the 12,678 dumb things they have done since the
franchise was founded, if you're keeping score.

"I've known that guy since 1950 when I was with the
Yankees. He was a linebacker then. At that time they had
Luckman and Lujack. George had to cover Buddy Young who
was the fastest back in the league in those days. He held him to
no touchdowns that day. In fact, he held him to very short
yardage. You wouldn't think of George as being that quick.

"But his speed was much better than you would imagine.
When he was young he could run as well as anyone and he could
cover anyone on defense. They had him playing cornerback and
safety, too, you know. His weight was down then. He's had
some physical problems over the years, but nothing too serious.
I go back with him a long time. I was his trainer as long as
anybody, I guess. The fact that he was never hurt badly except
for once with the Bears probably has as much to do with his
longevity in the game as anything.

"A lot of people complained about George when he was in
Houston. They said he was always trying to take over the team
and he wouldn't let the coach do any coaching. I was there on
the sidelines and I saw what happened. He was a coach-on-the-
field. That's a great attribute, but George made a lot of people
jealous. He had this great leadership ability. It was inborn, like
Eisenhower and Patton in the army. That kind of ability makes
a lot of people feel very small. So they reacted badly.

"The only athlete I've ever trained over the years who
reminds me of George is Arnold Palmer. He's the only one.
Palmer has that same great competitive spirit. He'll try and beat
you at anything, too. He'll beat you at anything, even drinking
whiskey. 'How much do you want to drink? I can drink more
than you. I can hit golf balls better than you. I want to win.'
It's something that the American athlete has lost. You don't
have the fierce competitor you had ten or fifteen years ago.
George may be the last of the breed.

"There are still great athletes, but little greatness in the athlete. George has that quality. That's what has kept him in professional football so long. Blanda knows how to stay in shape. He keeps his weight down. He watches his diet. I never had to give him a diet to follow like I had to some of those clowns. George just ate very little food. He was a protein eater and he watched starches. That simple. I watch him on television and it's obvious that he's still in splendid shape.

"He's still wearing the three-quarter shoes I developed for him in 1960. They're somewhere between low cuts and high cuts. They've got what is known as a Redskins' toe on the right shoe—the one he kicks with. It isn't a hard front on it. Rather, it's a spade-shaped toe. He had to have more flexibility than most kickers, because he had to play quarterback, too.

"People would come out to the Oiler training camp and they'd see George and they'd think he wasn't working hard, but he was. He had his own program of push-ups and calisthenics. And long after practice was over, he'd be running for an hour. All the kids would be indoors and he'd be running. You didn't have to train him, he trained himself. Some of the guys I've had would gain 30 pounds in the off-season and that would mean they'd have to lose 35 to get in shape. George would check in at 218 or, at the most, 220. Then he'd count on losing something so that he'd be down around 215 or 216 by opening day. The only time I ever had to needle him even a little was one year when he came in at 224. I couldn't believe it.

"He'd been making speeches for that trucking company he'd been working for and he was getting a little careless with his weight. I guess it brought him up short. Because he never came in that heavy again.

"Frankly, he can play quarterback until he's 50.

"And he could kick until he's 54, if he's willing to stick around as a specialist, which I would doubt, knowing the man the way I do. Look at Lou Groza, he kicked until he was something like 48. He was a big man, an ex-tackle, and if you remember the last few years of his career he had a big paunch on him. This man (Blanda) has no paunch and he's got a great leg. The only thing that might stand in his way would be getting hurt on the field.

"Of all the guys I've ever trained, George spent less time in the training room than anyone else. He was never a sympathy-seeker. I've always said that if you look in the dictionary you'll find 'sympathy' somewhere between 'shit' and 'syphilis.' I think probably George would agree.

"The funny thing is that, if you look real close at him, he isn't really built like a quarterback . . . at least not like a modern one . . . tall and rangy. He reminds me a lot of Ken Willard of the 49ers. In fact, I think if George were getting out of the University of Kentucky this year, teams would probably be thinking of converting him from a quarterback to a fullback. Don't forget, when he was 21 or 22 he had good speed. They'd want to make him a Ken Willard-style fullback.

"But I doubt if he'd let them. He's a proud man and a stubborn one. His overwhelming independence has probably cast reflections on his greatness as an athlete. I'm just happy that he's lasted long enough to get the kind of recognition he deserves. God knows he wouldn't have ever gone out sucking around for publicity."

On the walls of the Bobby Brown Athletic Club in Houston are large, photographic murals of football players—Y. A. Tittle, Charlie Johnson, Hoyle Granger, Bobby Layne. There is one picture of Blanda. It is hidden away in Brown's private office. It is autographed and mounted above his desk, right next to pictures of those astronauts he's worked on. A picture of an American flag isn't far away. It is not difficult to figure out where Blanda stands in his old trainer's estimation. George is right in there with apple pie, by God!

EPISODE 21

The awful truth appears in black ink and green paper. Sports fans wake up on the Saturday morning before Miracle V is due to occur at the Oakland Coliseum and discover that America's middle-aged folk hero has done it again. He has offended the delicate sensibilities of the Raider Booster Club. Confronted once again by mass absurdity, George Blanda has struck back with his own dazzling brand of blatant honesty.

As everyone but the members themselves are well aware, booster clubs have a dangerous tendency to be booze-drenched exercises in pretense. They can be nothing more than knothole gangs for the superannuated. A certain percentage of the people who attend meetings pretend that they love the dear old Des Moines Wildcats with as much passion as they reserve for the little blonde file clerk over in accounting. They get sloshed before the luncheon is served and proceed to stand up and either (a) bore or (b) embarrass their guest speakers and the majority of members who are actually serious about football. Some boosters are merely content to be just insulting and petty. On other occasions they will boo players, executives and newsmen covering the club.

For dark reasons which are never revealed, management considers booster clubs to be important, even though the stadium is sold out from here to eternity. Attendance at them is mandatory. It says so somewhere in the standard player's contract, ("Quick, get the lawyer for The Players' Association on the telephone!") and there is no way of getting excused from one, once the publicity man calls and tells you it's your turn in the barrel. For reasons too obvious to mention, the players absolutely hate the meetings. No one has ever spoken out against them . . . no one? Wait a minute, where's George Blanda?

The date is November 20, 1970—a day that will live as long as professional athletes struggle to breathe free. Ah, let the man tell you all about it:

"You have to realize what the setting was. We had just won four miraculous games in a row. Big, exciting stuff. We'd won those games in the last few minutes . . . well, one of them was a tie, but it was a game we were losing, so it was the same as victory. Now, every Friday I go to the track. I live by a routine. I don't honestly know if I'm just a routine kind of guy or whether I'm superstitious. I just feel everyone has to have some order to their lives. On Friday I go to the track. That's it. But this particular Friday I gotta go to the booster club.

"Now I don't say all booster club members act bad, maybe just ten percent do. The other 90 are serious about the Raiders. They charter planes and follow the team and that's good. But it's the other ten percent. They could care less about the Raiders. They just go to the booster club to sell insurance or make business contacts. Those people are boisterous and insulting. They ruin the meetings for the serious members and they're a real detriment to the team.

"So I'm sitting there at the luncheon. I'm going to make the most of it and then I'm going to the track. I'm anxious to get it over. I'm fidgeting. Anyway, they send up questions for me to answer. We've just had these four fantastic weeks and I've been lucky enough to play an important part in them, so I figure I'll get ten, fifteen or twenty questions. So what do I get? I get four questions. Four! There's 150 people there and you get four questions. Right away, it shows you what they think of you.

"You got four questions. Four! People are going to pay a fancy fee to hear you after the season is over. Here these damn people, your own alleged fans, have you come down for nothing and they got four questions to ask you. Four! That's all they have in their heads, outside of booze. Four questions!

"One of them is 'How good are you?' The second was 'Why isn't Kenny Stabler playing?' The third is 'Are you superstitious?' And the fourth one is some other stupid damned inconsequential question. So I get up and I say, 'It's nice to be here. I'm going to read these questions I'm supposed to answer. I want you to know I get more intelligent questions from 11- and 12-year-olds. I'll answer them real quick: How good am I? Don't know! Now here's a good question: Why isn't Kenny Stabler playing? This is what I'm talking about. Really intelligent.

" 'I just helped win or tie four games in the last four weeks and you want to know why Kenny Stabler isn't playing?' So I put that one down. 'Am I superstitious? If you read *Sports Illustrated* this week, you'll know I'm superstitious.

" 'This fourth question isn't worth answering. It's that stupid.' Then I sat down. I was teed off. I had spent two and a half hours going down there and getting bored. I told them so. Four questions. Four! I don't have to butter up to any of them. I'd do what I did again. Somebody comes up to me afterwards and says, 'I've got an intelligent question for you.' I said, 'Oh?' and he said, 'Do you think Kenny Stabler can beat out Daryle Lamonica?'

"What can I say to him? Hell, Kenny's just learning his trade. He's going to be a super quarterback someday. But he's young and that's why he isn't beating Daryle out. Besides if I say anything about either of the other quarterbacks, some writer is going to pick it up and it's going to look like Old George is blasting Daryle and Kenny. It's a plain, flat loaded question. No matter what I say I'm going to look stupid as hell, so I tell him I can't answer that one. I don't want to make any waves."

Surprise! Surprise! It happens just that way.

"George Blitzes the Boosters," says the headline in the *San Francisco Chronicle*'s Sporting Green. Seems that Blanda had been given a standing ovation by his loyal and loving boosters, and he had responded by telling them all how stupid they were. Quick, George, get a gun and shoot all those varmints in the press box.

EPISODE 22

It is the morning of a football game at the Oakland Coliseum, a vast concrete blob located within 16 miles of the coffee houses, pot parlors, crash pads and revolutionary seminars of Berkeley, where protest began. Hippies are humans, too, maybe more human than most creatures. A couple of them, possibly a male and a female, are standing next to the players' parking lot. A leased car comes easing around the corner and finds the proper stall.

The hippies, in magnificent unisex squalor, walk up to George Blanda, timorously.

"We don't want your autograph, Mr. Blanda," says the one with the beard, who must be the male. "We just want to say we admire you. We like the way you don't take any crap from anyone. That's good."

"Oh?" says George, the last rugged individualist. "I want you kids to know I don't much agree with your life-style, smoking pot and all that other stuff. However, that's your business. You do what you like with your lives."

"We don't care about that," says the girl, thin and blonde, pregnant and properly pale without a trace of makeup.

"Well, hell, I do like what you kids say about loving everybody. That's a fine idea. I hope you keep practicing that," says the Alpha Male, the lone wolf in winter. "I like it. Shows guts."

The three of them grin and nod nervously at each other. Worlds apart in style, they are still soul brothers of a sort, gentility and toughness combined for a brief second in one abstract frame of reference.

EPISODE 23

By their eyes and their voices, you shall know them. Quarterbacks are a different breed. They are not like ball carriers or pass receivers or defensive backs or linemen. They are more cerebral than most. They walk a certain way. They carry themselves a certain way. They act a certain way. They are prima donnas, absolute and unashamed. Daryle Lamonica is no different from other members of his breed. He is the grandson of an Italian immigrant who never learned English, who discovered Fresno, who started a peach orchard and who winced only slightly when his son married an Irish woman.

Daryle Lamonica has paid his dues, too. He is a genuine Alpha Male, a number of years away from true greatness because he has his flaws. George Blanda can empathize. He knows what Lamonica is going through—the criticism, the pain, the boos, the injuries. They say Daryle throws the long pass too often, that he sometimes panics, that he is too brittle.

It is a delicate and unusual balance that Blanda and Lamonica keep. Neither says an unkind word about the other in public. Both are careful to praise each other's special skills. There is a record of only one disagreement between them.

"Daryle's a good fellow in a lot of ways, but sometimes he gets carried away," says George. "One time he told me that I'd made my reputation in the early years of the American Football League 'throwing against weak defenses.' Now I just looked him square in the eye. Anybody else but Daryle and it would have really ripped me up. I said, 'Hey, I remember you at Buffalo, throwing against the same defenses when you were real young and you only completed 37 percent of your passes.' He looked at me for a minute and he laughed.

"He knew damn well he'd said the wrong thing. He's not afraid to challenge you. He sure as hell wasn't afraid to challenge me. He's got the physical skills to be a great one someday. He's a damn good one right now. He's had some bad luck and I'm glad I'm there to help him out of trouble. If I wasn't there, he'd probably get out of trouble himself. Either that or he'd learn a lot. He's got a real knack for coming up with the big play."

Lamonica is introspective, as inner-directed as George is outer-directed. Daryle lies awake at night, thinking of things he should do to improve. Blanda sleeps well, confident that when situations arrive, he will be able to cope with them as they happen. George is swagger and independence. Daryle is meticulousness and careful preparation. Blanda says the game plan is nice, but it doesn't always feed the bulldog. Lamonica does what science says is best. Both have a sense of the dramatic. When cornered, both are adventurous.

Lamonica thinks he can throw 60-yard touchdown passes every time. Blanda is convinced that it is foolish to eat the ball, that the best thing possible is to wing it into the end zone and don't worry about interceptions. Blanda is colorful in his simple, direct way. Lamonica is drab in his complex, hard-to-fathom style. One is a pedigreed Alpha Male. The other is an Alpha Male turned lone wolf. Behind them stands Kenny (Snake) Stabler, the Beta Male, just waiting, waiting, waiting.

"I know I'm not colorful," says Lamonica. "I don't pop off. I do try to stick around the locker room and talk to as many writers as come by my locker. I try to give them good, sensible,

logical answers. I don't wear mod clothes. I'm not saying I don't
like to have a good time. I like parties. I take a drink. But I'm
discreet. I work hard and when I relax, I guess I'd just as soon
hunt and fish as do anything. I like to let the old tissues unwind
in the open air."

George Blanda?

"What do you say about an immortal?" Lamonica asks, as
inscrutable as ever.

EPISODE 24

Ever since Al Davis came up the river from San Diego, there
has been a tribal feud between the Chargers and the Oakland
Raiders. It began with a little innocent merriment, the two
general manager-coaches lifting players off each others' injured-
waiver lists. Soon the players caught the general drift of things.
And, as the Chargers stopped winning Western Division championships, the Raiders began to. There was a vague affinity
between the two communities—freakish, really.

All those decades, Oakland had been playing Jersey City to
San Francisco's Manhattan and San Diego had been playing
Galveston to Los Angeles's Houston. It was the second city of
the south against the second city of the north; let's see who's
best among the have-nots.

Now the Chargers were in town and the newspapers had been
saying that this was George Blanda's chance for redemption
(same story, 129th verse). Earlier in the season, in San Diego, he
had missed that easy field goal and the newspapers had
described him as being "hesitant at field goal time," as ill-timed
a remark as any jock journalist has made in years.

"Redemption, hell!" he says before the game. "I get paid to
do my job. Sometimes I do it. Sometimes I don't. Lately, I've
been doing it. In the San Diego game I didn't. It's that simple.
I'm no miracle man."

Indeed, Miracle V belongs almost as much to Lamonica as it
does to Blanda. This time George is almost an automatic angel
of deliverance. It is Daryle who brings the Raiders close enough.
Still, the headlines go to the folk hero. It is part payment for all

the times Blanda did something that was forgotten 24 hours after the game ball was awarded.

But this is a miracle just the same and it is Blanda who kicks the winning field goal. The score is tied 17-17 and once again Oakland has to win to beat back the Kansas City Chiefs—who else? There is 4:35 left to play. Bill King, whose nervous system turned to strawberry jam three weeks earlier, is taking the whole thing so calmly that some listeners think he doesn't have a clear idea of what is going on.

"Well," he says, routinely, "it's cliff-hanger time once again."

Lamonica is setting the stage. George is waiting for his big entrance cue. Time passes slowly as Charlie Smith and Hewritt Dixon go crunching into the middle of a San Diego defensive line that will have to be almost totally restructured during the winter. But the important play comes with a kept football. Daryle, with a third-down-and-four-to-go situation on the San Diego 41-yard line, has his choice of receivers, either Dixon or Biletnikoff. Neither is convenient.

But Dixon, sneaking up the middle, gets open for only a second and then is sealed off forever. A defensive comes stomping after the quarterback. Wisely, Lamonica ducks and loses Biletnikoff. Instinct tells him to run. This is something that the old wolf admires in Daryle: his instincts. Someday, George thinks, he'll solve his other hangups and Lamonica will go on to become a great one. It takes time . . . so damned much time.

With no blocking to guide him, Lamonica gets down to the 27-yard line. Every football player's life is measured in chalk. Now Smith carries three times to the nine. There is an announcement: Jim Bakken has kicked a field goal. St. Louis has tied Kansas City, 6-6. Oh, wow! Now there's more incentive than there was a few seconds ago.

The sun, which has been hiding over San Francisco, naturally, comes sneaking out, ready to shine on old George. When you're hot, you're hot. When you're not . . . well, you're in Houston, you're throwing 36 touchdown passes in one season and Jack Gallagher is writing that you aren't good enough.

"The clock stops at seven seconds," says King, who knows . . . who absolutely *knows* . . . Miracle V is coming up.

"Could anyone . . . in the whole world . . . set the stage any more dramatically . . . to put any more heat on the shoulders of one guy than did the whole Raider Organization right there? They've put the ball where they wanted it, and they knew—everybody here knew—exactly what they were waiting for.

"George Blanda comes onto the field. Surely he must know what everyone expects. And that is—a miracle. This seems like a miracle he can deliver, as usual. The whole thing was placed on George's shoulders when Madden ordered Lamonica to run the clock down as close as he could. Good grief, there was a time when it appeared that perhaps Daryle didn't realize how close to the end of the game it was. Now only seven seconds are left.

"Madden is running along the sidelines, yelling at George. And now Blanda is calm. He knows pressure. He wants a good snap, a good hold, he'll get the field goal. The 16-yard line. Lamonica will spot it. He waits . . . the ball is snapped . . . it's spotted . . . it's kicked . . . it's good . . . *good!* George Blanda— oh, my God—George Blanda has kicked the Oakland Raiders into a three-point lead! Four seconds remain and this latest miracle may tie the San Francisco Bay Area up into a knot from which it may never extricate itself again!"

Again this is a stiff statement. The Bay Area extricates itself nicely. It is, however, awfully pleased by George Blanda. And why not? How much longer could this last? Is the man human? Is nature trying to overcompensate?

As the players rumble off the field, a woman leans over the side of the boxes and yells: "George, you stink!" Somebody from Chicago or Houston?

Now the Raiders lead their old friends the Chiefs by a full game. They are beginning to take miracle victories as their birthright. Nobody can afford the price of a pocket dictionary. ("Miracle—noun—an event in the natural world, but outside the established order, possible only by the intervention of divine power.") By now, St. Jude, patron saint of the Impossible, has probably decided that football is frivolous.

In another corner of the Coliseum bathhouse, the San Diego head coach Charlie Waller, who is doomed to strut and fret a brief hour on the NFL stage and then get reduced in rank again, is having convulsions. He claims that a 43-yard pass from Lamonica to Biletnikoff in the third quarter which set up a touchdown tying the game at 14-14 should have been ruled offensive pass interference. He does a nice job of complaining. Many people are impressed. Very shortly Sid Gillman will return as head coach and, a year later, get fired himself.

("Hey," says Freddie, who swears a lot, almost as much as Leo Durocher, "if they flashing call that flashing play flashing offensive flashing pass interference they are flashing out of their flashing minds. How the flash can they say that? Flash! Bob Howard, the flashing defensive back, gets there the same flashing time I do. We both go the flash up in the air for it and I come down more in the flashing control of it than he does. Flash! Flash! Flash!")

No question about Biletnikoff, he is a pretty good flashing football player. And anybody who doesn't think so can go flash himself.

Somebody asks Lamonica if he was worried about the field goal. He looks more serpentine than normal. He acts as if he's about to strike. He checks himself at the last minute. What he needs to do is study at the George Blanda Postgame-School-of-Honest-Replies. Instead, he is diplomatic.

"George would have had to scuff the ball in order to miss," he says. "I just can't believe he'd ever miss. Blanda doesn't scuff field goal kicks."

He puts a Blanda-for-Mayor button on his lapel, tactfully excuses himself and departs. Nobody can make anything out of that. Miracle V has arrived. There will be no Miracle VI, at least not in sequence. George is finally established as a folk hero. That's all destiny had in mind.

EPISODE 25

There is only one hotel worth a damn in Detroit. It is the Pontchartrain and it is a fortress, set aside by the hand of the

Establishment, against a sea of muggers. Detroit is crumbling. It is also dangerous. The white people long ago departed for the suburbs where they are building a new Detroit somewhere between Birmingham, Pontiac and Dearborn. They leave town in freeways, which are laid in trenches. That way nobody has to look at the decadence around them. This is one of the first places that poor blacks and Mexicans headed toward during the great cotton patch and lettuce field migrations of the 40s.

It is a victim of criminal civic neglect. The whole city seems to be composed of substandard housing. One newspaperman who worked there 13 months and then returned to California had two observations to make on Detroit: "First of all, if the blacks ever riot again and try to burn the place down, I hope they'll be kind enough to let a paleface join them. Secondly, the only way that I would ever return would be as the leader of a bombing squadron. To hell with Amchitka. The only constructive thing you could do with Detroit is to evacuate the civilian population and declare it an atomic test site."

So the Oakland Raiders do not leave the Pontchartrain, which is located in a narrow zone of urban splendor along the Detroit River, which ex-Mayor Jerome P. Cavanaugh, another Kennedyesque politician, redeveloped. While Al Davis lectures *Detroit News* reporter Jerry Green on faith and morals and quoting somebody out of context, an agent from the Hall of Fame shows up looking for George Blanda. This is a lousy week for George. His routine is smashed to hell because the Raiders must be in Detroit—of all ugly places—on Thanksgiving Day, which falls on a Thursday, when Blanda should be at the Grotto watching freighters pass by in the night.

Don Smith, publicity man for the hall, has come to pick up the jersey George has used in the last five games. He wants it, sweat and all. They plan to hang it in the front hallway.

"We saw something you wrote," he tells a guy from the *San Francisco Examiner.* "You said that it was inevitable that George would make the hall because he figures to retire with so many records. We felt he deserved some recognition right now. His jersey will go on display in the rotunda at the hall.

"George is going to be football's all-time scorer. It suddenly struck us that here is a guy who compares to baseball's Babe Ruth and his 714 lifetime home runs. What we want to do is show George what we think of him right now. He'll be voted into the hall someday, no question. But we want to honor him right now. That's why we have come after his jersey."

That's dandy. It is a nice gesture, one that George Blanda will eventually come to appreciate. But why in hell do they want it right now? This is the same shirt George wore through the games—Miracle I, Miracle II, Miracle III, Miracle IV and Miracle V. Why is Don Smith here now? There are still several games left. Blanda, who *absolutely* isn't superstitious, who just likes a safe, snug routine, would rather wait until after the Super Bowl. After much persuasion, he agrees to accept a new game jersey and send the miracle shirt to Canton.

You don't have to be a witch doctor, voodoo priest or east Texas conjure lady to know that this is a bad move. George knows it, too. It could only happen in Detroit, the city God never cared about in the first place.

In rust-ruined old Tiger Stadium, a structure so old that Ty Cobb's shade still seems to stalk the playing field, the miracles come to an end. Still, it is so close it is spooky. Oakland hits for two quick touchdowns. They are so convinced that no metal can touch them, they hoot and whistle at the Detroit Lions, most of whom are nearly as old as Blanda. This has a tendency to disturb the home team. It is a tactical blunder, one that old George would not approve of. Never rile the other side, he says.

"They thought the fact that we gave away two quick touchdowns was funny. Well, it sure as hell wasn't," says linebacker Wayne Walker, a geriatric marvel at age 35 himself. "It was like some stranger came into my home and shot my mother and tried to assault my wife. I just couldn't take it. I pointed it out to several other Detroit players. They were just as mad as I was."

It's bad enough you have to play football in Detroit, without a bunch of oafs from Oakland getting jocular about it. Even St. Jude could smile upon the Lions. And he does. Detroit scores three touchdowns and Madden turns toward George, respecting his elders as always.

"Get in there and change the tempo!" he says.

"Huh?"

Whatever happened to "momentum?"

Swiftly George works the ball down toward the Lions' 40. Now Chester slams his way past the free safety, Mike Weger, for a pass completion and a first down on the Detroit three. Beautiful! Here's Miracle VI coming up. But a yellow hankie flutters in the dreadful Michigan breeze. Oakland has gone offsides. George Blanda fights the decision for a few seconds and then turns and goes back to the huddle. The miracle streak is all in the past tense now.

"What happened, Raymond?" says Blanda, looking straight into the eyes of his tight end. George expected a logical answer. This was a very nice young man, very bright and very strong physically.

"I was watching the center," he says, as honestly as possible. "When he moved, I went with him. You gotta trust Jim Otto. He's been around so long. The rest of the line was behind him," he says.

"It doesn't happen often," Blanda says, "but I've seen it happen before. Okay, you're excused."

Now the magic is gone. The two teams drift off the playing field. The Lions are winners, 28-14. No miracles this week. No screaming headlines: "It's Blanda Again!" It is close, but George's game shirt is in the Hall of Fame rotunda, which is just as deadly as having to attend a booster club meeting and miss a day at Bay Meadows. The flight home is slow. The movie is God-awful. Never, never break routine!

EPISODE 26

After some deliberation, the chartered jet seems to know which side of the bay Oakland is located on. It comes to a creaking, grinding, moaning halt. Loved ones are present. There are no television cameras. No booster club drunks. Only friends of the family. Al Davis, wearing a white Lisbon-spy overcoat,

*gets off muttering to himself. Losing football games does awful
things to his psyche.*

*"What happened?" asks Mrs. Betty Blanda, who ought to
know better after all these years.*

*"Lost the damn game," says George, gritting his teeth and
marching straight ahead.*

So what did the lady expect? Miracle VI? Well, why not?

EPISODE 27

Now the long, long season is past. Now all that gaudy talk
about miracles is purely arbitrary. Somebody else is going to
Super Bowl V in Miami and that makes the nerve endings ache.
For several seasons, George Frederick Blanda has been saying
that if he could drag a team, kicking and screaming, into the
Super Bowl and win—say, in the last three seconds—he would
finally retire. It won't happen this year, because the Raiders
have come so perilously close and have failed. Besides, George
wants to play in 1971 and 1972 anyway.

It is late in January and George is on an airplane, flying to
Hollywood, of all plastic places. He is about to cut a record on
the Daybreak label, of all curious labels. The miracle season is
over. There was an unusual moment in New York. There was
Daryle making a miracle of his own, throwing a pass to Warren
Wells with seconds left to tie the score at 13-13. They asked
George to kick the extra point, of course, and the *New York
Daily News* headlined this automatic act as "George Does It
Again!" If a man can make miracles in places like Oakland and
Kansas City, he damn well better make them in New York, too.

"I guess that's what fame is," he says sardonically.

In the playoffs, the Raiders handle Miami easily and are
defeated by Baltimore, the eventual champion of the universe.
They stick George in there, with the idea that he might work
further witchcraft. It doesn't happen.

"Some afternoon! Ted Hendricks, that big gawky kid linebacker of theirs knocks hell out of me and then has the gall to
say, 'Sorry, Mr. Blanda.' And Bill Ray Smith, their tackle, who
is 35 or 36, is so happy to see somebody on a football field

older than he, that he takes shot after shot at me. Each time the bastard says, 'Sorry, old timer.' Old-timer, my Aunt Fanny.''

At the recording studio, they want George, who is wearing a white turtleneck sweater and looking very Hollywood, to talk his way through "This Old House," the country and western standard, and "Never Too Late," which has been written just for him. After two takes, they suggest that he try singing.

"His voice was excellent," says ex-bandleader Del Courtney, who now works for the Raiders directing halftime shows. "His voice is strong and firm. He seems to have a natural sense of cadence. I'm amazed."

Blanda isn't surprised when he hears the quality of the playback. It proves a theory of his: All great quarterbacks have superb voices, the better to call plays at the line of scrimmage with. Quarterbacks need to get everyone's attention. On the field, George has always had a drill instructor's baritone.

"Listen to John Brodie sometime," he says. "When John calls signals his voice fills the whole stadium. Listen to the 49ers' number two man, Steve Spurrier, if you can. Most people can't hear him, including his own center. That's probably one reason why he's still number two. Our Daryle Lamonica has a fantastic voice.

"When I was with Houston we had a kid named Don Trull playing behind me. He set all kinds of national passing records at Baylor. But he had a reedy voice. He was always coming out of the huddle, stammering and spitting. He never made it. He's somewhere in the Canadian League now, with Edmonton, I think."

George agrees to endorse the two products he really believes in. He also does a sales promotion film entitled, "Think Win!" It is similar to one that Vince Lombardi did. Blanda has no financial worries because of all those years with the trucking firm. In less than a year, he will also become the first active athlete ever to apply for his pension while he is still playing. It is $450 a month. He doesn't need it, he just wants to prove a point.

"I don't know if I can legally collect it, but I'm sure going to find out, because that's $50 more a month than George Halas gave me the year after I got out of the University of Kentucky," he says, lobo eyes gleaming.

He has seen the series of three articles that *Sports Illustrated* plans to run. He doesn't like the tone of the stories.

"The series covers a lot of material, but it doesn't show the real me," he says. "It makes me sound like some kind of cartoon character. I'm hardly that. I'm a simple, straightforward person. But those stories make me sound kind of simple-witted."

So George Blanda beats on against the current, struggling to show the world old verities aren't dead. Some kids still look up to football heroes. They still learn something from the game. Competition does ennoble a man. Isn't George Blanda living proof?

He cannot hope to be a first-string quarterback anymore, not at his age. It is unthinkable! So he hides his pride a little and coexists beautifully with Daryle Lamonica. He speaks well of Daryle at every opportunity.

"He and I have a great relationship," says Blanda. "He could have had an embarrassing year this past season, but he didn't. I try to help him. He asks me things and I try to do the best I can. He's a great quarterback. At my age, I'm just content to be No. 2 behind him . . . of course . . . if I was 31 again . . . it would be . . . heh! heh! . . . a whole lot different."

George Blanda grins wickedly. His hair is shaggy. His muzzle is gray. His eyes are luminous like those of a wolf following a sleigh. No man is ever too old, especially if he is an Alpha Male.

— End of Period —

SECOND PERIOD

Bear Bryant, Papa Bear, the Chicago Bears [*]

[*] And Other Wildlife

(Can a poor boy from a mining town in western Pennsylvania find happiness with two of history's toughest football coaches? Well, yes and no.)

TINTYPE 1

The scrapbooks are stored way back in the closet, behind the place where the winter coats go in the summer and the summer coats go in the winter. They crackle when they are opened, as if the pages were made out of onion peelings. The corners are totally decomposed and some of the stories pasted inside are no longer readable. They come from an era that is gone with the wind, when football helmets were still being made out of leather and more schools played the single wing formation than the T, which was considered just a little bit radical.

One of the great ironies in sports is that while athletes may be disturbed, annoyed or outraged at the curious things newspapermen write about them, they all clip out the stories and tenderly place them in scrapbooks. No active football player has more scrapbooks than George Frederick Blanda. His wife says she starts a new one every generation. And there is as much truth as humor in that remark. The first ones, though, are the most interesting. It seems incredible that a contemporary of

Doc Blanchard, Glenn Davis, Doak Walker and Leon Hart would
still be throwing his body around a football field more than a
quarter of a century later. But those four people were Heisman
Trophy winners during the four years that Blanda was an
undergraduate at the University of Kentucky. Think of it, and
enjoy the warm excitement of having your brain boggled.

Open those museum-piece scrapbooks and step way back in
time. It is 1945 again. The great crusade against Facism is
grinding to a merciful conclusion. Patriotism is everywhere.
There are flags behind the bar in Youngwood, Pa. There are also
gold stars hanging in mothers' windows. The movies that appear
in the town's lone picture show are so wholesome they squeak.
Lynn Bari is falling in love with some soldier home on leave or
John Wayne is being confronted by Sessue Hayakawa, who says,
with a rattlesnake sneer, "Ah, so, you are surprised I speak your
wrangwrige. I was enducated in your country . . . at UC-R-A."

Harry Truman fills the White House with piano music and
some of the choicest language anyone has heard in Washington
since Andrew Jackson was president. There is a drastic shortage
of athletes. So the Chicago Cubs and Detroit Tigers are winning
pennants with an incredible collection of old men and 4-F-ers.
When they come together in the fall, Warren Brown, the
Chicago columnist, will write: "I don't see how either team can
win this world series." Matters are so grim that the St. Louis
Browns—remember them?—have a one-armed outfielder and
everybody is saying, "Gee, he really isn't bad." Everything is
relative. At the moment, Pete Gray really isn't bad.

Television has not yet been inflicted on society, its develop-
ment held up by the war. So professional football does not
dominate Sunday afternoon. There are only a few teams, the
Pittsburgh Steelers, the Green Bay Packers, the Chicago
Cardinals, the New York Giants, the Chicago Bears, the
Philadelphia Eagles, etc. But they do not get much newspaper
coverage outside the cities where they play. So the men of
Youngwood spend their Sundays listening to Pittsburgh Pirate
games on the radio and drinking Polish Champagne—two shots of
rye whiskey in a glass of beer.

This is gritty, drab bituminous coal country. High school football takes everybody's minds off the low quality of their life-styles. Crowds are large at games. The entire town shows up. Stores close and houses empty for road trips. The traffic is bumper-to-bumper from Youngwood to Bentleyville and back. Only the police force remains behind. Players are named Stankovich, Kurowski, Stepko, Jurik, Puskarich, Ciereij and Blanda, the sons of men who spend ten hours a day crouched over where the rain never falls and the sun doesn't shine. Blanda is the tailback for the Youngwood High School Railroaders, of all exotic nicknames. He is what romanticists of the period refer to as a "triple threat," which means he runs, kicks and passes with equal skill. Not only that he plays defense. In one game he comes frighteningly close to kicking a field goal on the kickoff. The ball hits the crossbar and falls back onto the field.

"But my big sport is basketball," said Blanda, looking at the scrapbooks. "And I'm also crazy over track. In fact, I'm the whole track team. It's true. I was a discus and javelin thrower and I also put the shot. I didn't have a coach. All I knew I got out of books in the library and I didn't know much. I was so dumb that every time I'd throw the javelin I'd get this terrible whiplash across my back. I didn't know any better.

"I go to the interscholastic meets and they'd say, 'Introducing the Youngwood High School track team,' and George would be the only guy there. I didn't even have a uniform, just dungarees, T-shirt and sneakers. I guess it would have been funny as hell, except that I'd usually get firsts in all three events.

"In one big meet, I got 15 points and finished second in the team standing. I was a one-man team. I had a buddy of mine go with me to track meets. I'd carry the shot and the discus and he'd carry the javelin. He used to say that he was the manager for the Youngwood High School track team. Don't think track isn't dangerous. One day I'm standing around the field and somebody yells, 'Hey, George, watch out.'

"I look up and here's this javelin flying through the sky and it's headed straight for my middle. Anybody else jumps back, right? Well, I'm just a dumb Polack. So I jump up. That's right. That javelin hits me right in the upper thigh on my right leg. I came about this close to being the 'Queen of Pennsylvania.' That damn spear could have got me right in the groin."

So in May of 1945, George Blanda is recovering from his injury, the only athlete ever to be wounded in action at the Western Pennsylvania Interscholastic League track meet in Clairton, Pa. It has been his dream to go to Notre Dame. One afternoon he is on the playground, limping around, playing basketball and moving about as slow as you would expect anyone to move who has just recently been punctured by a spear. Along comes the Notre Dame football coach, who has a scholarship for this Slovak kid. Which one is George Blanda? The dark-haired kid with the defiant jaw. Him? The one that's moving so slow? When does the bus go back to South Bend?

"After that I just about made up my mind I'd go to the University of Pennsylvania and be a genuine Ivy Leaguer. I had offers from Purdue, Pitt, Penn State, NYU, William and Mary. I had received letters from lots of other schools. But I decided that I was going to go to the University of Pennsylvania. A fellow who lived over in the next town, a place called Greensburg, was an assistant coach at Penn and he hung around our place. Finally he talked me and Lou Kusserow, who ended up going to Columbia, into visiting the University. I'd played high school basketball against Lou. He was from another small town in the area, Glassport. We took our exams. I passed and I guess he did too. And it looked like I was going to go to Penn. I planned to enter in time for the summer sessions, which started in July.

"I'm home one day and this guy comes to the door. I don't know him from Adam, but he's a scout for the University of Kentucky. He's got a train ticket. He tells me it's a train ticket to Lexington and I want you to go down there and look the place over. If you like it, tell me and I'll get you a scholarship. Well, hell, I don't know anything about the University of Kentucky. In fact, I didn't even know where Kentucky was.

"I thought Kentucky was all the way across country. Up

until I was 17 I was never further away from Youngwood than Pittsburgh, which is about 30 or 40 miles away. I thought they were still fighting Indians west of Pittsburgh.

"I didn't want to go down to visit. But I don't know how to tell the guy I don't want his ticket. So I take it and thank him and close the door. I'm all set to go to Penn. I'd already told the head coach there, George Munger, that I was coming. They had some fine football teams there then. Chuck Bednarik was there. I guess maybe down deep in my mind I really didn't want to go there. I'd heard that you had to join a fraternity and keep up a social front. And I'm just a Slovak kid from a coal town and all I know is Polish sausage and boiled cabbage.

"The people at Penn had been impressing on me that there was a class structure there and it would be a good chance for me to move up socially. And that didn't really thrill me. I wasn't really looking for that, coming from my background. I wanted to get an education. I was good in mathematics and figured I might want to be an engineer. I didn't know what an engineer was, but it sounded good. I figured I'd go to Penn anyway, because their engineering school was supposed to be pretty hot. I figured I'd just learn to live with the society stuff. So I decided I wouldn't bother with Kentucky. One afternoon, my old man caught me by the scruff of the neck—he was a pretty hardnosed guy—and he says, 'When you going down to talk to the people at the University of Kentucky?' I told him I wasn't going. He said, 'The hell you're not . . . these people gave you an opportunity to see their school . . . so, go down there and look the place over.' Well, needless to say, if I hadn't gone he would have knocked the hell out of me.

"So I go from Pittsburgh to Cincinnati on the train. I'm a young, 17-year-old kid and I've got eyes this big. When I got to Cincinnati, I managed to get lost in the train terminal. Finally, I find my right train. I figure it'll be another long ride from Cincinnati to Lexington, so I better get some sleep. How did I know it's only an hour to Lexington? The conductor's shaking hell out of me and I'm trying to rassle him.

"I got off the train and looked around. Thank God you can

see the University from the station because there was nobody
there to meet me. Nobody! So I start walking and I feel like the
world is about to swallow me up. I keep thinking, 'I wish the
hell I'd never left Youngwood!' And, 'What am I doing in this
place?'

"After about an hour, I find the athletic department and I go
looking for the head football coach, who was Bernie Shively at
the time. He never heard of me! He never goddamned heard of
me! I said, 'I'm George Blanda!' He says, 'What are you doing
here?' I told him somebody gave me a ticket to come down and
visit the school. He wanted to know what I played. I said, 'I'm a
football player.' He said, 'Okay, this afternoon we'll have a little
workout. Take you out and see what you can do.'

"I told him I was a kicker and a passer—you know, a
single-wing tailback. So I went out and threw the ball around,
punted and place kicked. It wasn't a tryout exactly. They just
wanted to see what you had. At that time, in 1945, with the
war not over yet, they'd take you if you were breathing.
They're looking for anybody. I could always throw the ball a
long way. I probably could throw the ball better than I do now.
Maybe I wasn't as consistent or as accurate, but I was hell for
distance. I could really whip the ball. Immediately, they're
impressed.

"I told them I was going to the University of Pennsylvania.
Well, now Coach Shively knows my name. He has me stay
around for about five days. They took me to the Kentucky
Derby and I was impressed with that. I'd never seen horse racing
before. Somehow I let it drop that I really preferred to play
basketball. Now Coach Shively goes looking for Adolph Rupp,
the basketball coach. He asks me to come to one of his tryout
sessions. I guess Shively said, 'Give George some bull.' He knew
I could play football for Kentucky, but he guessed that I
probably wouldn't make the basketball team. Well, he was right.
So Rupp lets me work out and after it's over the Great Adolph
Rupp motions me over and says, 'I think you can make our
basketball team if you come to school here.' I always was a

better basketball player than I was a football player and I knew I was better than any of the guys he had in there for this tryout.

"That got me thinking about Kentucky. But you know what the clincher was? They decided to buy me two suits of clothes. I'd never owned a suit in my life. So I picked out two suits—one blue and one brown. Then Shively really went to work on me. He had all these big players coming back, bigger than guys I'd seen at the other schools. And he starts telling me how Kentucky is going to go to the Cotton Bowl and the Sugar Bowl and I'd get a chance to see the nation. When you went up East, the coaches and athletic directors didn't talk about a thing except how great it would be to go to their schools.

"I said, 'Well, this is the place to go. If they give me two suits and promise me we'll go to the Sugar Bowl or the Cotton Bowl, I'll go to Kentucky.' That's all I got. I was never a pampered high school athlete. If you played poorly in those western Pennsylvania towns, you couldn't run fast enough to get away from the lynch mob. If you did well, the people looked up to you and said, 'He's a good athlete, that George Blanda.' But there was none of this slipping you $10 for having a good game. They expected you'd have a good game. Nobody ever took you out for a meal. Hell, there was no place in Youngwood to buy you a meal anyway. You were better off eating at home. We weren't pampered at Youngwood and that was good training, because it got me ready to play for Bear Bryant.

"Bear Bryant! There was a wonderful coach and a wonderful man . . . a mean son of a bitch, but a wonderful coach and man. The Bear taught me discipline, respect and dedication. He'd run your fanny right into the ground. Those practice sessions of his . . . well, when they were over you wanted to collapse. But the Bear wasn't that merciful. He wouldn't even let you die. He'd make you run back to the locker room. He'd tell you to turn in your suit if you didn't sprint. I picked up a lot from him. He was just as mean as my old man. But they both taught me how to compete.

"All the pampering I ever got was those two suits. That's all I ever needed. Other than that I got just what the NCAA allowed, room, board and tuition. One time I thought I should be getting a little something under the table. I'd heard all these stories. I mentioned it to coach Bryant. He came up over the top of his desk and grabbed me by my eyeballs.

" 'You want what?' he yells.

" 'Just joking, coach,' I said and got the hell out of there. That taught me a great lesson about greed. After that I didn't care if other people got more than I did. I was getting my college education paid for and I was getting help finding summer jobs. So, I figured I was damned lucky.

"They hustle me into school in time for the summer semester, because they didn't want me going to Penn. Naturally, there was a summer workout for the football players. About the fifth practice session, I tore the cartilage in my right knee. I was pretty upset about it. But at the time they didn't know anything about knee injuries. I'm not so sure they know so much about it now. They just taped me up and I played my first year that way—freshmen were eligible for the varsity then. Needless to say, I didn't have a first-class year. My grades weren't that good because I was worried about my leg and I kind of let my classwork slip.

"Oh, yes, that first year . . . we didn't go to the Sugar Bowl or the Orange Bowl or the Cotton Bowl. We won one game and lost nine. I was mad at myself. I said, 'George, you damn fool. You made a stupid decision and now there's nothing to do but hang in there and make the best of it.' I figured maybe something good would happen. Then, flash! They brought coach Bryant in from Maryland. Well, that suited me fine. I'd heard a lot of good things about him. I had started out as a quarterback in the T-formation as a freshman and halfway through the season we switched back to the single wing and I played tailback. I didn't like all that switching around. Everything I had heard about coach Bryant led me to think we would go to one formation and stay with it.

"Wow! My first impression of him when he came down in January of my freshman year was, 'This must be what God looks like.' He was a very handsome man, tall and smooth. He was the most energetic man I'd ever seen. He'd walk in the room and you wanted to stand up and applaud. He gives this speech to the student body and I thought he was going to get elected president.

"He called all the players in, one by one. I got a little worried, because I figured that, having gone 1-9 the year before there wouldn't be too many of us around. He asked me how I felt and I told him my knee was killing me. He got me right to a doctor. I laid off spring practice, of course, and came back that summer. I went into that operation scared. I'd heard all kinds of stuff. A lot of guys told me that they might go in there and screw things up so bad I'd end up with a stiff leg. I made it all right. I had to drop out of school for the January-to-March quarter. I went home to Youngwood and I ran. I ran in that miserable weather for five or six miles a day. I figured I'd better work because coach Bryant didn't strike me as the kind who would run an easy practice. Then I came back in the spring quarter and they were working out. I just hung around and watched."

One interesting thing occurs because of the knee operation. George decides that it might be a good idea to take a tumbling class to build up the knee. It is co-educational. That is fine because there is this certain brunette that he is very anxious to get close to and she is enrolled. In the same class is Miss Betty Harris, a Lexington girl who does not happen to be brunette. She is a blonde, very bright and shiny. It is all right with her because she has her eye on another guy.

"Would you believe it?" she asks. "The girl George was after and the guy I thought was so cute fell for each other. In desperation, I looked around the room and here's this football player working out on the side horse. We made a marvelous couple. I was majoring in dance. That's why I took the class."

Did they tumble together?

"No," says Mrs. Betty Harris Blanda, "but we were involved in some wonderful pyramids."

They develop a meaningful relationship, long before the term becomes popular. There is one small hindrance: Paul (Bear) Bryant, who is now the sole proprietor of George Blanda's body and, he presumes, George's soul as well. Kentucky football players do not smoke, drink, curse or carry on with women, not even ones they are in love with and want to marry.

("Enjoy how warm and soft that little hand you're holding going across campus is," Bear is fond of telling his players, "because the memory of it is going to keep you company on the bench this Saturday.")

One afternoon, Betty Harris and another girl who is also dating a football player on the sly, leave their jobs at the University library, and climb to the top of the stadium where they can eat their lunches and get a little sun. It is summertime and even the bluegrass is begging for relief from the Kentucky heat. Suddenly they hear noise on the playing field below. Coach Bryant has driven the team out for a special practice, it being nice and humid and all. Now, the girls are aware that coach Bryant is aware that they are seeing a couple of his athletes. But nobody is letting on. However, if they show themselves, George and the other player will have to turn in their suits. So they figure they can outwait Bear Bryant. This is a tactical blunder, one which they share with numerous opposing coaches. The varsity scrimmages in the heat. Then everyone who is still alive goes through hours of special drills. By sundown when they all go sprinting off, the two girls are an inch away from a good sunstroke.

"I tell you that summer was hell," says George, who re-members it with more fondness than does his wife. "It was right after the war. You got all the returning servicemen who played in 1941 and 1942. You got all the kids from the 1945 team, freshmen and sophomores, mostly. And Bryant had people coming in from all over the country. He'd been the coach at the Bainbridge, Maryland training station and he knew where every stray athlete was hiding. Shoot, he'd fly them in. He'd get guys who had played on service teams and still had eligibility remaining. It was like you'd do now scouting and signing pro players.

"We must have had five hundred to a thousand kids come through there on tryouts. It was very competitive. It was the survival of the fittest, all right. It was like the old joke about having three teams—one there playing, one coming and one going. I think we practiced football eleven months that year. Coach Bryant brought in the Notre Dame box formation. I guess he figured he wanted to find the meanest Polack on the club and make him the blocking back. I qualified. I didn't like it. I'd always been a kicker, a passer and a runner and I liked the action. I didn't like moving around, blocking for somebody else.

"Hell, I sulked. He knew it, too. So he dropped me to the second string. Well, the first time we scrimmage the varsity, I'm at linebacker on the second unit. I tell myself, 'Okay, coach, you're going to see some action.' I kept hitting people and hitting people. I smacked one halfback so hard, he kicked me in the face when he got up. They were using Harry Ulinski, who later played with the Redskins, and Jerry Claiborne, who's a college coach now at Maryland, ahead of me as blocking backs on the varsity.

"I finally won the job late in the year. Next season we went to the T-formation and I became the quarterback. It was tough recruiting T quarterbacks in those days and I could throw the ball. Coach Bryant figured he'd better give me the job because I didn't want to hit anybody. He said he thought they had invented the position just for me.

"I wasn't what you'd call a skillful passer, I was a thrower. But I could get the ball up there. He wanted a quarterback who was a leader and he had found out I had a mind of my own.

"There was one pre-season scrimmage—they called it the Blue and White game—when we were still using the Notre Dame box. I was calling plays and we were down the two-yard line, getting ready to score. I get in the huddle and decide, 'Shoot, we aren't going to shift this time.' I'll just take the snap directly from the center, send a man in motion and throw him a pass. Make up my own play, in other words. I throw the ball in there and . . . no way it's going to be completed. We lose the ball on downs and by the time I get to the sidelines, coach Bryant, who had been watching up in the press box, is already there. He got down that quick. He's right there!

"He grabs me and he says, 'You little . . .' well, never mind what he called me. 'I'm the coach of this team and until you're smart enough to be coach of a football team, don't go making up any plays. If you do I'll have you back in that little Pennsylvania town you come from so damned fast you'll think you never left it.' That taught me a hell of a lesson. The year before we'd had this easygoing coach, Bernie Shively, who kind of encouraged individualism. And in high school we occasionally made up plays. But Bear . . . ooooh, boy! I never crossed him again. That man had you running so many 100-yard dashes. I think after my senior year, he had me down to 175 pounds. My mother thought I was sick or something."

During Blanda's senior year he gets some practice making miracles. Here's Kentucky with a 3-3 record heading for its worst season under Bryant. Here's the Bear making ugly noises at the troops. The Wildcats are matched against Villanova and they get the ball on their own 42-yard line with just 44 seconds left to play. They are behind Villanova by a 13-6 score. The customers figure it's time to leave. Naturally, Kentucky loses 11 yards in three plays. It is now fourth down and 21.

The Villanova line is charging with all the fury of Yangtze River pirates and Blanda can't find an open receiver. A tackle has one arm wrapped around George's funny leather helmet. Just as he goes down, he gets the pass off to halfback Jim Howe in the flat.

At midfield, Ulinski throws a block that gets Howe into the open. Only eight seconds remain when Blanda steps in and kicks the extra point that throws the game into a tie, 13-13. Kentucky does not lose another game all season. The morning after the Villanova game, the *Louisville Courier-Journal* mentions something about a miracle and says that George Frederick Blanda, age 20, senior, Youngwood, Pa., is probably the man most responsible for making it happen.

"You think that earns you any special concessions from coach Bryant? You figure that he's going to pamper you after that? Hell, no," says George, rubbing a finger over the clipping that tells about his undergraduate miracle. "At scrimmage the next week, I pitch out to a halfback, who just misses the ball entirely. It's a bad pitch and he's out of position, anyway. It just flops on the grass and neither of us make a move for it.

"So Bryant comes out and says, 'You bastards, both of you, start running around that track until I tell you to stop.' That makes me feel about that big. But we're both wrong, so we start running and running and running. Finally, this halfback leans over and says, 'Screw him, George, let's turn right at the exit by the gym and keep on going.' The Bear lets us run and run. About the fifteenth time around, I'm thinking, 'Is it really worth it?' I forget how many laps he let us run. It was way past sundown when he finally waved us in. And we were heroes of the game the week before. What do you figure would have happened if we had screwed up?

"The Bear was a demanding son of a gun. He still is, although he tells me he's mellowed some. I owe my longevity in the game to him and his coaching philosophy: Hard work equals success. That's the only way to make it. Hell, I didn't like his system at first. I wanted to be a goof-off like everybody else. But you could see Bryant get results. We were 1-9 the year before he got there. From that point we went to 7-3 to 8-3, his second year. There was proof that hard work would get you someplace. Bear Bryant laid the groundwork for my whole life," says Blanda. "The only thing he was wrong about was when he told George Halas I probably never would make it as a place kicker in the National Football League. Heh-heh!"

The yellowed clippings in the scrapbooks—their ancient ink fading fast with the stampeding years—show a meatless, almost callow face. The jaw juts. The nose is not as tangled as it will appear in later years with the Oilers and the Raiders. The hair is black and cut short. George Blanda was young once, sports fans. He really was.

TINTYPE 2

Come, close your tired little eyes and drift away on a golden cloud of fantasy. This is the part in the life story of every football folk hero where he (a) gets the girl (b) gets the degree . . . well, maybe . . . and (c) gets drafted on the first round by some high-powered professional football club. While he waits with lordly disdain, team executives scrape together a fancy financial package, which includes a $50,000-a-year no-cut contract good for four years; roughly $150,000 in cash bonus payments; a $250,000 life insurance policy; a portfolio of stocks worth $100,000, and a new Mercedes-Benz.

That's how it always happens, right? Wrong! You are guilty of living in the present. Return with us now to those penurious days of yesteryear. There are only a dozen members of the National Football League. The feeble candle that is the All-America Conference is about to be snuffed out. Great college quarterbacks can be had for as little as $6000 cold quid. George Halas rules!

Technically it is the spring of George Blanda's senior year. Actually it is the beginning of the winter of his discontent. The sun is about to set. It will not rise again for a full decade. When this dark period has ended, Blanda-the-enigma will be complete. Michael Blanda has taught him to compete. Bear Bryant has taught him the value of hard work and discipline. George Halas will have taught him to be suspicious of people's motives, to study his fellow man judiciously and put the good guys over here, the bad guys over there.

"I never gave professional football any real thought," Blanda recalls. "It wasn't something you thought about. I didn't read that many papers when I was a kid in Youngwood. I think the townspeople were afraid that if you read how well you were playing, you'd get a big head. I'd heard of the pros, of course. But I never gave them much thought."

It appears that Miss Betty Harris is serious about becoming Mrs. Blanda, so George starts hunting around for work. He qualifies for a degree in education, so he figures that he will get a job teaching and coaching football on the side. He even writes to a couple of high schools wondering if they could use an enthusiastic kid from western Pennsylvania on their faculty.

"Somebody had told me once about the Pittsburgh Steelers and I guess I'd heard of the Chicago Bears. But, shoot, I just wasn't oriented toward professional football. At Youngwood, we never read about it. We never heard about it on the radio. In fact, our family didn't have a radio until about eight years after radios came out. So I figured I'd better get me a job and forget about sports. My career was over when I graduated from Kentucky. At least that's what I thought."

So George Blanda wanders around the Lexington campus in the spring of 1949, watching practice from the sidelines, commenting on a sophomore named Vito (Babe) Parilli who is going to replace him at quarterback and wondering what to do with the rest of his life. One afternoon, he runs into a former teammate, Wash Serini, whom he has sort of lost track of.

"I asked him what he was doing and he tells me, 'I'm with the Chicago Bears now. Great team; great organization.' You saw so little about pro football in the newspapers that I honest-to-God didn't know Serini had turned pro. About the only pro players we'd heard of in Lexington were people who were real famous like Sammy Baugh and Sid Luckman. Well, Serini got me interested in the Bears. I start wondering, 'How do you try out for one of these teams?' The fall before I'd received about 15 questionnaires from the clubs in both leagues, but I really didn't know how to get a job with one."

In a few days the answer arrives. You don't volunteer, you get drafted. A letter arrives from—of all people—the Chicago Bears. They are so overwhelmed by Blanda that they have made him their twelfth-round selection. They don't bother to phone. They send a railroad ticket and suggest that George come north to Chicago to discuss signing a contract. Then comes a call from the commissioner of the All-America Conference. He tells Blanda that he has been drafted, on the fourth round, by the Los Angeles Dons. He asks that George not sign with the Bears until he is contacted by an agent from the AAC. Somebody from the Dons is on his way to Lexington. Suddenly, Blanda decides that teaching history and English and coaching a high school team can wait a year or two.

"I was so excited about the Bears, I couldn't think straight. Serini had convinced me that I should go to Chicago and that's what I wanted to do. Besides, the Dons used the same formation Kentucky had played when I was a freshman. They'd line up in a T-formation and, sometimes, they'd switch to the single wing. I had visions of myself trying to impersonate a blocking back again. I didn't mind taking the knocks. But I can see that if I go in that direction I might get killed."

Blanda is not aware of the fact at the time, but he has been recommended to the Bears by Michigan State coach Biggie Munn. Two years running, George has beaten the Spartans, passing, running and kicking. Munn informs Halas that this Blanda is still a trifle crude, because he hasn't quite matured physically, but has an interesting selection of talents. Halas has also written to Bryant. The Bear tells Papa Bear that George has not quite lived up to Bryant's expectations, but that he is a competitive fanatic. Obviously, he is worth squandering a twelfth-round draft choice on.

TINTYPE 3

The passenger train goes snorting through the Kentucky hills, hurling at the placid spring sky the residue of bituminous coal Michael Blanda might have dug. How does one act in the presence of a living legend? Even though sports writers have a habit of creating immortals and living legends rather frivolously, George Halas certainly qualifies for one designation or the other. It would not be possible to write an adequate history of professional football without mentioning his name. It might not be necessary to even mention the sport. Without Halas, professional football might have been stillborn in the early 1920s. He is stern, suspicious and ruthless. He is capable of great charity to fallen friends and ex-employees. He is also capable of committing acts of unreasonable ... er ... thrift. He is the son of Bohemian immigrants and he has become the first cousin to a

Jewish mother. He has become a Slavic father, a thunderous, sly, unreachable family ruler. He is an unquestioned patriarch.

Over the years he has mastered the art of survival. He has also seen many of his theories become popular. He insists that football is not entirely a physical exercise. It is so cerebral that Chicago Bear quarterbacks must commit to memory, literally, an encyclopedia of offensive formations. By signing Red Grange in 1925 he has instituted professional football's star system. He has kept his own franchise alive and prospering through an incredible series of intrigues. By socially ingratiating himself with their publishers, he has managed to keep Chicago sports writers properly cowed. Because he has not heard a discouraging word in so many years, he now has come to think that he is above criticism. He operates on that premise.

"George Halas, coach and owner of the Chicago Bears, has all the warmth of breaking bones," author William Barry Furlong will write one day. "He has a personality as daring as twin beds and—in the classic dramatic tradition—a strength that is his main weakness: He is a self-made man.

"That fact explains as much as anything why he is frugal, hardworking, paternalistic, utterly loyal—and why the juices of humanity seem to have been squeezed from him. The gracious arts seem as practiced in Halas as a pass pattern. He smiles as though it hurts. He pats a man on the back stiffly, like uncooked spaghetti breaking. 'The most human thing about him are his failures,' says one friend—and he turns from them as reflexively as blinking. Yet he has in him the ability to arouse a fantastic loyalty from certain personalities. He is a conscientious man religiously and a generous one privately. And he carries around with him the burden of his own success."

That is what a free-lance writer can say. When Halas picks up papers in his own city he is more apt to read: "George Halas is head of his household, and his word is law. He will tolerate no disobedience, no insubordination. And yet his boys love him. They'll go through hell and high water if he gave the word. He asks nothing of his players and assistants that he himself is not ready to do, and he is probably ready to do a bit more in addition."

(It is not until the 1969 season, with Halas approaching his golden anniversary in professional football and his team slopping through a 1-13 season, that the Chicago press really opens fire on the Patriarch. He responds with a godly wrath.)

Now George Blanda is traveling by train to Chicago to sign his first professional contract. The wolf is going off to meet the bear. Oddly, they have similar roots, a common blood. Both have jaws that dominate their faces. Their eyes have a lordly animal quality. Both are fiercely Slavic with parents who came from neighboring provinces of the same European state, Czechoslovakia. This will be one of George Halas's boys who will not love him. Over the next ten years, Blanda will mock, defy, obey, respect and admire Halas. But he will walk away from Chicago disliking the Patriarch intensely. And nothing, not even the passage of years or Blanda's twilight fame or Halas's dotage, will dull the intensity of that emotion.

Certainly, a psychiatrist might suggest that George Blanda sees in Halas all the fierce qualities he saw in his own father, but without Michael Blanda's deep, loving concern for keeping his son out of the mines. In the decade ahead, Halas will attempt to subjugate this harshly competitive young Slovak. He will make him a first-string quarterback, only to demote him time after time. He will place him in a symbolic coal mine and George Blanda will walk through hell to escape.

TINTYPE 4

With a certain tightness starting to spread through his upper torso, George Blanda gets off the train in Chicago and decides the only thing to do is act nonchalant. He picks up a couple of newspapers, hardly reads them and starts looking for a taxi. He is supposed to meet Halas that afternoon in the Bears' executive suite on West Madison. He arrives early and decides to have lunch in a nearby hamburger shop. It suddenly occurs to him that perhaps he might be better off with the Los Angeles Dons. Is it better to be a first-string blocking back in a league that seems doomed or is it better to be a fourth-string quarter-back with the Chicago Bears, an unshakable institution?

"I'm thinking while I'm waiting that I must be some kind of damn fool to want to sign with a team that already has Sid Luckman, Johnny Lujack and Bobby Layne around to play quarterback. If I don't watch out, they're liable to ask to put on some weight to see if I can't play guard. How did I know that Halas liked to stockpile quarterbacks so he could trade them off? I came to believe that the man honestly had a contempt for quarterbacks because he was afraid they might get too smart and show him out."

After debating the possibility of getting on a train and heading back to Lexington, a naive and nervous George Blanda presents himself in the Bears' throne room. The door opens and there is the Patriarch, looking properly dour and awesome. Blanda feels that, perhaps, he is rushing manhood faster than he would actually prefer.

"There are only three men in the whole world I was ever afraid of—my old man, Bear Bryant and, now, George Halas. I said to myself, 'This guy would screw you if he got a chance.' And he did, within an hour and a half, too. But I'm also thinking, 'What a privilege to be in the same room with this great man.' I called him 'sir' and I always called him 'Coach,' never 'George' or even 'Mr. Halas.' "

Blanda sits down and attempts to relax. He must listen to roughly ten minutes of Bear history and tradition. Then Halas takes a deep breath, clears his throat with a sound that re-sembles thunder on Lake Michigan, and says:

"What questions do you have?"

"Well, with all those quarterbacks, where do I fit in?"

"Now don't spread this around, but we're working on a trade for Bobby Layne, just to make room for you. Hm, Blanda, eh? Slovak? Polish? I'm Bohemian, myself. We'll have a lot in common. You're going to really enjoy being a Bear, George. Every year we'll be in the playoffs and that's extra money. I have a lot of contact with people in business and we'll set you up with an off-season job that will help you get started in a

non-football career, as well. Now let me tell you about the time
the Bears defeated Washington 73-0 in the playoff . . . we
kicked off.''

On and on, Halas drones, charming, cajoling and pampering
his victim.

"Now, in three or four years I can promise you that you'll take
over as our No. 1 quarterback. If we didn't have a chance at signing you, we certainly would never consider getting rid of Layne.
Now how much money are we talking about? . . . harrrrrrrrk . . .
well, we'll give you $6000. That's a lot of money.''

It is indeed a lot of money, especially since George Blanda
has been figuring on making about $3000 teaching, assuming he
can find the sort of well-paying job where the basic salary is
$2500 and you get $500 for coaching.

The figure rattles around in Blanda's brain. He realizes how
much college coaches are making. It strikes him that his father
probably never made more than $2000 in any one year of his
whole life. Why, Halas could have said $100,000 and not
shocked him any more. He does some figuring. Pro football is
four-and-a-half months' work. Players get $100 for each exhibi-
tion. That makes it $6500 really. And there's a chance to make
another $5000 more in the off-season. The poor Slovak kid
from Youngwood starts to feel exactly the way he did when
Bernie Shively offered him two suits, one blue and one brown.
Wait a minute, what about the offer from the Los Angeles
Dons?

("I tried to get suave and smart,'' Blanda recalls. "I settled
back and said, 'Yeah, that sounds good, but it's not a lot of
money. I might get more from the Los Angeles Dons.' Well, he
really got indignant.'')

As a matter of fact, Halas almost swallows his tongue.

"That is a lot of money. You don't want to go with that
Mickey Mouse league. It's going to fold and you'll be our
property anyway. You want to play with a team like the Bears,
a team that has tradition. You're a proud young man. You
don't want to be with a franchise that folds,'' says Halas. "And
$6000 is a great deal of money for a man just out of college.''

(Years later, Blanda discovers that the price really wasn't that bad. In 1954, a first-round draft choice tells George that he is only getting $5000.)

"Well, kid, tell you what I'll do. I'll give you $6000 in salary and a $600 bonus. That's $6600. I'll write you a check right now and we'll get this thing settled today."

So George Blanda, age 21 but growing older by the minute, figures he's outsmarted the Patriarch of professional football. He, whose family has never seen $600 in three months, is about to get that amount dropped in his hands. So he literally grabs the pen from Halas. After he signs the contract he gets a slip of white paper to sign. Why bother reading it? Hasn't he just hung the Chicago Bears up for a big bonus?

"Kid, I'm appreciative of the way you settled this like a man," says Halas. "There's nothing I wouldn't do for you."

Later on, Blanda will say that he turned to Halas and said: "Well, Coach, there's nothing I wouldn't do for you, either."

And for the next ten years they do absolutely nothing for each other.

TINTYPE 5

Now George Blanda is a legitimate professional. He has met the owner and coach of the Chicago Bears. And he has filched an extra $600. He stands in the hall outside of the club's executive offices. He glances down at the check to admire it, to feel the quality of the paper it is written on.

It is indeed made out to George F. Blanda. It is indeed for $600. Fondly, he turns it over in his hand. What's this? On the back it says: "Advance on 1949 salary." The other slip of paper says that if Blanda fails to make the final squad cut, the $600 will have to be paid back at one percent interest.

"I'd been screwed!" George tells friends back home in Lexington, after the long, empty, rattling train ride. "I went in there to screw him and he nailed me. So I said, 'Okay, you sly old son of a bitch, if I don't make your ball club, you're going to have to look all over Pennsylvania to get your damned $600 back.' "

The education of George Blanda, which he thought was coming to a completion at the University of Kentucky, has only just begun. He will not receive a raise for five years. And he discovers that in lieu of more money, Halas is fond of arranging to have Bear players appointed to the Pro Bowl roster in Los Angeles, where the promoters—not Halas—pay $500 a head.

TINTYPE 6

Famous quotation:

"Every time for the next five years that I went to Halas to see about getting some more money, he'd tell me the story of that damned 73-0 victory over the Redskins in the 1940 play-offs. I must have heard that thing 1000 times. And he'd start out every sentence with . . . harrrrrrk! . . . harrrrrrk!"

—George Blanda

TINTYPE 7

With one nasty little nagging exception, no training camp has ever been sweeter for an apprentice quarterback. The Chicago Bears are at their summer health farm in Rensselaer, Indiana. Where once they had three magnificent quarterbacks with impressive names and hand-embroidered reputations, they now have only a rookie whom no Chicago writer seems to remember from the year before. Gone is Bobby Layne, traded to the New York Bulldogs, whoever they are. Gone is Sid Luckman, who cannot practice because he is so slow getting over a thyroid condition. Gone is Johnny Lujack whose leg injury keeps him sitting around the dormitory.

Alone and throwing on the practice field is George Blanda, who looks distressingly young. One writer thinks Blanda came from Penn State, which is close enough. Another describes him as being "quiet and impressionable," a mistake in judgment no journalist will ever make again. Since one of the great quarterbacks is gone and the other two might as well be because of sickness, the press runs daily Blanda stories. They make charming errors in their enthusiasm to applaud what must be another marvelous move by George Halas, who does not sign just any young athlete.

"The Bears are just about the greatest team that ever was," one writer insists that Blanda has told him. Then he trips himself up in the next paragraph. "I was so anxious to play for the great George Halas that I never hesitated when they offered me a contract. I've admired coach Halas since I was a small boy in Youngwood, Pa. Coach Ray Flaherty of the Chicago Hornets called me later and said his team wanted me to be a blocking back. But I told him I'd signed with George Halas."

Does that sound like George Blanda, or even a young George Blanda? And when did the *Chicago Hornets* call? Aw, c'mon now, fellows.

Immediately, George falls in with a clique of elderly players. Possibly because of the way he seems to swagger when he walks, Bulldog Turner, Ed Sprinkle and the great Sid Luckman himself admit him to their presence. He spends some time pledging the fraternity. The scene might amuse Oakland Raiders rookies, who 20 years later will walk around him with such cathedral reverence.

On off-days, Luckman permits the rookie to chauffer his Chrysler Imperial convertible all the way to Luckman's summer home 100 miles away from the training camp. Jaw straight out, his hair now long enough to blow in the wind, Blanda drives while Luckman gets a suntan in the back.

"I was so impressed by Luckman and so thankful that he had befriended me, I would have worn a chauffer's cap if he had asked," Blanda recalls. "I got so sunburned doing that, the trainer was worried. But I felt like I was driving the president of the United States around. Besides, that was one hell of a car Sid owned."

But there is a fringe benefit. The Bears have about eight playbooks, all of which the rookie has to learn. It is more complicated than the formula for the atomic bomb, which Russian spies of the era were busily stealing. So Luckman gives Blanda private lessons. As a learning aid, the quarterbacks are supposed to copy each and every diagram. Blanda does his own and Luckman's too. But the postgraduate course is worth it.

"Now I begin to realize why Bear quarterbacks either go crazy or get traded," says Blanda. "Halas thinks enemy agents are out to destroy him. When we practice, which is next to a cornfield, he's got assistant coaches and second-string players out in the tall silk looking for spies. There is a fellow from the New York Giants—real big, fat guy—Jack Lavelle, who he always thinks is hiding in the equipment bags or something.

"This system of the Bears' is unbelievable. It's like Halas sat down and tried to destroy your mind. Football is blocking, tackling, passing, catching, kicking and hitting. If you knock the other eleven men down all the time, you'll win. But Halas thinks he's George Patton moving an army. The quarterback calls the plays for the Bears, he also calls the blocking assignments. We've also got fifteen options off the Statue of Liberty play. Every call was color coded and letter designated. There must have been 1000 pass plays and 1000 running plays in those books. I walk up to the line of scrimmage with my brain on fire trying to remember that.

"The thing destroys quarterbacks. Look at all the quarterbacks the Bears had when I was with them. It didn't stop after I left. It will always be that way. How many championships has Halas, the great innovator, won with this system since my rookie year? Just one. Professional football passed him by about 1954."

The weeks pass and neither Luckman or Lujack is that close to playing. And George Blanda is not that close to absorbing the truth and beauty contained in Halas's encyclopedia set. Just short of disaster, good old Bulldog Turner starts calling the plays in the huddle.

"What's it gonna be?" the quarterback would say to his center, of all people. Then the quarterback would march to the line of scrimmage and wow the Patriarch with his sudden and impressive knowledge of the play books.

Now Blanda begins to believe that he is the Bears' number

one quarterback. Hasn't he won the job? Aren't Luckman and
Lujack too sick to play? Well, not quite.

TINTYPE 8

Famous quotation:
*"At six feet, two inches, George Blanda is a precious two
inches taller than either Lujack or Luckman."*
                    —Jacke Clarke, *Chicago Sun-Times*, August 22, 1949.

TINTYPE 9

In the training room in Nippert Stadium on the University of
Cincinnati campus, the Chicago Bears' resident witch doctor is
looking at Johnny Lujack's right leg. He has several cans of
surgical tape ready and he looks exceedingly vexed.

In a few minutes he begins to wrap and wrap and wrap.
Sitting in the main dressing room a few yards away, Blanda
observes this little tableau and notices that his stomach has
dropped so low it feels as if he could step on it. Ready or not,
in sickness or in health, Lujack is going to start. Blanda is vexed.
No one needs to write out the message in a fiery hand on the
side of the stadium. Here is another great lesson in postgraduate
living.

"From that moment on, I knew exactly what I could expect
from the Bears and Halas. I'd done the work. I'd come a long
way. I figured I'd get the start. Hell, the Bears were playing the
Pittsburgh Steelers and all those people from Youngwood
would be wondering what George was going to do. So they
wrap up John and give him the job. I was mad as hell. I guess
maybe I never really got over it.

"I was disenchanted before I ever played a game. I could
sense something I didn't like about the situation. There was
something about Halas I knew I couldn't trust."

So the Steelers hold the Bears to a 0-0 tie with one minute to
play in the third period. Here begins a pattern. It will snake-
dance in and out of George Blanda's life for the next 22 years.
Somebody has put him down and he is angry. And out of anger

comes George's greatest strength. He must prove himself. And he does.

"I guess maybe that's true. I guess when I'm challenged I get angry and when I'm angry I play my damndest. It just seems to work out that way," he decides. "At Kentucky, when Coach Bryant dropped me down to the second-string defensive unit, I played so hard at linebacker, I nearly killed somebody."

Now Halas motions Blanda over to his side and says, "Go get 'em kid!" Here comes George escaping the coal mines. Standing on the sidelines, as if he is out of the line-up, is the great old halfback, George McAfee. This is "yellow-M-sideline fake-Z-purple-explosion-right-Jack," or some other jiggling nonsense straight from the Halas book of common prayer. McAfee wiggles his hand and Bulldog Turner turns to tell Blanda that the fake is on.

Pittsburgh thinks McAfee is on the bench, but he is in-bounds. Down the field he swoops and Blanda throws him a 40-yard touchdown pass that has Cincinnati stunned. The crowd of 24,000 doesn't know whether to cheer or go blind. Now here is George Blanda making his first miracle as a professional. He completes seven out of seven passes. He slams the ball into the end zone on every kickoff. Chicago gets five touchdowns in the final 18 minutes of play and George passes for three of them. He does miss one extra point. The place goes wild. A super star is born. Right? Wrong!

Afterwards, a *Chicago Sun-Times* photographer comes into the dressing room. Here's the Patriarch in his gray fedora pumping the hand of an amazingly shy-looking George Blanda.

"Harrrrrrrrk! . . . nice going, kid," he says. "You played great."

The next morning, a euphoric Blanda picks up the morning paper back in Chicago. He notes with interest that his modest comments have been recorded with some accuracy. Then he turns to see what nice things the master Bear has said. He grows swiftly ill.

"George is a good prospect," Halas has told his captive press. "His footwork is very crude and he doesn't really take the snap from center properly. I told him there were three things he had to work on. When he masters those, he'll be a good sound player. He's like a fastball-throwing baseball pitcher. He doesn't have much control on his passes."

Blanda cannot believe it. The same George Halas who referred to him as an "accurate long passer and a devastating man with the short flat pass," is now comparing him to some scatterarm pitcher up from Greensboro in the Cotton States League.

"That game was it. I didn't play any more until 1952. I started one more game that 1949 season—an exhibition. Oh, I got into parts of games and stuff like that. But that fourth period against Pittsburgh meant nothing . . . nothing. Luckman got well and so did Lujack. See, Halas was a mastermind, a great international genius. How would it look for him to have me come in, and after only five weeks look like a finished quarterback. He had these two high-quality guys he'd had around for years, Luckman and Lujack, carefully schooling them. They were his creations. I'd made the mistake, as much through luck as anything because they were hurt, of showing them up. So he had to find flaws in me that he could spend a lot of time working on. That's the way he was. There was no challenging his authority and by the way I'd played in that game I'd challenged his authority.

"I got to stick around as a third-string quarterback. I kicked off and kicked field goals. We had a great punter, George Gulyanics, so I didn't have a chance to do that. There was competition for the field goal kicking job. Oh, yes, Lujack kicked them, too. So Halas had him kicking from within the 20-yard line. He got all the extra points. I got the long ones, 35 and 45 yards out. Explain that one. If you have a veteran kicker and a rookie, who gets the ones in close? I had something like seven out of fifteen. I needed a special kicking shoe."

So, one afternoon, George, still wide-eyed and full of wonder, knocks on the Patriarch's office door. "Please, sir, may I have a little gruel?" asks young Oliver Twist. Halas appears shocked.

"Why, kid, if you want special equipment, you have to buy it yourself. The Bears are happy to . . . harrrrrrk . . . supply you with regulation equipment. But a kicking shoe doesn't come under that heading."

So Blanda peels $32.51 out of his $6600-a-year salary and buys a kicking shoe. It is several years before he discovers that all teams supply them to their place kickers as regulation equipment—everybody but the Chicago Bears.

TINTYPE 10

Significant social notes:

(a) For several weeks, Miss Betty Harris, spinster of Lexington, Ky., and George Blanda, bachelor of Youngwood, Pa., postpone their wedding, not knowing whether the Bears will get into the playoffs or not. Finally, the man printing the wedding invitations calls to say that he has started his presses rolling. The date has been left blank and Miss Harris can damn well fill it in with a pencil. It turns out to be December 17, 1949.

(b) The players are packing, getting ready to vacate Wrigley Field. In his locker, George Blanda finds a slip of paper. It is an autograph, the only one he has ever collected. It remains in his scrapbook years later, even when he is making miracles for the Oakland Raiders and turning on the Geritol-for-Lunch-Bunch. It says: "To my pal . . . to a real champion . . . to a real man (George Blanda) . . . from Sid Luckman." See, even folk heroes have folk heroes.

TINTYPE 11

During the winter, Blanda takes a married man's apartment near Lexington and finds a job—rolling wooden barrels around the warehouse at the James Pepper whiskey distillery. ("Where are all those Chicago business contacts, Papa Bear?") The next training camp is a little less glorious than the one before. Oh, nice things are said. Pretty headlines appear in the newspapers.

"I regard Blanda as one of the most promising young quarterbacks in professional football," says Halas in one of those voice-of-God quotations that always appear in the Chicago press. "Now that he has a year of experience under his belt, I'm sure he'll be taking over more responsibility." (How come those "harrrrrrks" never get into the *Chicago Tribune?*)

Somebody asks Blanda how he's coming with the complex, compound confusion of the Bear playbooks.

"Mr. Halas sure separates the boys from the geniuses," he says.

What he is really thinking is entirely different. Perhaps Halas can read minds, too. Lord knows he thinks he can do everything else.

"Everything is a big secret with Halas," the new bridegroom writes home to his wife. "He thinks that people are spying on us, so he has us up practicing at 6 A.M. This man wouldn't let his left hand know what his right is doing, for fear that his left hand might do something terrible to his right. It's weird being around him."

The quarterbacking job is awarded to Lujack. To his horror, Blanda discovers that he is not even going to be the third-string quarterback. A rookie named Steve Romanik has been moved ahead of him and the exhibition season isn't half over. He asks his coach why he isn't playing and gets what he considers to be a poor answer. Then, as his restlessness grows, his skill as a natural humorist gets him in trouble.

He locates Halas's limousine in the parking lot and plasters fraudulent parking tickets on the windshield. He discovers which route the Patriarch takes when he leaves the training camp. Halas comes to a stop at a red light, looks out the window and sees this leering Slovak face. Blanda revs the engine of his car in the style of the day.

"Hey, mister," he shouts like a black-leather-jacket-with-an-eagle-on-the-back-type, "you wanna drag?"

When the Patriarch isn't around, Blanda walks up to the blackboard and does his Head Coach Imitation routine, peering over the top of his glasses and clearing his throat hard enough to rupture a tonsil.

The owner and head coach of the Chicago Bears, the Fearless Pioneer, the Great Innovator (etc.) is not amused. Ridicule is

something that Halas's massive pride cannot handle. It bucks
and heaves under the strain. There is only one thing to do with
this wastrel in his midst: He must be traded. Deep in his soul,
George Blanda is willing to admit to George Blanda that
perhaps . . . just perhaps . . . that is what this sudden spasm of
relentless comedy is all about. Maybe he wants to get traded. It
happens within a week.

For some time, Halas has been openly coveting a guard
named Dick Barwegan, whose life is being wasted with the
Baltimore Colts, one of the smoke-covered survivors of the
All-America Conference. The new league has gone bubbling
beneath the waves and the National Football League has picked
up several of the shipwrecked members. The weakest of these is
Baltimore.

Obviously, the Colts need a quantity of bodies more than
they need one very expensive lineman. The price is not unreasonable, considering how badly the Patriarch desires
Barwegan—two linemen, a defensive back and that kid quarterback who kicks . . . ah . . . what's his name? Oh, yes, George
Blanda.

Play some traveling music, professor, the transaction is made.
First, George is happy. Then he's sad. The defensive back in the
deal is Bob Perina, late of Princeton, late of the All-America
Conference.

"George," he says, eyes full of fear, "we don't want to go to
Baltimore. It's an old All-America Conference team and I've
been through that before. The Colts will go bankrupt. Their
checks will bounce and we'll have to borrow money to get an
airplane ride home."

So Blanda figures this is not for him. Why, it's worse than life
under the Patriarch. So he gets on the telephone to Gene
Ronzani, a man who he remembers fondly. The year before
Ronzani was his quarterback coach. Now he is in charge of the
Green Bay Packers.

"While I'm dialing, it occurs to me that I probably wouldn't
have it much better with the Colts. If they're strong at one
position, that position is quarterback. They've got Adrian Burk

and Y. A. Tittle. So I asked Ronzani if he could use me. He's delighted. He says he'll call back after he's talked to the Colts about making a trade. In an hour I get the answer. The Colts want me. No deal. So Perina and I mess around all week and don't report. Baltimore is going to play Green Bay in Milwaukee on a Saturday night. Perina and I get there something like Saturday morning. We dress for the game and I kick off. It's all downhill after that. The Packers beat us something like 48-0. It's the last exhibition game. The team flies back to Baltimore, but Perina and I talk the coach into letting us drive Perina's car.

"All the way, Bob is saying, 'We gotta get out of this . . . we can't stay here with the Colts . . . we gotta get out of this.' I'm in a fine frame of mind by the time we cross the border into Maryland. I want to hop a freighter in Baltimore harbor and sail for Singapore or something. All the time it's, 'We aren't going to get paid . . . we're going to get killed . . . we gotta get out of this.'

"I start thinking if I can just get the Colts to cut me, I can go to Green Bay and have a first-rate shot at being the starting quarterback. So we go out to practice on Tuesday at Westminster. They had roomed me with Tittle and the word going around was that they were disenchanted with Y. A. and Burk was going to be the quarterback. I was going to be his back-up man. There was such a stink caused because the Colts had traded their captain, Dick Barwegan, that the head coach, Clem Crowe, doesn't dare get rid of Tittle. He's the only name player they've got and I guess he figures if he trades Y. A. the fans will string him up. He's already changed his mind about me. So from Saturday to Tuesday, I go from second string to third.

"First day, Crowe turns to Burk and says, 'Adrian, take Blanda and march him up and down the sidelines and teach him our cadence.'

"So there's Adrian making like a drill instructor, marching me up and down, teaching me how to count . . . hup . . . hup . . . hup. I feel like a real ass and so does Burk. No way I'm going to be in Baltimore now. So I screw up the cadence purposely. I even forget how to count. I just aggravated hell out of Crowe. He'd come over and look in my eyes to see if I was drunk. Pretty soon he figures here's just another dumb Polack who can't even count.

"We practice three days in a row and I never could get the cadence. It was just a mystery to me. Every time Crowe chews me out, I just shrug like I can hardly speak English. One afternoon, he comes over and tells me to forget playing quarterback. He says he understands I kick field goals, too. I tell him 'not too good.'

"I forget who was holding for me, but anyway, I kicked the center in the ass four straight times. Never got the ball over the line of scrimmage. So, back we go to throwing passes. I can't even tell which are the receivers and which are the tackles. I overthrow the ball, ground the ball, fumble the ball. One time I drop back and fire the pass right at one of my guards. Most surprised son of a bitch you ever saw. No way am I going to stay in Baltimore.

"So the Colts open up against the Redskins. I kicked off, put the ball out of the end zone and we lost that game 42-0. I'd been gone from the Bears about nine days, played in that Milwaukee thing and this one. So Clem Crowe calls me and he looks like somebody has died. He says, 'George . . . sniff . . . I've got some bad news for you. We just don't figure you can make it here as a quarterback and a kicker . . . so . . . sniff . . . we're trading you to Green Bay. Well, it's really not a trade. They're going to put this tackle on the waiver list and we got first pick, so we'll take him. Then we'll put you on waivers. They got second pick and they'll take you. I'm sorry.'

"They had to do it that way because Halas had this agreement that if the Colts didn't want me, they'd have to give me back to the Bears. To get around it, they would have to put me on waivers. So Clem says, 'You've passed waivers and you're now property of Green Bay. I'm genuinely sorry I have to do this to you.' I'm sitting back trying to look sad while I'm turning cartwheels inside. The Packers have Tobin Rote, but he's still young and unproved. They've got Indian Jack Jacobs and he's old. It's perfect. I run right out, put on my traveling clothes and fly out for Green Bay. I arrive Tuesday morning at the Packers office and Ronzani meets me. I want to know when we practice.

"Well, Gene says that Halas has called and he's raising all kinds of hell. He's called the commissioner and I can't practice until there's a ruling in the case. I'm expecting a little justice. How the hell do I know that whatever George Halas wants the commissioner usually lets him have. I can't see how they can return me to Chicago. I was very young yet.

"I get the word the next morning: Back to the Bears, back to the loving arms of my beloved George Halas. I have traveled from Rensselaer to Milwaukee to Baltimore to Green Bay. Now I have to fly to San Francisco, where the Bears are going to play. What have I got out of it? Nothing! I'm so unhappy I hardly know where to turn. I couldn't believe he was doing this to me. Halas has three quarterbacks. What does he want with me? He won't play me and he won't let anybody else have me."

So George Blanda gets on an airplane, flies to San Francisco and takes a bus north to the Sonoma Mission Inn outside of Boyes Hot Springs, Calif. The Bears are working out on a high school field and staying at the inn. He dresses and gets to practice five minutes late. The Chicago football club always forms a great circle for loosening up exercises. Any player who gets there late has to run around the circle as penance. Halas sees Blanda.

"Well, you smart son of a bitch, run around the circle," he yells. "You're late."

"Run around the circle? You've had me running around the world these last two weeks," roars young George. "No damn way I'm running around your circle. I tell you what, Coach, *you* run around the circle."

But Blanda runs around the circle, just as Halas has told him to do. And he runs and runs and runs. Years go by and George Halas, the Patriarch, still has him going around in circles. It is the old man's hobby, it seems.

Only two days after Blanda's return, the Bears play the 49ers in that moldly old repository for seagull guano, Kezar Stadium.

In the first half George kicks three field goals, a record for most field goals in a half. In the second half, Chicago has four more opportunities to kick goals from in close. Halas does not seem to know that Blanda is still in the ball park. How would it look to trade a guy and have him come back, only to kick seven field goals!?

The Patriarch is jealous of his image, just like any Slavic papa.

TINTYPE 12

"Looking back to those early years with the Bears, I probably was a wise-ass kid," says George Blanda, thumbing through a scrapbook with a blue-and-orange, Chicago Bears-color binding. "I had a strong personality. I knew where I wanted to go. George Halas had a strong personality. He knew where he'd been. I don't think I ever did anything detrimental to the Bears, because everyone on the team liked me. When I did get to play, they really played for me. From a management standpoint, maybe I was a liability. But from the players' standpoint, I was a positive influence.

"In that same year I got traded, 1950, Johnny Lujack got a separated shoulder, his right one. He had it all year and he played with it. He had a chain that kept his arm from going up too high. It gave him all kinds of pain. He threw something like three touchdown passes in the twelve league games and we were still tied for the division lead. We played off against the Rams and lost. Luckman was getting along in years. At least he thought he was. He was something like 31 when he quit. Some of the players went up to Halas and said: 'Why not let George play?' He told them to get lost. It was the ends, guys like Ken Kavanaugh and Jim Keane who were on my side. So I knew I had rapport with the players. But Halas thought I was a big jokester. Which I was. I know I was."

TINTYPE 13

Famous quotation:

"Well, I'm past 31 and I've had a long career, 12 seasons. I don't think it's wise for any quarterback to play much past his 31st birthday."   —Sid Luckman, upon retiring.

TINTYPE 14

There is an appalling lack of glamor in playing outside linebacker in the early 1950s. It is a fine place to hide while taking out feelings of repressed anger on enemy ball carriers. Hate your coach? Wait until Elmer Angsman tries to get out of the Chicago Cardinal backfield and rattle his bridgework with a good hard elbow in the mouth. Upset because somebody named Romanik is getting more playing time at quarterback than you ever did? Well, let old Bullet Bill Dudley come across the scrimmage line and sock him on his wishbone.

All his life, all 23 years of it, George Frederick Blanda has lived with the impression that a man who just kicks footballs for a living, no matter how clever he is at his art, isn't really an athlete. He is a shot-maker. But a man who kicks *and* plays a position . . . well, now, that's something. So Blanda chokes down his rage and goes to George Halas with a request:

"I've got to do something. I can't just hang around and kick. I feel like a civilian. I'm not a member of the team. I played linebacker at Kentucky. I wasn't the greatest in the world, but, hell, I made some tackles. I'm tall enough. I can move. Let me play safety. I'll even play on the specialty teams."

So George Blanda, apprentice quarterback, frustrated, goes into exile on the defensive platoon. Styles are changing in professional football rapidly. The Philadelphia Eagles have been frighteningly successful using four down linemen on defense, with three linebackers and four defensive backs. The middle guard is phased into oblivion.

"It wasn't as much of a comedown as people might think. Oh, the folks back in Youngwood weren't impressed. Although sometimes I think that because everybody's so poor and miserable in that town, they kind of hate to see you succeed. Anyway, I felt I was being paid fairly good money and I was happy to be playing professional football. It was a hell of a lot better than mining coal or working for the railroad or in the thermostat factory. It paid more than teaching school.

"My first play at linebacker, I faced Steve Van Buren. Now there isn't a tougher running back in the league than he is. His favorite play is off tackle and right over the linebacker—me. I

TINTYPE 15

Everything looks so dark, so desperate, so discouraging. It is dark as a dungeon way down in George Halas's mine. And a new problem has developed. A number of gallant old veterans have grown physically feeble and have slumped off into athletic oblivion. The ball club is losing consistently, causing the customers at Wrigley Field to get sullen and, then, mutinous. What's worse, the starving masses on the player roster don't even have the promise of playoff money. Poor George seems sentenced to hard labor as a linebacker-cornerback. Is there no hope? Is this almost the end of our story?

It is not apparent at the time, but a Blanda-watcher looking back from the vantage point of two decades in the future would know immediately what is about to happen. George's career is nearly dead. So what will he do? Well, he'll do something spectacular, probably in the fourth quarter.

"Death and Resurrection," mutters Betty Blanda. "Death and Resurrection. That's how it always is."

Williams starts the first few games of 1952 for the Bears. He is new and his mind is starting to short-circuit because of the dangerous overload inflicted by Halas's playbooks. He goes badly and the populace curses him for a knave and an idiot. Now it is Steve Romanik's turn. Sometimes he's good. Sometimes he's bad. But the Bears are getting whipped and it does no good to plead that Romanik isn't the only one to blame. Who do the varlets in the stands demand to see? Why, George Blanda, of course.

"Oh, I'm the darling of the crowd and the favorite of the press," George recalls. "It's always that way. The first-string quarterback is a jerk and a clown. Whoever is the second-string quarterback . . . well, he's a prince of a fellow. He can always do better. Everybody loves him—until he moves up to number one.

"Later on when I'm in Houston and Jacky Lee is getting all hot and bothered because I'm playing and he isn't, I have to have a little talk with him. I tell him, 'For Christ sake, Jacky, be happy where you are. You're making nice money. Nobody's asking you to get out there and screw up and get your head pinched off by the crowd. Relax for a few years, learn your business. Enjoy being popular. They'll boo you soon enough.'

"I was a great one to give advice. I knew exactly how Jacky felt. I'd been through it myself. Oh, how I'd been through it."

So the Chicago crowd howls for Blanda's scalp with almost the same fervor that a Houston crowd will use some 14 years later. George starts attending quarterback meetings again. He runs the offense some in practice. The stars are shifting again. The pattern is repeating itself.

"We're playing the Rams and Williams has an injury to his side and Romanik starts. I figure all I'm going to do is kick and play some defense, maybe. This Los Angeles club is great . . . really great. They got more players than you can count, all of them outstanding. They've been champions two years running and they are busily stomping hell out of the Bears. It's 42-7 going into the fourth quarter and one of our assistants, Luke Johnsos, goes over to Halas and says, 'Please, let's put George in.' I guess he figured I couldn't be any worse.

"Halas has run out of excuses why he can't use me. So he shrugs and sends me in. I complete ten passes for two touchdowns. Suddenly the great George Halas has discovered a quarterback. Me!"

At a midweek press conference, it is announced that Blanda has been given a battlefield promotion. He is going to start his first league game that following Sunday. It has all been part of a careful program designed to bring young George to this momentous point in his career. Who has designed this program? Do you have to ask?

It is fortunate for Blanda that the Patriarch has taken credit for bringing Blanda along so scientifically, so thoroughly. The wandering Dallas Texans—not the club that Lamar Hunt starts out with in the American Football League, but a one-year NFL miscalculation—are the Bears' next opponent. This was an early attempt at bringing professional football to the land of collard greens and chicken-fried steak. The college game is next to cleanliness in Dallas and every southern Baptist from Waco to

Lufkin knows what cleanliness is next to. Come to think of it, college football might even be ahead of cleanliness. The poor ignored Texans become a traveling tent show since no one will pay to watch them play at home. They are discouraged and disorganized. They are also capable of devastating Blanda's first genuine, official start. They beat him. Now comes a delicious irony. Halas has no choice but to keep young George in the starting lineup. It is just as well. George is ready to work his first documented miracle in a league game.

He is matched against the Detroit Lions. Before the game, Halas gives a flawless performance. He becomes Knute Rockne at Notre Dame. It is pure, uncut birdseed. He goes into a long sermon. His text is a familiar one: Bear tradition. He throws in a couple of excerpts from the 73-0 victory over the Washington Redskins. Then, with tears growing fat in the corners of his eyes, he says, "Harrrrrrk . . . Let's dedicate this one to the loyal Bear fans. Harrrrrrk . . . I don't mean the ten percent who come out here to boo . . . harrrrrrk! I mean the 90 percent who love us and encourage us. They're faithful. Let's win this one for them." Bob Williams and Steve Romanik wonder where the loyal 90 percent have been hiding all year. They sure as hell haven't been at the ballpark.

Television cameras, those one-eyed, affluent intruders, are located in strategic positions around Wrigley Field—on the grandstand's second deck, behind the bench, in the ivy on the walls, everywhere.

Blanda is superb. The Lions put a sturdy rush on him, but he does not throw an interception all afternoon. The crowd of 37,508 applaud him heatedly every time he brings back his right arm to throw. He is their darling boy, the second-string quarter-back being given a chance to prove his manhood. He is also fresh meat, so he can't make any mistakes.

With 1:09 seconds left in the final period, he has a 17-16 lead. From his own 20, Blanda orders a punt. Detroit has a dandy punt return specialist, Jack Christiansen. But that's no problem. Chicago has a dandy punter, Curly Morrison.

"Just get that damn ball out of bounds," young George

whispers to Morrison as he trots off the field, making room for
the punting team. "Don't let that son of a bitch Christiansen get
near it."

"No sweat," says Curly, who sends the ball floating straight
down the middle. Christiansen takes it on the Detroit 21
and . . . don't bother to guess. He brings it back 79 yards for the
score.

"They kick off with 1:35 to play," Blanda recalls. "We get
the ball on our own 30. I pass to Billy Stone, our halfback, and
he gets 15 yards."

Here is an interesting fact. Up until a couple of weeks before
the Detroit game, Stone is serving time as a defensive halfback
on the same unit with linebacker George Blanda. Now both are
breathing free.

"Now I'm excited as hell. I drop back and gun it to Morrison.
Same play only I go to the fullback instead of the halfback. He
goes 55 yards to their two. My blood is pounding through my
head so hard it hurts. There's George sneaking—I used to be a
runner—to the one."

There are nine seconds left. Assuming that the Patriarch has
some great mystical message to pass on, Blanda goes over to the
bench. What does Halas want him to do?

"Shit, you're the quarterback," says the Great Innovator.
"You keep telling me what a great quarterback you are. You
call the play."

"I run back and Bulldog asks me what the coach said. I told
him. He says I better think of something. Well, we do pretty
much the same thing modern teams do when they're down
around the goal line. We put in two tight ends. When it comes
to basic football, styles don't change that much. I got a full
house backfield. They send in Ed Sprinkle, a defensive end, to
block on offense when we get in close. He was a very strong
man."

So the rascals make up their own play. There are 2000 plays
in the Patriarch's encyclopedia. And here is George Blanda
calling for suggestions.

The offensive captain, George Connor, thinks he remembers a

play that might work in close. But he can't remember what it's called. Undoubtedly it sounds like "azure-left-H-jack-up-and-down-purple-right-flex." But it is cold out and there are only nine seconds left. Finally, Bulldog Turner speaks.

"Let's cut out the screwing around and do something. Why don't we send Bill Stone ahead on a dive play. You fake to him, George, and hit Sprinkle in the end zone. They won't be expecting that, because he's a defensive guy."

There is no one in Chicago that Blanda admires more than the Bulldog. Sounds fine, he says. The play begins. Stone dives. Blanda fakes. Suddenly, Lion defenders notice that Sprinkle is running, not blocking. He is almost, but not quite, covered when the ball falls into his arms. Touchdown! The final score is 24-23, favor of Chicago. Later on, in the dressing room, with Halas weeping large Bohemian tears, Blanda will say Turner called the play; Connor will say it was Blanda's idea and Turner will put the finger on Connor.

"Hell, we didn't have the play. Bulldog made it up. I agreed to it and Connor swore to it. We all got a little scared. As I ran off the field, Halas grabs me and says, 'You son of a bitch, where did you get that play?'

"I said, 'I came over and asked you what to do. You wouldn't tell me. It was a golden chance for you to guide me. Hell, we made up that play. We got 1000 plays in that damn book of yours and we made that play up."

The press comes in to meet the conquering warriors and to grovel at the Patriarch's toenails. Halas is up to the occasion. He always is.

"These kids were superb. Every Bear season has its high point. This was one of those times. It made up for a season of heartache. As for the winning touchdown," he says, "well, Blanda called that play himself. Give the kid credit. It was a great play. It worked. It created an element of surprise. And if it hadn't worked, it was the only play in the book that would have given us another chance to score before time ran out."

What play in what book?

Now the press leaves and Halas has a private word for the

young quarterback. It is actually several words strung together in a simple, well-formed declarative sentence: "Don't you ever pull that shit again."

At his regular weekly press conference, Halas is at it again. Blanda has been brought along slowly, carefully, logically. When the lad came up four years earlier he was simply a wild passer, just like a baseball pitcher with a fastball that he can't throw to spots. Now George has control. He has poise. He also has an immortal genius for a coach.

It is customary for Halas to call his loving children in for little private confessions when the season is over. Once again George Blanda disappoints him by not being properly servile. The boy never learns.

"The same old nonsense started all over again after that miracle game against the Lions. The papers said the Bears had finally discovered a great quarterback. So the next week, I didn't even start. I played a little bit the rest of the way. But he went back to Romanik. He felt that if any quarterback had a great year it would cost George Halas and the Chicago Bears too much money. I had that hunch. Maybe I was dead wrong. But I doubt it. Halas was like that.

"We had a fullback from Mississippi, his name was John Dottley. He was first in the league in rushing in the first six games. He needs something like 300 yards to break the all-time league rushing record. They bench him—for no good reason. It broke his heart. Look it up. His name was John Dottley. *D-O-T-T-L-E-Y.* He only played two or three years. Halas didn't want to pay him. I don't think Halas was in bad financial condition. He was just cheap. He made all his money himself and he was jealous if somebody else wanted to share in his prosperity.

"After my first year when I got in trouble by being a smartass, I just took it. I popped off, he traded me, and got me back. If this was the way he wanted to run his football team that was fine with me. I had to feel I was the best quarterback. You have to feel that way, otherwise you don't belong out there. But Halas, he didn't want you to be anything but low-class labor, so he could pay you that way. By 1953 he didn't give a damn about winning championships. He just wanted to run an inexpensive operation. Why? I don't know, except that he was naturally cheap. Hell, he was selling every seat in Wrigley Field."

What's a fellow to do? The answer is simple. If he can't play and he can't get traded, he can go to Canada. Where? Why, the Canadian League, just across the border. They have this funny game, see, no downfield blocking, a dozen men on a team instead of 11 and three downs to go five yards. It's a living. And George Halas can't have you extradited. He can't? Oh, is that so?

TINTYPE 16

Halas likes to call his players in for little lessons in faith and morals and low finance. He has persuaded some of his under-lings to take $50 a week in salary and put the rest in a large account, payable when the season is over. Everyone thinks this is fine. After all, $3500 in a lump seems comforting. For those who do not have stable off-season jobs, it is a means of lasting from January to July, when camp opens.

It strikes George Blanda, in December of 1952, that all Halas is really doing is holding on to a big piece of money which he, the owner and head coach, can use for working capital during a four-and-a-half-month period. He can even invest it and collect interest. Henceforth, George Blanda will take a full $500 a week. And, oh yes, a couple of other things.

"Coach Halas, sir," says George. "I am going into my fifth year in the league. I have demonstrated that I can play quarter-back by beating the Lions, a team which has just won the league championship. I have been making the same salary for the past four years and . . ."

Ah, kid, don't worry about a thing, Halas replies. There's plenty of time to discuss this matter—after the college draft.

The winter days drift by with a sleepwalking monotony. One

afternoon, George saunters downstairs and picks the *Lexington Leader* off his front steps. His eyes wander from the front page to the sports section. Good God, the man's done it again! He's drafted Tommy O'Connell, Illinois's Rose Bowl quarterback. Oh, the dangers are many, the pleasures are few. It's dark as a dungeon in the damp, dreary mine.

"My whole life flashed before my eyes," Blanda says, looking back. "I just stood there, numb as hell. O'Connell had been the most valuable player in the East-West game one year and he'd been to the Rose Bowl another year. And I could see the headlines forming in my mind: 'Tommy O'Connell Answer to All Bear Quarterbacking Problems.' I'd been looking forward to 1953. I figured I'd get a solid chance and I'd get more money. Now this."

Blanda has outlasted Lujack. He is struggling to outlast Romanik and Williams. Now along comes Tommy O'Connell. And what do George's wondering eyes read in the *Leader* only a few weeks later? Halas has signed O'Connell for—gasp!—$14,000.

That does it.

Before Blanda can get out the door of his home, 222 Norway Drive, Lexington, and point his car toward Chicago, destiny blows him a kiss. There is a long-distance telephone call from someone named Carl Voyles. He identifies himself as the commander-in-chief of the Hamilton Tiger-Cats, members in good standing of the Canadian Football League. It seems that the Bears have signed Bill Gregus, a linebacker-fullback from Wake Forest, who also has a valid contract with Hamilton, where he had played the previous season.

Voyles immediately called Bert Bell, commissioner of the NFL, to protest. Since it was Halas who had done the pilfering, no action was taken. For reasons too vague to go into, Bell did not recognize the option clause in Gregus's foreign contract. Why? If you have to ask, don't ask.

"They seem to think that it is perfectly all right for the Bears to pick up an option in a contract Gregus signed with us,"

Voyles tells Blanda. "That seems to make it open season on each others' players. Now, have you signed your 1953 contract yet? Good, we've decided to pick up your option year with the Bears. Are you interested?"

A bonfire starts to crackle noisily in George Blanda's brain. Before he signs with Hamilton, he'd like to talk to dear Mr. Halas first. Ooooh, boy!

"I had never dreamed of the Canadian League. But now I've got me an outlet. If Halas won't do anything for me, I can go to Hamilton. Why in hell hadn't I thought of this before?"

Into the Patriarch's office steps George Blanda, lupine eyes blazing. Halas begins to discuss the past season, pointing out Blanda's virtues, which he minimizes, and stressing Blanda's sins, which seem so vast the athlete ought to be begging the front office to be merciful and give him only a small pay cut.

"As for the coming season, kid, we've got Tommy O'Connell coming on and he looks like a first-rate prospect. Since you've been fairly valuable as a place kicker, I think we can give you a $700 . . . no, $900 . . . raise. Now if you'll just sign here, kid, where you usually do," says George Halas.

"Just a minute. I read where you're giving a kid coming out of college $14,000 and I'm going to get about half of that for doing all your kicking for you and for trying to win the quarterback job. Is that what you're telling me?" says George Blanda.

"That's all we can afford," says the Patriarch.

"That's ridiculous. I can't play football for you for so little money," says the ballplayer, getting ready to set the hook.

"That's all we can afford, kid."

"In that case I better take that offer from the Hamilton Tiger-Cats."

"Whaaaat!"

"I've worked hard and just when it looks like I'm getting somewhere, you do this to me. Goodbye, I'm going to Canada."

End of dramatic confrontation. Let the curtain down with a thud.

TINTYPE 17

The telephone is palpitating like a loose nerve when Blanda walks back into 222 Norway Drive. Long distance, Mr. Halas calling from Chicago. There is a fatherly tone in his voice.

"Kid," he begins, "I've treated you decently and I'm offering you a good raise. Remember $900 is a lot of money. You don't want to leave the Bears do you? You'll hate Canada! Let's be reasonable."

Something in George Blanda's psyche starts to vibrate. He hears Halas's words as his thermostat starts to rise. He is no longer one of the Patriarch's loving sons. He is mad as hell is what George Frederick Blanda is. He proceeds to curse George Halas with a warm and picturesque flow of language that ends, rather prosaically, with: "And don't you ever call me or talk to me again. I've had all I can take of you. You can stick your football club in your ear."

Slam! Click! Bzzzzzzzzz!

Figuring that the Patriarch will never talk to him again, Blanda calls those warm, wonderful people in Hamilton and tells them he's ready to emigrate. There are massive chunks of ice bobbing on Lake Ontario and the Canadian winds are flapping like chilled bedsheets, but George's heart is full of warmth. Voyles gives him a three-year contract at $14,000 a season and promises him that the Tiger-Cats will keep no other quarterback before him. So it isn't the National Football League! So the rules are a little weird! So the Canadian dollar is worth six cents less than its American counterpart! So what?

Flying back from Ontario, Betty Blanda wonders if all this is legal. Well, it seems that George has been to a lawyer and there is a precedent. Two years earlier, Dick Huffman had jumped the Los Angeles Rams and gone to the Winnipeg Blue Bombers. Naturally, a California judge was quick to issue an injunction. It was sustained by a Canadian court. But when Huffman appealed, he won his freedom and played with the Blue Bombers.

"Don't worry about a thing," says George. "No problem."

Back home in Lexington, the phone rings again. Halas has seen the morning papers. Blanda tells the Patriarch that since he

1. There are Blandas and Blandas and Blandas . . . more than you can count, it seems. The children, from left to right, are sister Helen, cousin Mary, sister Margaret, cousin Helen, brother Joe, little George himself (note stubby legs; square shoulders; dear reader) baby sister Irene, brother Mike. Mathmatics students at West Point will be interested to know that Major Tom Blanda is still several years away from being born. Blandas · Blandas · Blandas · Blandas · Oh, yes . . . the adults, from left to right, are: Uncle Steve, Aunt Christine, Father and Mother . . . Blandas . . . Blandas . . . Blandas . . . Youngwood, Pennsylvania, is full of them.

3. Once upon a time, long before you were born,
you college seniors, there was a young George Blanda who played
tailback (an obsolete position now) . . . here he is stomping around
right end for an impressive gain . . . who says quarterbacks never
run? . . . They do when they are 16, just like everybody else . . .

2. Coming at you, ready to trample you into the dust, are the Youngwood High School Railroaders . . . these vicious-looking brutes who
look as if they just stepped out from behind the altar after serving 6
A.M. mass at Holy Cross Roman Catholic Church are, left to right,
naturally . . . George Blanda (No. 25 in your programs, No. 1 in your
hearts) . . . Gerald Mertz, Milton Brdar, Eddie Robertson, Jimmy Allen
and Henry Hart . . . the leather helmets are not shown . . .

4. *You may find this difficult to believe, but when George was young he dreamed of going to college on a basketball scholarship and playing in Madison Square Garden . . . football was fun, but basketball was the game . . . poor kid, he never made it . . . here he is leading a second-half rally against good old Sewickley High . . . for people who are absolutely bugs over records and cannot sleep if they don't find a new one everyday, the final score was Youngwood 51, Sewickley 19 . . . (it was a bad year for Sewickley, a good one for Youngwood) . . . George led the Railroaders with 471 points . . . there! Now you have two records . . . see what a lovely day it is?*

6. *Return with us now to tho* *thrilling days of yesteryear . . . the k* *quarterback is our own George, fre* *out of Kentucky and posing for t* *Chicago Bears' publicity man . . . goo* *looking passer, Charlie, how long do y* *figure he'll last? . . . Well, if he tak* *care of himself and doesn't get hurt,* *might be around for five or six years .*

5. *Ever wonder what kind of a* *photo the wife of a football player* *carries in her wallet? Is it a mug shot sent* *out by the ball club's press agent? A minia-* *ture action shot, perhaps? What? What?* *. . . And now, direct to* *you from Betty Blanda's wallet, is this* *picture of young George, down by the* *old mill stream . . . romantic, huh?*

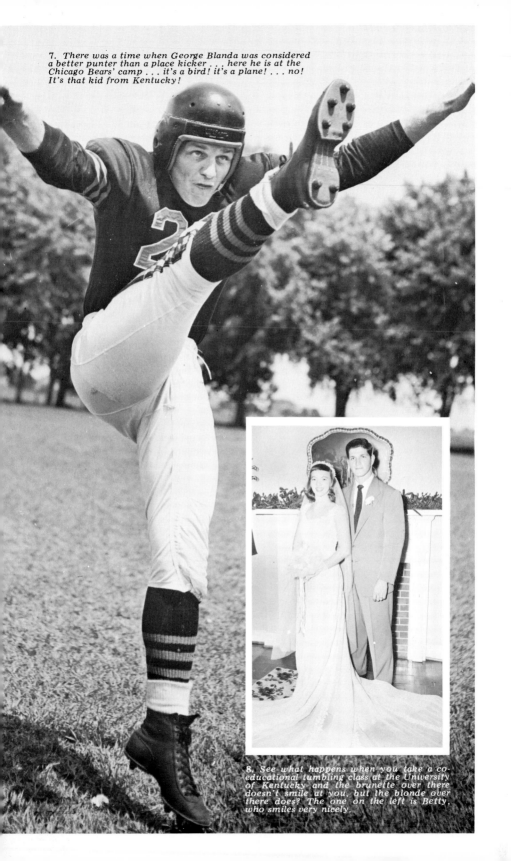

7. There was a time when George Blanda was considered a better punter than a place kicker . . . here he is at the Chicago Bears' camp . . . it's a bird! it's a plane! . . . no! It's that kid from Kentucky!

8. See what happens when you take a co-educational tumbling class at the University of Kentucky and the brunette over there doesn't smile at you, but the blonde over there does? The one on the left is Betty, who smiles very nicely.

9. *One commodity the Chicago Bears always have plenty of is young quarterbacks . . . the ones in this particular mob scene are (left to right) Bob Williams, Steve Romanik and George Blanda . . . they come and they go . . . they come and they go. . . . Over the course of one decade, George poses with so many other young quarterbacks that one day he looks up and discovers that—surprise!—he's not young anymore . . . he's also not a Bear.*

10. *The years go by and there are still Blandas all over the town of Youngwood. . . . Posing with the lady who helped make it all possible are Joe Blanda . . . Pete Blanda . . . George Blanda . . . Paul Blanda. . . . Now, Mama Blanda, aren't you proud of yourself?*

11. There are a couple of excellent methods for avoiding big Ben Davidson, defensive end for the Oakland Raiders, whose aggressive tendencies are well documented. A quarterback like George Blanda can always try to run away . . . failing that, he can get himself traded from the Houston Oilers to the Oakland Raiders and let someone else worry about getting . . a lobotomy from Ben . . . and that's just what George did. (Oiler–Raider game played November 7, 1965.)

12. *Proof positive that if you go to the racetrack enough Fridays, you'll eventually get the urge to buy a horse. . . . That's My Dad George on the left and Leslie Blanda's dad George on the right . . .*

13. The one on the left who looks like country singer Eddie Arnold, is, in reality, John Wayne, that's the only cowboy ever to come out of Youngwood, Pennsylvania . . . no! no! . . . that's not Wayne, the Miami Dolphins and Pete Banaszak of the Oakland Raiders.—George Frederick Blanda . . . That's also Garo Yepremian of What's everybody doing? Well, it's the Dade County, Florida, Youth Fair . . . The man behind the microphone is not Howard Cosell. Blanda, who kicks field goals, against Yepremian, who kicks field goals . . . Well, why not? . . . and somebody thought it would be a great idea to match Maybe he just likes fairs . . . So what's Banaszak doing there? . . .

14. *There's Lamonica holding and Blanda kicking. . . . They're warming up before Miracle Game IV on November 15, 1970 at Denver. . . . To get ready for the game, Blanda practices from 37- and 47-yard lines. . . . It is fine exercise . . . every man past 40 ought to try it . . .*

15. It's time out in Miracle Game III . . . there's 1:34 left and George is getting a little refreshment from the modern-day version of a water boy . . . That's Raider coach John Madden on the right, who is too nervous to drink. When play resumes, Blanda throws a 14-yard touchdown pass to Warren Wells and kicks the extra point to give Oakland a 20-20 tie with Cleveland. . . . Quick, find out what brand of bottled water that is, and order a gallon each for the rest of the players . . .

16. *It is a mile high in Denver . . . so where's a better place for a summit conference? . . . This is Miracle Game IV . . . Blanda is getting ready to go back out on the field, hit Rod Sherman and Warren Wells for two passes good for 62 yards and then pass 20 yards to Fred Biletnikoff for the touchdown that wins it 19-17 for Oakland. . . . But first, a word from your friendly head coach, John Madden . . .*

17. Up, up, up and awaaaaaay! . . . and with this field goal, on October 31, 1971, Lou Groza disappears from the National Football League record book. . . . It happens against Kansas City at the Oakland Coliseum. . . . Now George Blanda is the greatest scorer the game has ever known. . . . The customers give him a standing ovation. . . . Did you read the story, George Halas?

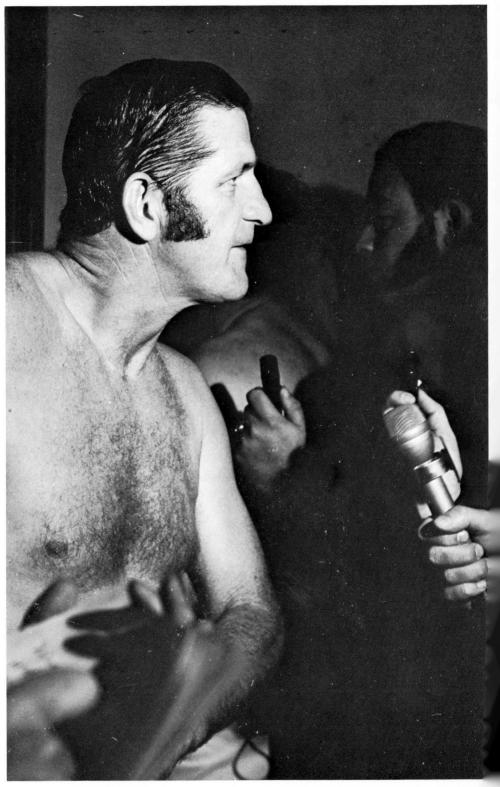

18. *One of the great things about being a football folk hero is that you get to meet so many fine people. . . . You also have to talk to newspapermen. . . . The game is over and George answers questions with enthusiasm . . . and take that $%+&'('%$+% microphone away from my mouth . . .*

19. *Great quarterbacks are supposed to cooperate, but this is ridiculous.... That's Daryle Lamonica on the left and George Blanda on the right and some defensive back on the other team is about to catch hell ... so, where's Kenny Stabler?*

20. *Nobody's tougher than George Blanda, right? . . . Wrong! . . . There's somebody as tough as. . . . Name's Paul W. (Bear) Bryant. . . . See, you knew it all along. . . . "Greatest college coach in the country," says George. . . . So who's going to argue?*

21. *What do most football players do in the off-season? . . . Well, Chip Oliver insists they smoke grass. . . . George Blanda doesn't smoke grass, he plays golf on it. . . . That's George and that's Betty, and there's a golf tournament going on someplace. . . . Grass is good for you, but only if you putt on it.*

is now an employee of the Hamilton Tiger-Cats, he doesn't think it would be wise to talk contract with the owner and coach of the Chicago Bears. He doesn't want the commissioner of the Canadian League to think he's considering jumping to the States. Oddly, Halas does not see the point of Blanda's humor.

Brrrrrrrrring! Hello, George? This is Bert Bell. Yes, the commissioner. You've got to talk with Halas.

"Why do I *have* to talk with him? I don't work for him anymore."

Because . . . because . . . because you *have* to. That's all.

Slam! Click! Bzzzzzzzzz!

"Hello, George?" says the next phone call. "This is George Halas."

"What the hell do you want? I told you never to call me again."

Slam! Click! Bzzzzzzzzz!

"Kid, this is Halas again. Dammit! Don't hang up on me again. We're going to sue you. You have an option year left on your contract and you are going to play it out with the Bears. If you don't, I'll take you into the courts. The damn case will drag out until you're 35. There aren't many 35-year-old quarterbacks around. You're not going to Canada."

Some of the joy began to drain out of George Frederick Blanda's heart. After all, he is still young, only 24, and he does want to play football. Maybe he was a little hasty with this Canadian adventure. All right, he says, he'll go to Chicago and talk things over.

That's better, Halas roars.

Slam! Click! Bzzzzzzzzz!

"It turned out there was a lot of talking going on between the two commissioners. They're afraid that if I go to Canada, there will be wholesale raids back and forth across the border and that would be bad for The Establishment, because player salaries would rise. Then Voyles calls me from Hamilton and says he doesn't want to get tied up in a lot of court costs and he'll release me from the contract I signed with the Tiger-Cats.

"So now I sit down with Halas and I think, for the first time, he realizes he's not dealing with some stupid Polack kid from Pennsylvania. I really think he's starting to respect me a little. He raises me to $11,600. When Halas signed that contract there were little tears in his eyes. Honest-to-God, there were. I had him and he knew it. It just tickled hell out of me to see a grown man cry. I'd finally screwed him.

"I was a whole lot different then. All I cared about was me and Betty and my boy. I didn't really give a damn about the game. But the more you play it, the more you come to love it for itself. It becomes a part of you. Even a man like Halas can't knock your love for football out of you."

There comes now an end to the winter of George Blanda's discontent, a brief period of balmy weather, unseasonably so. The darkness rolls away. The snows cease to swirl. The sun begins to break through the clouds. Too good to last, you say? Right! Right! Right! You are on your way to becoming an experienced and skillful Blanda-watcher.

TINTYPE 18

Important historical items:

(1) George Blanda, who has lived in Kentucky since his graduation, finally permits himself to be dragged out to the race track. He has $20 in his pocket. He notes that Calumet Farms usually has horses that can outrun racing cars. There is an entry from that stable running in a Kentucky Derby prep. So George fearlessly backs the two Calumet colts. They run fifth and sixth. A week later one of them, named Ponder, wins the Derby. Blanda vows never to bet on a horse race again. Never? Really? Well, never is a long, long time.

(2) With the idea that he is about to become the Bears' first-string quarterback (finally) and with the idea that it might be profitable to stop wasting winters rolling barrels in old Kaintucky, Blanda moves his family to La Grange Park, Ill., just outside of Chicago. He takes a job as a sales representative with a trucking firm. Eventually, he will become a stockholder in REA. He never even misses those whiskey barrels, either.

(3) Bulldog Turner retires as an active player and becomes an assistant coach. He feels it is safe to do so, because George has now memorized all 1000 passing plays and all 1000 running plays.

TINTYPE 19

It has finally happened. There is no question in anybody's mind. The bona fide, uncontested, absolute number one quarterback of the Chicago Bears professional football team is George Frederick Blanda, whose face is starting to get fuller, whose physique has become slightly more stocky. There are a few character lines around his lips and eyes, placed there by his feudal lord and master, George Halas. He is in charge. The newspapers, ever faithful to the Patriarch, says he is.

Missing is Bob Williams. Still on the premises, but no longer a threat, is Steve Romanik. Waiting is Tommy O'Connell. But the Chicago journals are adamant. They show George studying those damn playbooks, talking with Clark Shaughnessy and showing his passing grip to the fading Romanik. The headlines do not waiver in their support.

"Blanda Gets Nod as Bear QB," screams the *Sun-Times.*

"Mr. Blanda Builds a Dream House at Quarterback," sings the *Daily News.*

"Bears To Let George Do It," intones the *Tribune.*

So the 1953 season opens and . . .

"Needless to say, I didn't start the first league game," recalls George, looking at those agonizing clippings. "Yeah, O'Connell starts and I thought, 'Oooooooooh, God!' So I'm angry as usual. That's how I started every season with the Bears, angry. They stick me into the opener against Baltimore and O'Connell had already lost it. About the third game of the year, they started me and I finally got my chance. Finally.

"We'd got rid of all the old fellows who were veterans when I was a rookie and we don't really have a real good team. Maybe that's why Halas finally gave the job to me. We start losing. Ended up 3-8-1. Beat the Rams and they were a good football team. And we held Detroit to within six points twice. It looked like we were going to have a better team in 1954. Even so, I led the league in completions that year. Didn't do too badly. Of course, I started feeling as secure as you could feel in those days.

"There was no such thing as no-cut, non-release clauses in contracts in those days. You do poorly and you'll be cut—like that. They cut guys before the first game, they cut guys after the tenth game. Hell, they might cut you at halftime if you screwed up in the second quarter.

"Anyway, I'm all excited about 1954. I'd eliminated O'Connell from further competition. I'm in Chicago as a permanent resident now. I'm getting set up in life now. For the first time I'm going to camp without real competition. I'm it. I'm the regular quarterback. All I have to do is play well and I've got it made, me, George Blanda!"

Everything is beautiful. The trucking company is paying George $125 a week, all year around. He has an expense account and a $20 car allowance. He is making more outside football than he did his first four years with the Bears.

"I figure there's no way they can screw me now. Right? Wrong! They drafted Zeke Bratkowski from Georgia and Ed Brown from the University of San Francisco. I got to go through this *again*. I tell myself, 'George, you gotta relax. You've been around for five years. You've got experience. You know the system. They can't screw you again. They can't.'"

Oh, but they can. The season starts. It is like all other season openers. The Bears are in Detroit's tinny old Tiger Stadium to play the Lions. And George Blanda has a seat for all the action. Yes indeed, Blanda-watchers, you *knew* it was coming, didn't you?

"Off my performance in the exhibitions I knew I'd start. So who goes against the Lions? Zeke Bratkowski—a rookie! I wanted to quit right then. I was white hot inside. It's hard to explain the feeling. Halas won't let you have any security at all. You make your move and he chops you down. He didn't tell me until the morning of the game that it was going to be Zeke. He's sadistic as hell, that man. I called Betty and told her how sick to my stomach I was.

"So they start Zeke and he can't move the club at all. Finally, he gets straightened out some. It's 24-23 and Chicago's moving the ball slowly. So Halas waves me in to play quarterback. It's the fourth quarter and I move the team. I *move* the team! I drop back to pass and I get rushed. So I run around end for about 15 yards. I'm out of breath. So Halas pulls me out. Zeke throws an incomplete pass. I tell Halas, 'Coach, I got my breath back now.'

"He looks at me and yells, 'Sit down, dammit.' On the next play, Zeke throws an interception and they run it back for a touchdown. Now the game turns into a rout. They get 24 points in the last four minutes. Next week I'm a starter. Halas has no other choice."

By midseason, the Associated Press runs a story on George. The headline that appears over it in the *Chicago Daily News* is awesome: "Blanda Appears Headed for Acclaim as No. 1 Quarterback in NFL."

How's a guy going to be the number one quarterback in the league if his coach just won't let him be the number one quarterback on the team?

It is October 24, 1954, an invigorating, smog-smeared afternoon in the Los Angeles Coliseum. Early in the afternoon, Blanda throws his first pass. It is to Jim Dooley for a touchdown. Surprise! The Bears have a 7-0 lead. This only antagonizes the Rams. They come back for two quick scores. The first period is coming to an end and Chicago has the ball on its own five-yard line. George glances over toward the bench, always protecting his flanks. There is Ed Brown getting ready to come into the game.

"Halas has gotta play Ed Brown, because Ed is from California. It doesn't make any difference that this is Southern California and Ed is from Northern California and it's like two different states. He's going to stick him in the ball game.

"Well, Clark Shaughnessy is there, too, thank God. Here was a great man. I learned more from him than I ever thought of learning from Halas. That's because Clark was the real genius behind the Bears. Well, he liked me and I liked him. He was always pushing for me, urging Halas to use me more and to stop horsing around with me. He sees what the Great Innovator is up to and he steps right in. 'George,' he says, 'you can't send that rookie in with the ball on our five-yard line.' Halas always listened to Shaughnessy. It was one of the few *really* smart things he did."

Blanda trots back to the huddle, shaking his head and trying to repress his anger. The other Bears are curious. What is it now? Blanda grins, weakly.

"Fellows," he tells the troops, "if you ever blocked in your lives, do it now. We gotta move this ball 95 yards for a touchdown. This is my last series of plays today. He's going to come and get me. So if you think anything of me—please! please!—help get this damned ball in the end zone. Do it for George. Please!"

With the Patriarch waiting for the smallest excuse to send Brown into the ball game, Blanda completes five straight passes, the last one to Harlan Hill in the end zone for the touchdown.

"Now, you son of a bitch," he mutters, "you can't take me out."

In all he completes 28 passes for 338 yards and four touchdowns. This makes him a good little boy. So Papa starts him the next Sunday in San Francisco as a reward. As it so often happens, anger turns Blanda into superman.

"I actually play the whole game this time. I throw three touchdown passes to Harlan Hill and it's 24-24. They have a third down on our 15-yard line with 35 seconds to go. They take a time-out and, instead of running one more play, they ask Gordy Soltau to kick a field goal. No way he's going to miss. So now it's 27-24."

Darkness has come creeping into Golden Gate Park, where Kezar Stadium rests like an elderly frog on a lovely lilly pad. The wind is blowing and the lights are gleaming on San Francisco's perfect hills. Most of the customers get up and head for the nearest saloon. Here is Soltau kicking off. Somehow he squibs the ball and Ed Sprinkle takes it on his own 34, stepping out of bounds to save valuable seconds.

There are eight seconds left and Brown comes in at halfback. Blanda hands off and Ed throws the ball to Hill for the touchdown.

"I've got to block on the play. I look up and there's Leo Nomellini bearing down on me with that big dirt-eating grin of his. I handoff to Ed. There's Leo coming in and I just kind of stand in front of him. He's laughing and laughing. Before he can wipe me out, he turns downfield and sees Hill catch the ball on the San Francisco ten-yard line and coast into the end zone. Leo's face hits his socks, it drops so low. An unbelievable game."

It comes at a perfect time. It is Halloween in San Francisco and George Blanda, along with some friends, has produced another in a long, long line of spooky conclusions to football games. In another decade, in another era, writers will insist that they are miraculous. Could be.

TINTYPE 20

Another famous quotation:

"George Blanda is the best quarterback in football today. Blanda is having such a great year that we haven't had a chance to use our fine rookie quarterbacks, Zeke Bratkowski and Ed Brown. In fact, in Los Angeles, Brown begged me not to put him into the game because George was playing so well. They wanted to give me the game ball after the victory in San Francisco, but I insisted they give it to Blanda. He deserved it."

—George Halas, speaking before the Bears
Alumni Fan Club, November 3, 1954.

TINTYPE 21

Let the good times roll! Even the Patriarch is forced to admit that George Frederick Blanda can play quarterback as well as any living man. To celebrate his anointment, Blanda comes back the following week at Wrigley Field and throws a scoring pass to John Hoffman with two minutes left that beats the Green Bay Packers, 28-23.

"George Blanda pulled another incredible last minute come-back yesterday," writes the *Tribune's* George Strickler. "It was a regular miracle."

There's a real newspaperman for you. That lead paragraph will stand up for 17 more years, right into the 1970s, in fact.

TINTYPE 22

Now the dark clouds come rolling back. Snow dots the grass. Winter is returning. The headline, all thick type and om-inously black, jumps up off the page of the scrapbook. It is like something out of one of those God-awful 1940 football movies (something called "Jim Thorpe, All-America" or "The Spirit of Notre Dame" or "George Gipp, Immortal") where the progression of a season is shown through a series of newspaper pages superimposed upon game action film.

"Blanda Throws Four Touchdown Passes against L.A.!"
(jaunty football marching music)
"Blanda Hero in Last Minute Victory over 49ers!"
(more jaunty music, growing louder)
"Halas Says Blanda Best in League!"
(jaunty music growing unbearably loud)
"Blanda Jars Packers in Last Two Minutes!"
(jaunty music starting to sound vaguely somber)
"Blanda Hurt! Browns Crush Bears!"
(end jaunty football music; begin jarring funeral music)

"It's fairly close at the half. And in the third period, I dropped back to pass. I didn't see anybody open and here comes Len Ford and Don Colo. Oh, Len would go about 250 and Don about 265 or 270. They sandwiched me and tore my shoulder. I go trotting off the field with a complete shoulder separation. I miss the Cleveland game and four more," says Blanda, the recollection grinding at his tongue, slowing his words down to a pain-stricken pace.

"Up until that time, I'd thrown 16 touchdowns in seven games. I'd passed for 2200 yards and I was leading the league in completions. Every passing record in the National League was within reach, if I'd played those last five games."

Cut to the operating room of Illinois Masonic Hospital: There is Dr. Theodore Fox, a man with a reputation for successful repair work on damaged athletes, saying that there is nothing to worry about. This is a simple shoulder separation, easily fixed. (But it's not your shoulder, Doc!)

Fade now to the office of George Halas, owner and head coach of the Chicago Bears: He presents a contract calling for a $1000 raise to George Blanda, who hasn't even asked for more money. Isn't the Patriarch a nice man? Too bad, Blanda can't sign the contract. His throwing arm is in a cast.

Now time starts to drag. Hopelessness overwhelms George again: "In 1955 Ed Brown's the quarterback . . . plays all year . . . in 1956, Ed's the quarterback again . . . we won the division . . . in 1957, Zeke Bratkowski gets out of the army . . . I'm a number three quarterback again . . . in 1958, I'm third again and I'm 30 years old . . . only good thing that happened those years, I ran my extra point streak to 156 straight . . . oh, yeah, and my daughter Leslie was born . . . other than that I was sleepwalking . . . just sleepwalking . . . George Halas stole those years from me . . . and he left me with a dead sparrow and a piece of string."

There is an obvious enigma here. Why did George Halas suddenly decide in 1959 he didn't need a perfectly good place kicker and quarterback when such a specimen still had a healthy market value?

"I have a highly personal opinion on the matter," Blanda says. "I can't name names because I'm not really sure it happened just that way. But I have my suspicions. There was an assistant coach in the organization who was afraid I was going to take his job. Maybe he had good reason to think so.

"I really don't think Halas wanted to get rid of me. Despite the differences we'd had, there were still a lot of good points to our relationship. For one thing, we respected each other. We didn't take anything from each other. When it came to following orders in a game, he was the boss and I didn't question him. When it came to other things, I didn't mind telling him when he'd been unfair. And George Halas didn't mind telling me to shut up when I had it coming. To show you what he thought of me, he called me in before the 1957 season and said, 'You're getting close to 30. Have you thought about coaching?' I told him I had and he said there might be an assistant's job opening up with the Bears real soon. That sounded good. I'd always given him an honest day's work and he liked that quality in me. He had no reason to expect I wouldn't be a hardworking coach.

"They used to say in the Chicago papers that I was a 'troublemaker.' That wasn't so. I was a team man. But this one assistant thought I was causing trouble with the other two quarterbacks. It wasn't so. I'll tell you how it started. This assistant came up to me one day and said, 'George, who do you think the best quarterback is?' I told him I thought that I was. I also told him that since I wasn't going to get a chance to play, that I'd have to say that Ed Brown was better than Zeke Bratkowski. Now that's no cheap shot at Zeke. All I meant was that Brown had just taken us to a divisional championship. Shoot, we might have won the league championship if the game hadn't been played on ice. Halas was too cheap to buy us rubber-soled shoes. So we slipped and slid on our cleats and got bombed by the Giants, 47-7.

"So this assistant tells me I'm crazy, that Zeke is the better quarterback. The coaching staff likes Zeke because he doesn't smoke or drink. And they want to find an excuse to get rid of Ed because he's always looking for a way to have a good time. I told this assistant that Zeke was just too nice a guy to be a successful pro quarterback at that point. He was a fine person, but he wasn't mean enough yet. He was always walking around saying 'gosh' and 'gee.' So, this coach didn't like what I said. But, hell, he asked me for an opinion and I gave him one.

"I came back to Halas to sign my contract for the 1958 season and I told him I'd talked over the possibility of coaching with my wife and it sounded pretty good. He said, 'Oh, forget about that.' So I did. We had a lousy year. We kept losing and I

hardly played at all. So when I went in to see Halas after the
season, he said, 'Kid, it doesn't look good for next year.'

"I knew right then that I had told that assistant coach the
wrong thing. I'm sure that was my fatal mistake. It cost me a
possible coaching job and it cost me a year as an active player.
It damned near finished me in professional football."

Try to picture the Chicago Bears' front office suite as a
Byzantine palace. Sitting upon the throne is the Patriarch himself. He has his lines out all the time. No one can afford more
than one little error and George Blanda has been challenging the
royal authority too long. Now he must pay. The final act of
intrigue is coming closer . . . closer . . . closer . . .

TINTYPE 23

For the umpteenth time, the career of George Frederick
Blanda, professional football player, is lying very still and very
cold in the market place. Can its resurrection be far away? Of
course not! The Patriarch, now nearing his 65th birthday, will
make two serious blunders during the year 1959. One will be in
his capacity as head coach and owner of the Chicago Bears. The
other will come because he is both lord high executioner and
expansion committee chairman for the National Football
League. One will have a direct bearing on the other. Both will
affect George Blanda. (Ah, see how intrigues come back to foil
the master intriguer of professional football?)

Some historical information is necessary at this juncture in
the plot. It has been forgotten by 1959, due to the clever
manner in which Halas manipulates the Chicago press, but the
first pro team in his city—the city he consents to share with
Richard Daley—was the Chicago Cardinals. They were founded
by Charles Bidwell, who, during the stock market crash, saved
enough money so that one day he would be able to give Halas a
loan to keep the Bears alive.

By 1959, Charles Bidwell was in his grave, his widow had
married Walter Wolfner and the Cardinals were in a steep
decline. They were trying very hard to vacate Chicago, a prospect that pleased Halas so much that he almost smiled without

forcing himself. Wolfner had contacted Lamar Hunt, son of the multi-zillionaire H. L. Hunt, about the possibility of bringing professional football back to Dallas. Well, that was fine with Hunt, except this disturbingly mild young man of 26 wanted to buy the whole franchise. No, Wolfner, told him. Only 49 percent was available. The family wanted to retain controlling interest.

Now the Cardinals sniffed around Houston, an even larger Texas town, located 264 miles further south near the Gulf Coast where men are men and they sweat a lot, too, because of the humidity. He contacted K. S. (Bud) Adams. His papa was chairman of the board of Phillips 66, which is the biggest oil company in Bartlesville, Oklahoma, as well as being one of the biggest in the whole blamed nation. Adams had been pushing AAU basketball for years and was looking for a larger toy. But alas, he, too, wanted 100 percent of the Cardinals. These Texans are notorious for not wanting to share their trinkets, especially with Yankees from Chicago.

In their mutual grief over not being able to get their very own football team—hurry, kids, be the first one on your block, etc.—they have joined together to form a new league. There are four other people or syndicates who are also interested: Bob Howsam in Denver; Barron Hilton in Los Angeles; Harry Wismer in New York, and Max Winter, H. P. Skoglund and William Boyer in Minneapolis. Everybody has posted a performance bond of $100,000 and earnest money of $25,000. They have been shopping for two more franchises. Ralph Wilson, the Detroit insuranceman, wants Miami, but if the Orange Bowl is unavailable, he will settle for Buffalo. And a group of ten businessmen have inquired about Boston.

While the American Football League has been struggling to breathe, the commissioner of the National League, Bert Bell, has pledged to do nothing to inhibit its birth. In other words, he will do nothing that violates the antitrust laws and gets congressmen to fretting over the legality of the common draft or the option clause.

In the midst of this peaceful atmosphere, Bell drops dead and

Halas, the power behind the throne all these years, becomes prince regent, only in fact, not in name. There is an attempt to buy off the new league before it becomes a threat. The possibility of franchises for Hunt and Adams is mentioned. And Hilton is informed that he can buy stock in an existing team.

Halas, the self-made man, summons Lamar Hunt, the son of a self-made billionaire, to an audience in Los Angeles, where the Bears are playing an exhibition match.

"What's all this talk about a second league, now?" he asks.

Hunt explains that he would be very pleased to have the NFL expansion team in Dallas. He knows exactly how Bud Adams feels about getting the same thing for Houston. But what about the other members of the new league?

"What about them?" snaps Halas.

"Well, they've already put up performance money."

"That's your problem," says Halas. "We'll take in two of you and no more." Hunt is summarily dismissed, after agreeing to meet with Halas again in Chicago with more of his colleagues in a few days. The second conclave is no better. Even though a rival group, bidding for an NFL franchise, has failed to rent Rice University's 70,000-seat stadium, technically the only suitable playing field in Houston during those pre-Astrodome days, Halas is unmovable. He secretly is opposed to expansion and he is willing to fight this newest Mickey Mouse League. The war has begun. This takes place in August, just three months after his other big blunder of 1959. Unwittingly, he gives the American Football League an athlete with a recognizable name. And that name, sports fans, belongs to George Frederick Blanda. Take it away, Bill Stern! Portrait of an old man and his mistakes.

TINTYPE 24

It is May and in another few days it will be time to pick up Blanda's option. The Patriarch calls George into his office. Never again will he be empowered to do so. Halas looks up gravely. He is wearing an expression suitable for use at funerals and firings.

"Kid," he says, clearing his throat, "we just don't think we can have you back this year. I just doubt you can make our club."

"Well, that's all right," says Blanda, who isn't exactly overwhelmed by the news. "I'm not real upset. If that's the way it has to be, that's okay. Would you mind telling me what your reason is?"

"You're a troublemaker," Halas answers. "You've been creating friction between the quarterbacks."

"Well, I've tried to help the ball club. If that's being a troublemaker, I guess I'm a troublemaker. One of your assistant coaches came up and asked me to talk about the other quarterbacks, which is an area I'm involved in. He asked me who the best quarterback was and I told him. If he's coming back telling you I'm a troublemaker, that's bullshit and I'll tell him to his face. I've tried to help Ed and I've tried to help Zeke."

Blanda assumes that he is about to get his release. His mind is already moving. Where will he go? Let's see, there's Canada and there's this new league they're talking about. And, surely, there must be a club in the NFL that could use a 31-year-old quarterback, who has been up on blocks for four years, who has only been injured once and doesn't really have that much mileage on him.

"Oh, no, we can't give you a release," says the Patriarch. "I'll give you three options. You can come back and work, but I don't think you'll make our team. We've got Rudy Bukich and he'll be number three behind Brown and Bratkowski. Secondly, you can be traded. But you don't want that. Your home is here in Chicago. You have a fine job with that trucking company. Now the third possibility is the one I want you to study.

"We don't know about our kicker for next year. We got this kid, John Aveni, coming in. Now you go home and keep yourself in shape. If our kicker doesn't come through, if one of our quarterbacks gets hurt, we'll call you. You can skip the training camp, stay at your regular job, spend some time with Betty and the kids. If anything goes wrong, we'll get you back before the first league game. If we don't need you, we'll pay you $6000 just to stay in shape."

On the way out the door, it strikes Blanda that the Patriarch simply doesn't want him around. Someone has told Halas he's a troublemaker. So don't call us, George, we'll call you. Bye-bye!

TINTYPE 25

See the ex-football player. See him run. See him play handball. See him sweat. See him watch his weight. After being screwed with an unrelenting regularity by his curmudgeon coach for ten whole years, he still thinks he can trust George Halas. See the ex-football player wait by the telephone, hoping for a call. Nasty old Mr. Halas is having one last, sadistic laugh. See the ex-football player. Funny ex-football player. Color him blue. Color him sick to his stomach. Color him retired-and-doesn't-know-it.

"I spend my afternoons on the high school field in La Grange, kicking until it gets too dark to see. The kids think I'm crazy. I run every morning at the YMCA. I really think Halas is serious. I make the mistake of believing he'll call me back."

It turns out that Aveni, a highly excitable lad, late of Indiana University, cannot hit the side of a zeppelin even if he stands up real close. Desperate, the Patriarch himself goes out and gives him lessons. That ought to turn him into an immortal, but it doesn't.

"The truth is starting to sneak into my brain—my stubborn Polack brain. Halas is paying me $6000 to retire, so nobody else will pick me up and use me as a kicker. So I call him and say I want to be traded. He tells me he can't do that. So I start resigning myself to my fate. Still, I keep thinking maybe he'll call me back.

"I go out to see their exhibitions and this kid is terrible. He misses every field goal he tries and he can't get the extra points. In the last exhibition game, Aveni misses three extra points and the Bears lose to the Giants by a 21-18 score. I figure if I'm not called back after this rotten performance by the kid, I just

won't come back. There's no use me working out. So I sit by
the telephone on Monday and on Tuesday, figuring he's going
to come crawling."

Finally, the indecision becomes oppressive. Blanda calls
another assistant coach who is amazed that Blanda even has to
ask.

"They aren't going to call you back. They think you are a
troublemaker and they want you out of the picture," the
assistant says.

Now Blanda is ready to chew concrete, he is so angry. This is
the final, towering insult, the unkindest cut of all.

"People wonder why I'm still angry at Halas a dozen years
later. In this case he just lied to me. The kid is just a bad kicker.
None of the quarterbacks can move the ball. I'm better than
any three of them. I'm not a dummy. I may talk like one, but
I'm pretty smart. This trucking company I work for has a
terminal manager in Baltimore. I called him and said, 'Why
don't you call Weeb Ewbank, the Colt coach, and tell him you
know a guy who is a quarterback and a kicker. I know they
need both.' So he does. He calls me back the same day and says,
'Hey, they're interested.' "

There are some technical problems involved, as George plots
this one last glorious counterattack on Halas. When he accepted
the Patriarch's $6000 deal, he was supposed to write to the
commissioner and officially state that he had retired. Blanda
hadn't done that.

Ewbank calls and says that he needs a kicker desperately and
he wants somebody to play behind John Unitas. "All you have
to do is get away from Halas and we can use you."

Now isn't that an understatement, one you can stitch on a
sampler and hang over the fireplace? "All you have to do is get
away from Halas." For ten years, George Blanda has been trying
to do just that. Might it have been wiser to have signed with the
Los Angeles Dons and gone down with the ship?

"How in the hell do you expect me to get away from Halas?
Tell me Weeb. I'll do anything you say," says George, a sense of
helplessness chewing on his large colon.

"Do whatever you have to do. Buy up your own contract and we'll reimburse you. Beg him. Plead with him. Do what you have to do," is Ewbank's reply.

Blanda calls Halas and gets a sermon. Why, the Bears have an understanding with George, who in turn has a moral obligation to stand by in case he is needed. Of course, he may be waiting three days past his own funeral, but how dare he go back on a solemn agreement which the Patriarch himself shook hands on. Doesn't Blanda have any conscience?

"Oh, cut out the bullshit, Coach," screams Blanda. "Give me a chance to go to this team that wants me."

"What team?"

"Why, Baltimore."

"Hang on, I'll try and make a trade for you."

Slam! Click! Bzzzzzzzzz!

An hour later, Ewbank calls Blanda.

"George! He wants two first-round draft choices for you," says Weeb, absolutely demoralized. "I guess we'd better forget it, unless you can get a release."

Off George drives, looking for his lawyer. The time has come to assault the Establishment with pitchforks and pruning hooks. The palace revolution is on. The lawyer instructs Blanda to write letters to Halas and to the commissioner, announcing that he is coming out of retirement. It comes down to a matter of: Either take me back or release me.

"I am coming out of retirement and reporting to Wrigley Field for practice," says the letter, which goes registered mail, special delivery.

Years later, Blanda explains what was going through his mind.

"Bert Bell was in Halas's pocket. Now, Pete Rozelle would have stepped in as soon as he heard about this damned illegal deal that Halas had arranged. That man had me trapped. I wanted to go out of pro football my own man, if that's the way it had to be. If I had to retire, I didn't want to remain the property of the Chicago Bears until I died. I wanted to say, 'Screw you, George Halas, you don't own my soul.' "

Blanda gets a telegram right back from Halas: "You can't report. You have a legal and moral obligation to stay where you are." On Tuesday afternoon, Blanda marches down to Wrigley Field and walks in the dressing room. Halas orders him out.

"You can't come in here, you son of a bitch," Halas screams, ordering someone to eject Blanda and lock the door.

"All right," says George, "you are depriving me of my livelihood. You have to either take me back or release me."

"I don't have to do a damn thing I don't want to."

So Blanda walks back to his car, finds a telephone and calls Bert Bell. The commissioner is horrified. Somebody has been befouling George Halas's nest. One of the Patriarch's boys does not love him.

"You can't come out of retirement any time you want," Bell says, as if he is lecturing a second grader who has suddenly gone berserk in the middle of *McGuffey's Reader*. "What if everybody in the league wanted to come out of retirement the same day? It can't be done."

"Halas forced me to retire. If he can call me back whenever he wants to, why can't I come back when I want to? Besides, where's my formal letter of retirement? Do you have a copy in your files?"

"That just isn't the way we do things," shouts Bell.

Slam! Click! Bzzzzzzzzz!

On Wednesday, the lawyer informs Bell that George Frederick Blanda, who has nine years on professional football's pension fund, is going to file suit against the Chicago Bears and George Halas and against Bert Bell and all the other teams in professional football. Now the season is well along and Baltimore says it is no longer interested. Bell calls back on Thursday to say that he will take the case under advisement and will render a decision soon. On Sunday, Bell is watching an Eagles game in Philadelphia and . . . drops dead. The case is now in limbo. On comes an acting commissioner, Austin Gunsel. He deliberates for a week and comes back with an answer: "Go ahead and sue the National Football League." This is one poker bluff George loses. A court case could drag on interminably. He does not sue. At the end of the season, Halas calls.

"I want to send you a check for sitting out the season. Now you don't want to sue me. Nobody has ever done that to me. Now what do you want?" he says.

"I've got a hell of a case and I know I can win," Blanda replies.

So Halas writes out a form letter, saying that his unloving son can go to the American Football League if he wants to, without fear of a suit. As far as the National League was concerned, he would be forever retired.

Once again, George Blanda's career had cardiac arrest. Which is a sure sign—all together now—that resurrection is coming. Back home the telephone is ringing. John Breen, former Cardinal executive, now personnel director of the freshly minted Houston Oilers, is on the line. The number for George to call is RI 8-2780. It has just been installed.

This howling winter of discontent is over. George Blanda is 31 years old. No longer will the Patriarch be a factor in his life. And where the hell in Texas is Houston, anyway?

— End of Period —

Epilogue:
"I think we'd all have to agree that George Blanda is one of the all-time great pro football players."   —Sid Luckman, 1970

THIRD PERIOD

Are those coyotes howling on the plains? Shucks no, them's Houston football fans, podnuh!

(Which might be subtitled: It's fun to live in Texas if you happen to be a native Texan.)

EPISODE 1

The sunshine, which the tourist bureaus get so lyrical about, lies in great golden pools on the patio, symbolic of the money that is about to be spent. While expensive firewater is being ladled out to reporters and sundry other freeloaders, young ladies in puffy chiffon things move through the crowd passing out press releases detailing the start of the great adventure. Everywhere in the room, men with vast amounts of cash reserves are laughing. Within a few months their mood will have changed. Within a few years they will be biting blood boils on their lower lips.

For the moment, everyone is optimistic, mostly because no one has spent much more than $100,000 for a performance bond and $25,000 to help set up a commissioner's office. For weeks and months there have been rumors and half-truths and shaky truths appearing in the newspapers. Now it appears that, for better or for worse, ready or not, there will definitely be an American Football League. Press conferences are being held in each of the eight league cities. This one is at the Sheraton-West

Hotel on Wilshire Boulevard in Los Angeles. Every writer, columnist and photographer present knows what is going to happen. Some of them even care.

Barron Hilton, son of the international innkeeper and a millionaire on his own hook, has been granted the right to lose money in Los Angeles. Everyone hopes this doesn't mean daddy will have to sell the Baghdad-Hilton if the new league crumbles in the dust. A public relations-type creature points toward a draped easel and, yakking away in well-oiled standard English, says, "Gentlemen, I give you the Los Angeles Chargers." A cloth falls away, revealing a promotion poster. Only the name of the club is spelled cHargers (sic). Why the small "c" and big "H"? Well, they're owned by Hilton and Hilton starts with a large H and . . .

Never mind.

What exactly did the nickname mean? The question seemed academic, because no one in the room outside of the new owners ever expected to see a team called the Los Angeles Chargers actually take the field. Anyway, "Chargers" brought no image rapidly to mind.

"Well, you know how people go 'dah-dah-de-dah-de-dah—*charge!*' at the Coliseum," explains Press Agent Number One. "We are the Chargers. When everybody yells 'charge' they'll be advertising our football team. Clever, yes?"

Clever, no. But fairly typical of a flack's sense of logic.

"Actually," interjects Press Agent Number Two, "a charger is a large war horse . . . you know, big and powerful . . . like the knights used to ride into battle on. Get it?"

Not really, but try again. There has to be more to it than this.

"Ahhhh, you see, Mr. Hilton is president of a new charge-card firm, Carte Blanche," says Press Agent Number Three, flouncing ever so slightly. "So we felt 'Charger' was appropriate."

Ahah! Someone points out that since the Buffalo team is to be known as the Bills, there is no reason why the Los Angeles club can't be called the Chargers. After all, the two seem to go together. Arf! Arf!

Of such bad humor and gentle confusion is the American

Football League born. Before a football is thrown in anger, the humor will get worse and the confusion more rampant. Within days, the Minneapolis-St. Paul group will drop out, bribed with a National League franchise. Someone will find a new location for an eighth team. Atlanta will be the first choice, but Hilton will insist on a second California site and Oakland will come blinking and bawling into the sunlight. At any rate, the AFL says it is alive.

A reporter, present at the creation, is gripped by a curious sense of posterity. Before he returns to the *Pasadena Star-News* to write a column on what he has witnessed here today, he checks his watch and discovers that it is 2:31 P.M. (PST). The date is January 7, 1960. The new league is a Capricorn, which is good. Capricorns are stubborn, materialistic, occasionally foolish, but always ready to work to correct faults. They are also accomplished at the art of survival. A Capricorn? But this is the dawning of the Age of Aquarius. There have been second leagues before, and the NFL has crushed them all. History barely pauses to note the fact, but three other organizations calling themselves the American Football League have failed in the 1920s and 1930s. The poor, brave All-America Conference required only four seasons to disintegrate. The odds-on success for this latest adventure are a little better, though. For one thing the owners—well, some of the owners—are incredibly rich.

The story is unquestionably apocryphal, but it is charming just the same. Someone allegedly tells H. L. Hunt that his boy could lose as much as a million a year in professional football. Since Lamar has plenty in his own bank account, independent of daddy, the elder Hunt snorts.

"At that rate, he can't last much past the year 2135 A.D.," old H. L. is supposed to say.

The television networks have been giving the public professional football for some time with indifferent results. But in 1958, the whole nation gets turned on when Alan Amache, Baltimore's big fullback, goes slipping and sliding over the frozen turf at Yankee Stadium, scoring a touchdown that gives the Colts a playoff victory over the New York Giants in a highly theatrical overtime period. Football is becoming a hot item on the tube and revenue is rising fast. By 1959, the NFL is collecting $200,000 for rights to televise its games. In 1961, the newly crowned commissioner, Alvin (Pete) Rozelle, will astound his barons by getting them a contract with the Columbia Broadcasting System that will fetch $9,300,000 for two years. The spiral is just starting. If the new league can just get on the field and survive for a few years, it might be able to catch the updraft of a trend, too.

So much for the good news. The bad news is: There ain't no place to play in Houston, Boston and Oakland. And Harry Wismer, the sportscaster who owns the New York Titans, ain't got anywhere near the money he says he has. Also, the owners have only a vague notion of where the players are going to come from. What's more, the commissioner of the American Football League does not seem real. His name is Joe Foss and surely some fourth-rate author has hacked him out of pure pulp. He is a worn but still rugged little piece of leather. His hair is curly and his face is handsome, only his features look like they were left out in the wind and snow all winter. He wears a rawhide thong on his right wrist. Most of the time he is hiding in a duck blind back home in South Dakota. Either that or he's tromping across Africa, doing something about the elephant population explosion.

That is only a small part of it. He flew for the Marine Corps in World War II and did as much damage to the Imperial Japanese Air Force as he currently does to mallards and canvas-backs. He machine-gunned 26 of the Emperor's best airplanes and dropped them into the Pacific. They gave him the Congressional Medal of Honor, which helps him get elected governor of South Dakota twice. He seems uncomfortable in offices and probably is. He has an amazing habit of making a $200 suit look as rumpled as a gunny sack when he wears it. Even though he is cowboy to Pete Rozelle's public relations man, it is Rozelle the Super Flack who will win the gunfight and send the cowboy into an abrupt retirement from the AFL commissioner's position.

There is a folksiness about Joe that is absolutely impossible to hate. He is fond of drifting into training camps and saying things like, "Criminy, fellows, stay away from gamblers. If you're approached and you don't report it, remember you're out of work for life, as far as the American Football League is concerned. Criminy, fellows, don't make me take steps. Be careful for old Joe's sake."

Instead of a gunslinger, which they think they have hired, the AFL owners have bought themselves an honest, earnest range hand—a solitary cowboy who yearns for the feel of a good pony under his behind and the sound of a herd bawling in the ravine. The owners call themselves, with as much accuracy as humor, "The Foolish Club." Reading from left to right, they are:

Lamar Hunt of the Dallas Texans—Cool, inscrutable and loaded with money. He is frail physically, or at least he appears to be. His eyes move slowly. His jaw slides back, on heavily oiled ball bearings, into a silent grin. He has the confidence that comes with having a father who earns $200,000 for the family every day. He has the great good sense not to be conceited. He is the mediator and the swift, slick negotiator. He moves on little cat's feet.

K. S. (Bud) Adams of the Houston Oilers—What do you say about a man who wears a black cowboy hat? Loaded, although not really in Hunt's super star category financially, he is apt to do almost anything with his money. No scheme is too large, no scheme is too small. He is the sort of plunger who brings 500 copies of the *Houston Chronicle* to New York on an Oiler charter to sell to New Yorkers who are suffering under a newspaper strike. He is pound wise and penny foolish. What's more, he is given to grandiose gestures. His face is broad and his smile is uneasy, as if somebody is watching him. His uncle, W. W. Keeler, is the great chief of the Cherokee, and some of his players will come to refer to Bud as "Crazy Horse's Revenge."

Barron Hilton of the Los Angeles Chargers—Tall, boyish and gosh-awful interested in professional football. A power in league meetings in the early years, the pressure of non-sweaty Hilton enterprises pulls him further and further away. Cautious and something of an enigma. When the customers in Los Angeles blatantly ignore his club, he almost weeps when San Diego sends a petition with 20,000 names on it begging him to move down Highway 101. An intriguer on the surface, but something of a Hamlet underneath, he makes sure all American Football League teams stay at Hilton hotels, where they get a rate.

Wayne Valley, the power among the general partners who have the responsibility of keeping alive the Oakland Raiders—A former college fullback who never really took off his jock. Blunt and direct, he has a lumberjack's skill when it comes to cutting through the heavy layer of bullshit present at all American Football League meetings. When indecision threatens the AFL, he is a virtuoso at bullying other owners into actually doing something. Quiet, gruff, lacking in pretty parlor manners, he gets more done with a growl than most of the owners do with eight hours of oratory.

Billy Sullivan, front man for the Boston Patriot syndicate—A stereotype lace-curtain Irishman come to life. Billy has fruit on the table when no one is sick, but watch out, the fruit is wax. No one ever knows what Billy's mood is because his face is almost always camouflaged by a door mouse expression that seems to be a smile, but isn't. Very "in" with the Boston Irish elite. He always listens intently, as if he means to repeat every word to James Michael Curley himself. Determined, unimaginative and always short of funds, he never really competes for first-round draft choices, but always has a good reason why they got away.

Ralph Wilson of the Buffalo Bills—An intelligent, serious, efficient man who has more class than the company he keeps. His physical appearance makes him seem out of place. This is no sportsman, no crawling, grasping club owner. This is an Episcopal bishop making a tour of the parishes. His word is good, and when the NFL barons insist that all American Football League owners are devoid of good sense, it is possible to point to Wilson and say, "not all of them." The straight man in a heavy comedy.

Bob Howsam of the Denver Broncos—A baseball man out of his element and not heavily burdened with cash of his own, although his in-laws have a dollar or two. He hires a general manager who spends $350,000 building end zone stands and buying socks with vertical stripes. He is soon gone and replaced by Calvin Kunz, a funeral-parlor type, who is always slithering around trying to secretly move the Broncos to (a) Philadelphia (b) Atlanta (c) Chicago (d) Montreal (e) Miami (f) two of the above (g) some of the above (h) all of the above.

Harry Wismer of the New York Titans—A book in himself, which he threatens repeatedly to write and then makes good on the threat. Jowly and unwilling to let anyone else talk, he is the mad pitchman of the league, which survives in spite of him and also outlives him. Only one of those feats is an upset. Some promoters operate out of their hats. Harry literally sells tickets out of his bathroom. There are no Titan offices. The executive staff works in Harry's apartment and the ticket manager . . . well, you get the picture. An immortal name-dropper, Wismer is likely to interrupt a league meeting with, "As I told Jack Kennedy when he called me this morning, I don't think the Pope is going to go for this . . . and believe me I know what the Holy Father is thinking." His players have a phrase that adequately describes Wismer's paychecks: "Don't cash them with anybody you like." He and the Polo Grounds are well suited to each other. They are both falling apart.

Now that the Foolish Club is assembled, with all members of the association present and accounted for, let us take a scenic tour of the botanical gardens where the new league will conduct its games. Or, as Spiro Agnew will say one day, "See one slum, you've seen 'em all."

It appears that the Patriots have pulled an astounding coup, because Billy Sullivan has prevailed upon Boston University to let the new professional club use its 27,000-seat stadium, which is really old Braves Field in drag. Soon, Billy learns why the Braves moved to Milwaukee. And the Patriots wander all over Boston before they settle in Fenway Park, which isn't much for

baseball and is even worse for football. They really covet
Harvard Stadium, which resembles a place where the British
would be apt to bury their kings and poets.

No sweat in Buffalo, because the Bills can use War Memorial
Stadium. This seems fortunate, but the place is one of the last
of the great WPA projects and from the way it is built it looks
like the best thing the workmen did was to lean on their shovel
handles. Worst dressing rooms since the Roman Colosseum and
the surliest crowds since Caligula was emperor. What's worse?
Thumbs down in Rome or a beer-can barrage in Buffalo?
Tackles develop 4.4 speed getting off the field. A marvelous
conditioner, War Memorial Stadium.

The Dallas Texans are booked into the Cotton Bowl
where the seats are hard and bats live in the end zones because the lighting system never bothers them there. The Texans
cohabitate with the Cowboys of the NFL. No parking on the
Texas state fairgrounds, but that's all right because only 7000
come out for the games and they are the sort of un-Texan
cranks who drive Volkswagens. Oh, yes, the drainage system
stinks and don't think it don't rain in Dallas in the wintertime,
y'hear?

No one can find the Oakland Raiders because nobody in
Oakland can see them play without crossing a bridge. There's no
stadium in the East Bay except the one owned by the
University of California which objects to professionalism in
athletics and is sworn to combating it right down to the last
athletic scholarship. So the Raiders hide out in Kezar Stadium.
They could all be convicted axe murderers on the lam from San
Quentin and nobody would find them there.

Ah, the Polo Grounds! This is where Bobby Thomson hit the
home run and Sal Maglie pitched all those beautifully tough
baseball games. But the football Giants long ago jumped across
the river to Yankee Stadium and the baseball Giants found
peace and prosperity, if not a better stadium, in San Francisco.
The Polo Grounds are haunted by ghosts, most of whom kick
the girders, causing rust to fall in your coffee up in the press
box, to select the best-populated section of this sagging Vic-

torian ruin. The Polo Grounds are the home of the Titans. A wrecking ball is getting closer ... closer ... closer. Hurry, before the joint falls down.

The Los Angeles Chargers have a lease on Memorial Coliseum, that graceful swirl of early 1930 concrete. Happily, it is not a long one. They have the best stadium in the league. They would be better off in the Hollywood Bowl with its 5000 seats for stage shows and concerts. They might have a fighting chance of filling that. The Chargers are an NFL-quality team from the start, but this is Ram territory.

The logical place to play in Houston, despite the humidity, damn the mosquitos, is Rice University's architecturally elegant football stadium. It resembles nothing so much as a red-brick-and-concrete butterfly with its two stands spread toward the skies like huge wings. But Rice is zonked on culture and football players who get paid in broad daylight are not cultured. So Adams discovered an open sewer adjacent to the University of Houston campus. It is a high school stadium named after somebody whose surname seems to have been Jeppesen. It is cramped, uncomfortable and it reeks of doggie doo-doo. The Oilers paint the joint Columbia blue—the club owner's favorite shade. They erect new stands that get the attendance possibilities up around 38,000. It still smells as if a little kitty crept in, crapped and crept out.

It is bearable because the Oilers are another team that could stand eyeball-to-eyeball with, say, the Chicago Bears, and because some big-talking Texans are getting ready to build an air-conditioned indoor stadium way over on the other side of town, down in the south meadows where blackbirds fly and oil wells pump in the distance.

"That damn Mickey Mouse league doesn't even own a football," says George Halas, echoing one of the slogans that helped win the war against the All-America Conference. But he is an old general who doesn't understand that times have changed. Television is getting ready to spend big. The AAC didn't have that jolt in its veins. The war is on. Old soldiers never die, Mr. Halas, they just fade away ... they just fade away.

EPISODE 2

Great lines from other books:

"When considering George Halas, it is helpful to think back to the classic Patriarchal character in our Western movies. The role is usually played by Spencer Tracy or John Wayne, who early in the script is braced by his progressive son about giving the newly arrived sheepherders or sodbusters a chance on the vast acreage he claims is his. The answer, always the same—and it would not sound strange coming from George Halas—is, 'When I came here thirty years ago, there was nothing here. I fought Indians and the plague and I have a wife and two brothers lying in that cemetery in the north forty. If you think I'm going to give up an inch of that land to some sniveling sodbuster, you don't have the right to call yourself my son.'"

—Bob Curran from *The $400,000 Quarterback,*
Or, the League That Came in from the Cold.

EPISODE 3

The irony is so delicious that George Frederick Blanda keeps his face stretched out into that eerie lobo smile of his. He is in demand. Honest!

It appears that this new league is at least going to get one season in. And guess who the hottest commodity in America is right now? Aw, c'mon. Lie down, give yourself plenty of chance to enjoy this, because you'll get these awful abdominal pains laughing. Here's the situation: For a decade George Halas, the Patriarch, has been trying to suffocate George Blanda. He has done everything to make him feel cheap, alone and unloved. He has literally plucked the best years of Blanda's life away from him. Why? Who can tell? Now in the classic tradition of romantic literature, he has made two gigantic blunders. He had challenged the American Football League to a duel to the death at a time when there is an interregnum between commissioner Bert Bell, who listened very carefully to every word he said, and commissioner Pete Rozelle, who will call the Patriarch in and explain that his power has now been broken. And he has agreed to give Blanda his freedom at a time when a new league—with real money behind it—is forming.

Here's a quick quiz: What does a new league need most? Answer: Players with recognizable names, athletes who won't make readers squint when they pick up their sports sections in the morning. And what do football teams have to have before they can seriously think about winning games? Answer: Why they need quarterbacks.

The people who are getting the American Football League together are aware that, for a few months in 1953 and 1954, George Blanda was a genuine super star. They are aware that he is a very forceful, very independent person who eats beans only when he feels like it. This man is now free to sign with any American League club. And Halas has expressly forbidden him to join a National League team, even though there are several who might like to hire him. In effect, the Patriarch has released him to the new league.

This is one of the least intelligent moves any great power has made since the Americans sold scrap iron to the Japanese, who in turn made bombs, which in turn fell on the battleship Arizona. Every owner in the new league has been calling. The Houston Oilers were first because their personnel director, John Breen, is smarter than anyone else and he was around Chicago, first as coach at Lake Forest College and later as an executive with the Cardinals, when George was having that brief flicker of fame in the mid-1950s. How many quality quarterbacks are available? Count them. There's Jack Kemp, the Giants and 49ers and Lions dismissed. And there's . . . there's . . . well, Kemp and Blanda seem to be it. Oh, you can get guys out of college. You can find people like Cotton Davidson, Butch Songin, Al Dorow, Frank Tripucka, John Green, etc. anywhere. But Blanda and Kemp are the only ones worth owning.

"Every one of those teams has called," Blanda tells a friend. "All I have to do is wait and take my pick. Can you imagine that? What I have to do is sit and evaluate the owners, the cities, the personnel. It's unbelievable."

Indeed it is. If somebody hadn't invented the American Football League for George Blanda, surely he would have invented it for himself. They have been made for each other. Here is a league that everybody is laughing at, making stupid jokes and minimizing the odds for survival. It is a quaint outfit, one that has so many flaws that it is difficult to take it seriously. Yet, it has a certain jaunty quality about it.

And here is the forgotten quarterback, the buried-alive quarterback. Here is the man who challenged the unchallengeable George Halas. Here is a league that seems to be doing the same thing. If one can succeed, so can the other. It is just a question of where George will go and destiny seems to be pushing him toward Houston, where glass-and-steel towers rise daily, where money comes gurgling up through the sandy soil. There are several less romantic reasons.

"Houston brought in John Breen, whom I always thought had a lot of sense. He got them off to a great head start. They were out signing players when everyone else was talking about where they were going to play. John was after me from the very start," Blanda recalls.

"I was almost signed by the Oilers when a lot of the clubs came calling. Shoot, Oakland wasn't even in the league, yet. Buffalo and Boston were so far behind the others, it wasn't funny. Houston really put the rush on me. Then Los Angeles came in. It was wonderful. Here I had been sitting around, begging that damn Halas for a chance—just a small chance—now a whole new league was courting me."

Sidney Gillman had just jumped to the Chargers, which was just as well because the Los Angeles Rams had decided they needed a new head coach anyway. The first man on his shopping list is George Blanda. The second is Jackie Kemp.

"Come on out here, George, we really need you," he says, breathing heavily into the mouthpiece like somebody making an obscene phone call.

Several years earlier, during a Ram-Bear game at the Coliseum, someone had misplaced Chicago's kicking tee. Before the Bears could kick off, someone went over and asked Gillman if he could borrow his. That someone was George Frederick Blanda. "Screw off," said someone from Los Angeles. That made someone from Chicago damned angry. And Blanda never forgets an injustice, remember, no matter how trivial it may seem to somebody else.

"Sidney," Blanda says over the long-distance phone in January, 1960, "I won't play for you. I don't like you. I barely got away from a man just like you, George Halas. What do I want to play for you for?"

"Come out anyway and bring Betty. Have a week in Los Angeles and then we'll talk some more," says Gillman in that avuncular tone he affects.

Having warned Gillman well in advance that he does not love him very much, Blanda finds an airplane and seven hours later falls out of a smog in time to be greeted by Gillman. The man's smile is so warm, his manner so jovial that George decides right away that he isn't making any mistakes going to Houston.

Also on the trip are a couple of other ex-Bears, Stan Wallace and Rocky Ryan. They, too, are being rushed by Gillman. Like Blanda, having played for Halas, they have no desire to get in the same sort of situation again. Everyone stays at the Hollywood Hilton for a week and has a dandy time. George buys everybody in the bar drinks, running up an impressive tab. At the end of the week Uncle Sidney drops in, polka-dot bow tie and all, and asks Blanda what he thinks about the Chargers now.

"Same thing as week before last," says George, who is genuinely enjoying all this freedom from oppression by owners and general managers. "I wouldn't play for you under any circumstances. I'm going to sign with Houston."

And he does.

EPISODE 4

Having gone through the wrenching pain of being born, having stood up to the awesome thunderbolts of the Patriarch, without flinching more than a little bit, having located some structures vaguely resembling stadiums, the new league now decides to sign some players, which seems logical. Adams has had a man in the field for some time. It is one of the first truly intelligent moves he makes with his franchise. It is also one of the last. The agent is John Breen, a tall man with the carriage of a United States senator and the face of a defensive lineman who has blocked several field goals with his nose. He eats cigars by the box and talks tough, mostly to disguise an abnormally irreverent sense of humor that can only get him into trouble. He is one of the few competent football executives that Adams ever hires. Breen's sin is that he knows what he's doing, which frightens the club owner who prefers to dress up and play general manager himself while conferring the title—in name only—on a parade of wooden soldiers. While the other clubs are still trying to figure out what color uniforms to wear, Breen is out signing as much NFL-quality talent as he can find. The first man he goes after is Blanda.

"My first thought was if you're going to play in a new league, go get the best-throwing quarterback you can find and have him put the football in the air, because it will be a year or two before anyone can get the kind of defensive backs that will be able to stop him," Breen recalls.

"I told Bud Adams that this was the man we needed to build our offense around and Bud said, 'Go get him.' I'd seen him when I was with the Cardinals and I admired his toughness. I used to tell people that he learned to kick field goals by kicking people in the head. He's done that, too. He's kicked a few in the fanny. Anyway, I always thought he was a terrific guy and I called him just as soon as I heard—through the grapevine—that Halas was willing to let him go to the American League.

"It took me two weeks to sign him. Bud started to wonder what had happened to me. He called me in Chicago while I was negotiating with George and I told him, 'Mr. Adams, we just have to have this man.' He'd talked to everybody in the league. I had to go to him and I had to go to his lawyers. He had us over a barrel. He could have really stuck it to us if he had wanted to. But Blanda was just interested in making a fair deal.

"I was aware of his situation with the Bears. I knew he was a great competitor and that Halas just plain didn't like him. Halas never wanted to give him any money, to teach him a lesson, I suspect. He didn't like Blanda personally, that's all there was to it. Every time Blanda would go in there, he'd look good and Halas was afraid he was going to have to pay him a little money. Blanda and Halas were too much alike, in their personalities, ever to get along. Blanda would never knuckle under and Halas hated that.

"One day, in a Cardinal-Bear game, the crowd was yelling, 'We want Blanda! We want Blanda!' So Halas turned to George and said, 'Hey, kid, you better get up in the stands. They want you.' They were both so outspoken, those two men. Blanda wasn't above walking up to Halas on the sidelines when things were going bad and saying, 'Why the hell don't you put me in, you're such a great coach?' Halas always felt that he didn't want to have Blanda, but he didn't want anybody else to have him. If it hadn't been for the AFL, I don't think Blanda would have ever played again.

"At any rate, he was very reasonable in his demands. I think I signed him for right around $20,000. Salaries weren't tremendous in those days. I gave him a small bonus. There was also some stock he wanted. George was very smart about the stock market and he asked us for some stock he knew was going to grow. We didn't give a car or anything. In those days we wouldn't even buy you gas for a car."

Blanda has several sound reasons for going to Houston. A former Bear colleague, Gerald Weatherly, had moved there and kept praising the city's remarkable growth potential. It strikes George, who never forgets a lesson, that going to some of the other franchises might not be too different than going to the old Baltimore Colts in 1950. Who knows how long the New York Titans are going to last? And who wants to sprint to the teller with a Denver Bronco paycheck?

Should the American Football League collapse after only one season, it is reasonable to suspect that the Oilers would be taken into the NFL, as the Cleveland Browns and San Francisco 49ers were when the AAC went down.

Besides, the head coach in Houston is going to be Lou

Rymkus, whom George has known for years. Rymkus is tough, hyper-competitive and thoroughly dedicated to the principle that victory is worth skinned elbows and an occasional broken collarbone. Besides, his jaw juts way out. He's a second-generation American, born of Lithuanian parents in southern Illinois's dismal Little Egypt region, where people mine coal and salt, work on the railroads and tell their sons to play football so they can get a college scholarship and get the hell out. Lou Rymkus is a Slavic soul brother! George Blanda knows the type.

EPISODE 5

The glass towers rise majestically from the monotony of the coastal plain. They glitter in the morning sun like the turrets of Oz. This is the first major city whose architectural style is strictly mid-twentieth-century modern. When the wreckers arrive to make room for another skyscraper there are no lovely old Victorian curlicues to mourn over, no gothic gargoyles to remove to the safety of the civic museum. In Houston, tradition is being made tomorrow. Oil gurgles to the surface in the suburbs. The petroleum companies have their headquarters here and they each try to erect a taller building. When men talk about their "interests," they do not refer to petty things like golf or yachting or keeping a mistress. Interests are financial diversification—oil, cattle, cotton, restaurant chains, insurance, banks, television stations.

Houston does not come close to Hollywood fiction. There are no swaggering blowhards in ten-gallon hats who drive Cadillacs with cattle horns jutting out of the hood. Their car horns do not play "The Eyes of Texas." Hell, that's a University of Texas fight song and a lot of the really important people in Houston went to Texas A&M and they would rather vote Republican than be associated with that infernal tune.

As the sixth decade of the century opens, the rest of the nation is bracing for racial strife, looted stores, antiwar protests and sexual freedom. Houston has none of these problems. Its only worry is where to put the freeways so that more glittering glass towers can be built, further and further out. While

America convulses, Houston expands. People come pouring out of the decay that is Detroit and Cleveland and New York and head for the Texas coastal plain.

Air conditioning is turning Houston into a paradise. The humidity is still there, but it can't get at the population.

A man rises in his air-conditioned house in Spring Branch, showers in his air-conditioned bathroom, goes to his air-conditioned garage, gets in his air-conditioned car, drives to his air-conditioned downtown parking garage, walks through an air-conditioned tunnel beneath the pavement and takes an air-conditioned elevator up to his air-conditioned office.

So many northerners settle in this semi-Western, semi-Southern town that the natives come to refer to the Humble Oil Building, the tallest of the towers, as Yankee Stadium. The city is the sixth largest in the nation, but it remains pleasantly folksy, which disarms the immigrants who have been pelted and pushed across the sidewalks of New York. Visitors, though, hate the place. Because of Texas's curious liquor laws there are no open saloons. Vice is all underground, but it is there, brethren. Every Southern Baptist knows it is so.

Already they are hollowing out a crater to hold the lower levels of the first covered sports stadium the world has known since the Emperor Vespasian stretched a purple canvas across the top of the Flavian Amphitheater to keep the midday sun out of the lions' eyes. It will be called the Astrodome by its implausible creator, Judge Roy Hofheinz.

Into this enthusiastic, competitive atmosphere steps one of the most enthusiastic, competitive athletes in the Western world. An instant love match, right? Wrong! No one can really say why the city built on oil explorations, roughnecks and wildcat wells never fully appreciates this aggressive, gambling, victory-oriented quarterback. Faulty chemistry? Bad karma? What? For seven seasons, George Blanda is to remain a stranger in Houston, a man who drops out of the sky every summer, is either a great football player or a terrible bum, depending on the viewpoint of the particular fan, and departs in the winter. He is more of a personality than a person. The press writes

about him endlessly and rarely talks directly to him. The city
doesn't understand him and he doesn't understand the city. In a
sense they admire each other's style, but fail to find anything
deeper. It is a puzzle.

EPISODE 6

The side room of Glenn McCarthy's opulent saloon, The
Cork Club, is crammed with hungry newspapermen whose well-
insulated abdomens are growling with pain. It is well past their
feeding time and they are starting to suspect that the Houston
Oilers, or whatever this new football team is called, need to hire
someone who can get a press conference started on time. After
much bitching (you can't call yourself a journalist, if you don't
bitch) some food arrives. Now a press agent enters the room,
followed by Bud Adams, John Breen and a stranger.

"Gentlemen," says the flack, "I give you the new first-string
quarterback of the brand new Houston Oilers—George Blanda."

Blanda's overpowering stare is missing this afternoon. He is
wearing an expression that is closer to that of a small boy at
Christmas. He could almost pass for an acolyte, he is so serene
and happy.

Now the press agent is reading off some statistics. George is
31 years old, has led the NFL in pass completions one season
and holds the record for most consecutive extra points kicked.
George says something pleasant in a voice that soars so high it is
almost a falsetto on this momentous occasion. Now, any
questions?

"Isn't 31 a little old to be a quarterback?" somebody asks.

"Now I wouldn't say that, because I'm 31," he says, his voice
dropping several registers, his gaze growing more intense. "I feel
I have at least six or seven good seasons left. The Bears didn't
use me much, so I didn't take that much physical abuse. There's
no telling how long I can last, not really. Charlie Conerly of the
New York Giants made it to 39."

"You kicked 156 straight extra points," says another writer.
"Was that all in one season?"

Blanda's eyes become mere pen strokes. When they open

again, he is glaring like a wolf. Does this writer really think it is possible for a team to score 156 touchdowns in one season? Why, that would be 11 touchdowns a game—77 points every Sunday.

Jesus Christ!

George Blanda has just met the Houston press corps!

EPISODE 7

Great quotations, continued:

"Keep ancient lands your storied pomp. / Give me your tired, your poor, / Your huddled masses yearning to breathe free, . . . / Send these, the homeless, tempest-tossed, to me: / I lift my lamp beside the golden door."

> —From the inscription on the base of the
> Statue of Liberty, by Emma Lazarus.

EPISODE 8

Way up in the tall piney woods, an odd couple is throwing gear into the back seat of a car that looks like it is mentally deranged. Its headlights stare feebly. Its sides are battered. When it goes, it makes weird and irrational noises. All it has to do, says the taller of the two, who is built like a flamingo, is get from Robeline, La., to Houston, Tex., where the tryout camp is being held. Wrong, says the shorter one, who could pass for a bowling ball with legs, it may have to get the two of them down and back.

The flamingo is named Charlie Hennigan. He is a school-teacher and he likes money, which is an impossible combination. He has a slip in his pocket that shows he made exactly $2734.18 flinging knowledge at small children. Hennigan is sleepy-faced and his voice moves with all the fury of a snail stampede. Behind that drifting rural image is a palpitating brain. Eventually he will get a doctorate in education. At the moment he is anxious to make some money playing football. He has been inspected and found to be too careless catching a pass to be of further interest to the Edmonton Eskimos of the Canadian League. In the couple, Hennigan is the optimist.

The bowling ball is Charlie Tolar. Would you believe a 5-6,

210 fullback? Well, neither would the Pittsburgh Steelers. They took Tolar to camp, used him in a few exhibition matches, including one against the Chicago Cardinals in Houston. Then they looked at his height. Then they closed their eyes, gritted their teeth and sent him back to Louisiana. Tolar is almost as wide as he is tall. He smiles constantly, possibly even when he's taking a shower. He is the pessimist.

"Somebody told us about this new league," Hennigan recalls. "I hadn't seen a single word in our newspaper. News kind of trickles up to Robeline. Anyway, I called the sports editor of the Shreveport paper and he told me that Houston was the nearest franchise to us. I doubted if the car could make it to New York or Denver, so I figured we'd better go. I called the Oiler office. Lou Rymkus said they were interested in anybody. So I got on the phone to old Charlie Tolar and asked him if he was interested."

In college at nearby Northwest Louisiana State, the odd couple had played in the same backfield. Incongruously, the lean Hennigan had blocked for the overly muscular Tolar. A sprinter with flat palms, Hennigan would ultimately be taught how to catch a football with his chest. At the moment, though, he was actually a man without a position.

"All the way down, Tolar keeps telling me how foolish this all is, that the pros aren't interested in guys like us, that we ought to turn around. On and on. But danged if we both didn't make good once we got there. It was a little tougher for me than it was Tolar. He could always run hard. It was just a matter of not letting his lack of height bother you. But I had hell holding on to the football. One of the Oiler assistants, Mac Speedie, kept working with me. Every time the other coaches would insist that I ought to be cut, Mac wouldn't hear of it."

It is fortunate for the new league that (a) Hennigan doesn't listen to Tolar's grumbling pessimism and (b) the car doesn't break down. Hennigan will set an all-time professional football record for most passes caught (101) in a season. And in 1962, the bowling ball, Tolar, will roll for 1012 yards.

"I'm not being maudlin when I say 'thank God for the

American Football League.' I mean it sincerely," Hennigan says.
"You know damn well that if it hadn't been for the AFL, even
our neighbors back home in Robeline wouldn't have heard of
us."

The athletes are pouring into the Oilers training camp at the
University of Houston in a flow that looks like the retreat from
Caporetto. It is raining. It will continue to rain, day after day,
until the turf at Old Buff Stadium, where workouts are held,
turns into quicksand, sucking up a man's strength even as he
tries to run away from the elements. When the rain retreats
down the ship channel and out past Galveston Island, the
choking humidity shows up, sneaking over the outfield wall
while everybody is turned around waving goodbye to the rain
clouds.

Some of the players have names the public knows. Blanda is
there. So is Billy Cannon, the Heisman Trophy winner, the
running back from LSU that the Los Angeles Rams thought
they had signed, too. The Oilers have won him in a legal brawl.
And there is Jacky Lee, pinto-faced and palomino-haired, a
quarterback from the University of Cincinnati, who just a few
months earlier threw six touchdowns in the North-South Game.
He likes to throw long and he has a live arm. He is a competitor,
too, almost as strong a one as George Blanda. He isn't quite and
it becomes his personal purgatory, trying to beat George at
anything—football, golf, cards, anything. He fails.

There is Johnny Carson, not the television performer, but a
pass receiver who has some mileage on him, picked up mostly
with the Washington Redskins. There are other name players,
fresh from college—Dan Lanphear of Wisconsin, Charlie
Milstead of Texas A&M, Don Floyd of Texas Christian, Bob
White of Ohio State and Doug Cline and Bill Mathis of Clemson.
All of them have had national publicity.

Then come the second-class citizens, the people who would
have been discarded or never given a chance in the first place:
guard Bob Talamini of Kentucky, split end Bill Groman of
Heidelberg College, fullback Dave Smith of Ripon and a tight
end named Al Jamison from Colgate. The latter is really a tackle

in disguise. He hides his intellect and his polish nicely (he is an honor student who attended college on an academic scholarship). And he becomes the league's first legitimate character, a brawler and a masterful holder, Dirty Al Jamison. They are the tired, the poor, the homeless, the tempest-tossed, the huddled masses yearning to breathe free. For every cheerful story about a Bill Groman, a Charlie Hennigan, a Dirty Al Jamison, there are dozens of tales of hardship cases given a plane ticket home.

Over 150 individuals are Oilers briefly this first year. Some barely last through one practice. A few show up in uniform, watch the calisthenics and drift sadly back to the dressing room. Some are totally pathetic. There is a guy who had played guard only during his junior year in high school. He barely knows the rules. There is an alleged defensive end who has stuffed himself with milk shakes and beer to get his weight up to 335 pounds. He understands that the professionals like their linemen large. He passes out in the Houston sun.

There is a flankerback from the University of Mexico. He has flare and promise, but he consistently goes AWOL. There is a lad from a small southern school who doesn't know from chitlins about the outside world. He asks to sign a "verbal contract." They come. They strut and fret their one brief hour and are gone.

One morning there really is a Houston Oiler football team. It has uniforms and cleats. It even has a quarterback with a reputation. No one really knows what kind it is. Does Houston own the George Blanda of 1953-54? Or does it own somebody who couldn't even make Rudy Bukich obsolete? It is an academic question, good for hours of boozy conversation in neighborhood beer joints. The important thing is: The American Football League lives!

EPISODE 9

Three interesting viewpoints:

(1) "The American Football League can't be anything but a Mickey Mouse League. How can it be anything else? Isn't George Blanda a first-string quarterback over there?"

—George Halas

(2) "No player on the Houston Oilers could break into the starting line-up of any of the top four teams in either division of the NFL, and only one or two could break into the starting lineups of any team in the NFL. The only reason George Blanda, who threw only 50 touchdown passes in ten years in the NFL, can hope to succeed in the American Football League, is because he can expect to find his receivers less adequately covered."

—Hamilton Prieleaux Bee (Tex) Maule in his weekly *Sports Illustrated* hachet job on the American League (circa 1960).

(3) "Damn right I was bitter about the way Halas tried to shelve me. I became pro-AFL right from the start. I still am. Even when the Oakland Raiders became an NFL team officially in 1970 with the completion of the merger, I was an AFL man in my heart. I always will be loyal. That first damn year, the Houston Oilers or the Los Angeles Chargers could have beaten— repeat, beaten—the NFL champion in a Super Bowl, despite what the detractors were saying."

—George Blanda, looking back in December, 1971.

EPISODE 10

Nothing in the real world mirrors Lou Rymkus, the first and, possibly, the most successful of all those Houston Oiler head coaches. He could not exist outside of fictional literature. He belongs with Dink Stover and Jack Armstrong and Milo of Corinth. He is not just a simple anachronism. He isn't out of step. He isn't out of tune. The drummer he hears never lived. Big Lou is something that could never have been.

Once upon a time there was a pseudo-heroic image of athletics. They were supposed to be noble and uplifting, too similar to religion to be criticized. Victory meant joy and no sacrifice was too large to insure victory. It was a fraudulent philosophy, born of America's rampant, turn-of-the-century Anglophilia, this preoccupation with the spiritual side of sports.

Lou Rymkus grows up in a coal town, too, in Royalton, Illinois. His family life is tragic—a broken home and an only brother who dies in his teens. But Lou believes in the American dream, every soggy bit of it. He lives it as fully as any human

can, because hard work is the only route to success. And Lou
desperately wants to escape from southern Illinois. He goes to
Notre Dame on scholarship and bawls like a fool whenever he
hears the Victory March. He believes that all his life fellow
alumni will look out for him, as he is pledged to look out for
them. The beautiful legends, the charming lies all sink into his
soul. Frank Leahy's honeysuckle rasp will always echo in his
medulla oblongata.

After graduation—and he is extremely proud of the fact that
he has a degree—he plays one year for the Washington Redskins
and goes into the wartime navy, umpiring softball games between teams of vacationing sailors in Honolulu. When that ends,
he is exposed to the aggressive tendencies of Paul Brown and
the Cleveland Browns. He is a hard, fierce player, a tackle who
goes both ways. Some people, George Blanda included, think
that he is a whole lot tougher than he really needs to be. By
God, he gets the job done. Victory isn't everything. It is the
only thing. Win any way you can, he thunders, until all the
bravado is beaten out of the slogan. That's okay. Big Lou
understands. All he wants to do when his playing career is over
is to spread the gospel. He wants to be the equal of Leahy and
Brown and, later, Vince Lombardi. Trouble is that some of the
infidels don't have Big Lou's devotion to the one true faith.

Some of them think football is merely a pastime, an exercise,
a vehicle to a less violent career in mercantilism. Big Lou has no
use for such heresy. He tells overbloated halftime stories,
because that is what Leahy says Knute Rockne did and Leahy
should know. Leahy was on Rock's last team, the one that
graduated the spring after the great coach died.

He has been preparing to be a head coach, preparing to
ascend to the glory that he is sure is due him, for nearly a
decade. As an assistant with the Rams, he has his choice of two
teams, the Los Angeles Chargers and the Houston Oilers. He
makes the same choice George Blanda does, for almost identical
reasons.

Rymkus is tall and ominous. His neck crooks forward slightly and he has a habit of closing his eyes until it appears that they are hooded like some bird of prey. He could pass for a turkey buzzard turned human. He wants his athletes to know immediately that they are doing more than just playing a football game. They are on a holy mission, a war to the death.

"Football was mother and father and home and family to me," he is fond of saying, using a voice inflection that Leahy must have previously thought was his private property. "I want you players to think the same way I do."

It is a trifle excessive, but hardly unworkable. In another place, another time, with another club owner whose heart is less tinny, this could easily be a highly successful head coach. But it is not to be. Lou Rymkus and George Blanda leap from the same ethnic sources, the same social class. One sees the real world and adjusts his personality. The other sees exactly the same thing and decides to convert everyone. The willingness to challenge from within the system saves George Blanda. The unwillingness all but destroys Lou Rymkus. One Slav is counterpoint to another. The competitiveness that lifts one ruins the other. No sociologist could ever adequately explain it.

Rymkus decides that his refugees and Billy Cannon must exist on one plane if the Oilers are to be successful. One cannot let a $100,000 halfback think he is that much better than a $10,000 wanderer from Ripon like Dave Smith, who plays just about as well. So Rymkus attempts to bring the Heisman Trophy winner down to the level of the locker room proletariat.

"Until you prove yourself on that football field, you're just another football player to me," says Rymkus, with some logic.

The words fall heavily on some eardrums. Cannon, who has had some teenage scuffles with law and order, has enjoyed thinking of himself as aristocracy. And Bud Adams starts to wonder about a coach who would put down one of the three or four legitimate big names in the new league. No one will ever truly understand the passion that snaps, crackles and pops in Big Lou's chest. It may be unrealistic, but it is uniquely his own and he is willing to die with it.

EPISODE 11

It is late afternoon and Lamar Hunt, who is somewhat fretful over this new venture, is driving home in the mud-thick Dallas freeway traffic. He flicks on the radio and hears football odds quoted.

"In their first exhibition game this weekend in Tulsa, the brand-new Dallas Texans of the brand-new American Football League are two-and-a-half-point favorites over the Houston Oilers," the voice curling out of the radio says.

For several astonished seconds, Hunt simply sits there. Then the whole impact strikes him, right between his heavy bifocals. For crying out loud, they're talking about us, he says. Swiftly, he gets Bud Adams on the telephone.

"We've arrived," he reports, coming about as close to raising his voice as he ever does. "The bookies made odds on us. I heard it on the radio, Bud. They have made us two-and-a-half-point favorites over you. They know about us in Las Vegas. Isn't that wonderful?"

Hiring players, buying uniforms and calling yourself major league does not make you that in fact, as George Blanda will discover when this first season is over and he attempts to talk to all those people back in the VFW Hall in Youngwood. First you have to get a reputation. And that is exactly what the Dallas Texans and Houston Oilers are trying to do on this pasteboard-dry night in Tulsa. The newspapers have been wonderfully kind.

"24,000 expected to See First AFL Exhibition Match," says the *Tulsa World*.

With the exception of the game itself, the production is almost a total fiasco. There is supposed to be an open-car parade through town, so that the public can see these freshly minted professionals. The civic booster in charge takes the cavalcade through the wrong section of town. The three or four thousand curious spectators who will show up at any parade never see the athletes. At the stadium that night, the Oilers discover that roughly half of their Columbia-blue home jerseys have been stolen. They borrow blazing red shirts from the Texans, who are scheduled to wear their white road suits.

Visually, the Oilers look badly bush. Artistically, they aren't much better.

Cannon fumbles twice. Blanda completes only nine of twenty-five passes and gets two intercepted. The public address system doesn't work. The crowd is not much more than 10,000. Whereas Dallas looks excellent, Houston gets nothing but boos. The plane ride back is long and mournful. So the AFL has been discovered, eh?

"Say this for George, he had some problems in those exhibitions," Rymkus recalls. "He had been a hell of a quarterback for a couple of seasons with the Bears, but George Halas damned near ruined him. He hadn't really thrown much in five or six years. So his arm was a little weak from inactivity. At first, I wasn't sure how to treat it. You know, was his arm dead or was it just out of shape? I got the answer eventually. But I was worried for a while."

For those obsessed by statistics, the final score is 27-10, favor of Dallas.

It is September 18, 1960, a day that will live as long as rich men dream of having sweaty toys they can call their own. The weather is suitably humid. In fact, Barron Hilton, owner of the visiting Los Angeles Chargers, wears a drooping white shirt that will have to be taken out behind the Shamrock Hotel and buried at midnight under a full moon.

"I didn't recognize you, dressed like that," says Rymkus. "You're usually wearing those $500 suits."

"In this heat," says Hilton, "I'm just happy to be able to breathe."

There are three 17-year-old girls, all of them equipped with modest bosoms and discreet smiles, standard equipment for beauty queens in heavily Baptist Texas. Miss Diane Scroggins—Oooooh! Me? You mean me?—is the first Miss Houston Oiler. She gets $500, a bunch of roses which promptly commit suicide in the awesome heat and a kiss from Bud Adams. There is a pregame invocation long enough to make Oral Roberts weep. Then there is a kickoff. Are you listening, George Halas? The American Football League owns a football. There are 20,156 customers on the premises. Sorry old Jeppesen Stadium looks almost festive in its new paint job. If you stand upwind, the odor isn't too fierce, either.

These are George Blanda's salad days. His arm is growing stronger, stronger, stronger. The Oilers win the opening game, 38-28, and move swiftly through the season, whipping the Eastern Division handily. Behind Blanda stands Jacky Lee, who looks young enough to be throwing papers on George's front doorstep.

"Wow, you sit down in a bull session with George and you realize how little you really know about the game of football. Wow!" he says. "Every move George makes and everything he says gives you a new insight into the game. He'll probably be retiring in about five years and when he does, I'll be ready because I've had the opportunity to be around him. Wow!"

Part way through the season, Blanda twists an ankle and Lee throws a record 92-yard touchdown pass that helps beat Denver in the rain. His eyes twinkle. His heart flutters. He still thinks he can beat George Blanda. Poor boy! He has more to learn than he imagines.

George has not wrestled with destiny all these years in order to surrender to the first blue-eyed, lollipop-faced child who comes along. In his heart, he rather likes Jacky's enthusiasm. But as far as George is concerned, on the surface this is just Steve Romanik and Bob Williams and Rudy Bukich all over again. Lee had better be super. He is a Beta Male and George will not let him advance until he is absolutely ready. Such is the law of the pack. Blanda has been taught to obey it faithfully. After he beats Denver as George's surrogate, Lee tells the press: "I feel as if somebody way up high was calling the plays. Somebody higher up than the press box."

Blanda reads the quotation, lifts one eyebrow, shakes his head and takes a deep, bemused breath. Even after all that abrasive realism with Halas in Chicago, it has never occurred to him to tell reporters something like that. Amazing! Has he lived so long that he has actually witnessed a distinct change in the life-style of professional athletes? Have the charming recreational habits of Ed Brown been replaced by voices from the great beyond? For the first time, George Blanda is starting to feel as if he is past 30 and that he will probably never get excited ever again over the senior prom at the University of Kentucky.

EPISODE 12

A fascinating dialogue, which may even have taken place:

Houston sports editor: *"What? You're bringing me another picture of George Blanda? Do you realize that this paper has run more pictures of Blanda than it has of President Eisenhower?"*

Oiler publicity man Jack Scott: *"That's because Blanda is having a better year."*

EPISODE 13

The days have dwindled down to a precious few and the only teams left in contention for the American Football League's very first championship are (a) the Houston Oilers and (b) the Los Angeles Chargers. They have clinched the Eastern and Western divisions and now they are meeting before 32,183 to settle this thing. There are some empty seats at Jeppesen Stadium and only a secret agent reporting directly to George Halas—and who says there isn't one present?—would notice.

Clearly it is time for an inspirational speech. Where in Lou Rymkus's vast storehouse of gallant football oratory is there a proper text for the sermon? It should be something straight out of the Book of Frank Leahy, Chapter IX, verses 22-29. Like a lay reader, he clears his throat and looks over the congregation in the Houston dressing room.

"Gentlemen, after all we've been through, the heat and the mud and the mosquitos, we deserve to be champions of the AFL. We do. They don't. Nobody is going to beat us. Let me tell you why . . . we . . . are . . . Great Northern Buffalo! Yes, men, that's what we are. When I was at Notre Dame and Frank Leahy was the coach and Angelo Bertelli was the quarterback, we had this late November practice and it was snowing real hard in South Bend. We're getting ready to play Northwestern and the snow was coming down so hard we couldn't see.

"There's Coach Leahy on the sidelines. We could hardly hold onto the football, our hands were so cold. We figured he might take us into the fieldhouse. So we go into a huddle and Bertelli says to me, 'Lou, why don't you go over and ask Coach Leahy and see if we can't go inside.' So I go over and say, 'Coach, we just had a little meeting and we'd like to finish up the practice indoors.'

"So Leahy looks at me and says, 'Just one second. Last night I happened to be reading a book about the northern buffalo and the southern buffalo. That book was so interesting I couldn't put it down. I read it chapter after chapter, with no regard for the lateness of the hour. Let me just tell a little bit of what I learned about the northern buffalo. He stands out there with his head into the wind and the rain and the snow. He has a big strong neck and a big strong chest. The weather doesn't bother this northern buffalo. Now you take the buffalo of South America. He's in a warm climate. The breeze is blowing off the ocean.

" 'The weather is nice . . . so he has a small neck . . . small legs . . . small body. I made up my mind after reading that book all night. Now I want you to go over and tell those lads that we will continue to practice out here in the snow because we are Great Northern Buffalo.' "

Rymkus pauses in the narrative to make sure that his words have had the proper impact.

"Now get out there and show them you are Great Northern Buffalos! Don't stick your asses to the wind like puny southern buffalos!"

(There is no record of how many Notre Dame players actually believed that George Gipp had begged Rockne on his deathbed to have the team win one in his memory someday. The Irish did, indeed, go out for the second half and defeat Army. A few cynics may have snickered at the Great Northern Buffalo Speech, but history indicates it did not have a poor effect on the Oilers.)

If this first championship match is below National Football League standards, the difference in quality is not that obvious. It is a showdown between Charger quarterback Jack Kemp and running back Paul Lowe on one side and George Blanda and Billy Cannon on the other. A television crew is on the premises. The customers are so enthusiastic they probably don't know they aren't watching the Chicago Bears beat the Washington Redskins 73-0. (No defense in the NFL in those days, eh?)

There is a lovely brawl on the field. Julian Spence, a former army sergeant who is one of the original Oilers' few black players, is asked to leave the field. He is a 153-pound defensive back with a crackling sense of humor. He dresses in an outrageous imitation of owner Bud Adams, from the black cowboy hat and blue tinted glasses down to the white leather Rommel coat.

On this occasion, Sgt. Spence has hit Lowe hard enough to loosen a few cotter pins in the latter's neck. Several Chargers take offense at this enthusiastic act. The punching is brisk. The crowd is vastly entertained. Also asked to go cool his psyche under a shower nozzle is Maury Sleicher, defensive end for Los Angeles.

The lead switches three times. Then, in the fourth period, with the Oilers leading by a single point, 17-16, Blanda figures that enough is enough. With a third-down-and-nine situation on his own 12-yard line, George notes that the enemy is tightly bunched. He calls "Pass Z, slant four, swing and go." The object is to isolate Jim Sears, the strong safety who is assigned to cover Cannon. Out on the flank stands the lean and money-hungry Hennigan, his teacher's salary slip still inside his helmet. He is the responsibility of a cornerback named Charlie McNeil.

Hennigan takes several steps downfield, then swerves to his left, taking McNeil with him at a 45-degree angle. Cannon slants for the sidelines at the same angle. This is where it gets oh-so-technical. Now Cannon swings upfield. Sears, who charged for Cannon at the snap, now discovers that both McNeil and Hennigan are between him. He will have to take two steps to go around and get at Cannon. Suddenly he is aware of exactly what it means to isolate a defensive back. Cannon is by him and, presumably, gone when Blanda puts the ball in the air. The reception occurs on the Houston 35 and Cannon has the distance he needs to make it 88 yards from the line of scrimmage into the end zone. Now the score is 24-16 and it stays that way.

"If that wasn't just as good a brand of football as they play in the other league, I'll kiss your ass," Rymkus tells one reporter, who obviously does not care to risk having his buttocks smooched by arguing.

Now George Blanda is the master of his fate, the captain of his soul. There is no George Halas telling him to shut up and go stand in the corner. He is the acknowledged Alpha Male, the undisputed number one quarterback. Pride swells up and bubbles. He has had a magnificent year with 169 completions, good for 2413 yards and 24 touchdowns. American Football League pass defenses aren't superb exactly, but they are better than anyone thought they would have had a right to be. The players swirl around George Blanda. He fits in exactly the same place Sid Luckman did when George was a rookie with the Bears.

"I've waited eleven years for this moment," he shouts in the Houston dressing room. "I've waited eleven lousy years. This is my first championship. I've waited all this time for one. The damn Chicago Bears never won one during my ten years. Maybe if Halas had let me play, they might have. How about that?"

Champagne, which had been ordered for the division clinching by Adams and prohibited from use until after the final championship game by Rymkus, is brought out. Blanda wallows in euphoria.

"Bud Adams pays a man what he's worth," says George taking one final, mighty blow against the Patriarch. "And Coach Rymkus treats you like a man. I'm going to enjoy getting used to both in the years ahead. This is just the first of a lot of championship teams in Houston."

The next day one newspaper refers to George as the greatest living Texan, a line which the senate majority leader, Lyndon B. Johnson of Johnson City, apparently does not read. A week later, George Blanda flies home to Chicago. He has redeemed himself. Now everyone knows how shamelessly he was wasted with the Bears. They do?

"Hey, George," says a familiar voice, "you sure had a great year down there in Houston. Congratulations."

"Thank you," he says, in that tinny voice all athletes affect when they are listening to compliments.

"God, what a shame it is you have to play in that other league. You belong right up here in the big leagues—right here in the National Football League. I sure hope you get your chance again someday."

Arrrrrrrrrgh!

EPISODE 14

One interesting quote and one news item:

"Some forty or fifty million people saw the best professional football playoff game of the season. The American League game was far better than the one between Philadelphia and Green Bay in the other league. I'd say that the Houston Oilers could easily beat the Chicago Bears, the Los Angeles Rams, the Washington Redskins and the Dallas Cowboys, to name some of the weaker clubs in the NFL. And the Oilers could play a representative game against either of the NFL divisional championship teams. Our prestige is on the rise."

—Harry Wismer, owner of the New York Titans.

"San Diego, Calif.—(UPI)—Barron Hilton, owner of the Los Angeles Chargers of the new American Football League, announced that he is moving his franchise here in response to a petition signed by 22,000 San Diegans. The team will operate in Balboa Stadium in time for the AFL's second season next fall. The Chargers are defending champions of the AFL's western division."

EPISODE 15

For courage in the mouth of the enemy's cannon, nobody deserves a military decoration more than John Breen, who agrees to speak in Chicago during that first off-season.

The members of Chicago's American Quarterback Club have just come lurching in from the bar. While they pluck at the plastic chicken and concrete peas on their plates, Breen pulls himself up to the dias and sprinkles some ashes—Groucho Marx-style—on potted palms in front of him.

"You never expected to see me back here representing the Houston Oilers, did you?" he says. The members roar. "Well, we fooled you bastards, didn't we? We're going to keep on doing it, too. It will take four or five years, but we'll catch the NFL in all phases of the game. I'd like to say it would happen sooner. It takes about four years to develop a good lineman. Maybe that's how long it takes to teach them how to hold without getting caught.

"Now, I want to say a word about George Blanda—whether you like him personally or not, he's a great player. That's right, a great player. You can boo and hiss all you want, because George Halas has you brainwashed. But that's what Blanda is and if the Bears had hung on to him instead of doing the stupid damn thing they did with him, they'd be leading the league."

It is the most unpopular thing Chicago has heard since somebody phoned the fire department to suggest that there seemed to be a warm glow in Mrs. John T. O'Leary's barn. They boo Breen for fully ten minutes.

EPISODE 16

These are the pre-dawn years, just before everyone in professional football is due to get rich through the blessings of the Great God Video. The check for winning the league championship arrives one miserable morning in snow-saturated La Grange Park, Illinois. It comes to $1016.42 per person. Television money has not gone into the players' pool. If it had, the sum would have risen to $2016.42. Very shortly, the postal department will bring everyone diamond rings commemorating the Oilers' glorious victory. At least, that is what Bud Adams has promised. So everyone waits and waits and waits. Years later they are still waiting.

Times are cruel-bad all over. Adams announces that he has

spent $710,000 more than he has taken in from his professional football interests. Why, the legal costs involved in taking Cannon away from the Rams amounted to more than $70,000. Things are looking up. One day alone, there were 25 applications for season's tickets. So the rings may be along any day now. Now Adams is after the University of Pittsburgh's brutal tight end Mike Ditka, the Oilers' first-round draft choice. He will fail. Here is the Houston club's fatal flaw: It will pay big money for all the expensive bonus players who aren't real good pro prospects—guys like Don Trull, Lawrence Elkins, Scott Appleton, etc.

It will bid for, and subsequently lose in a wave of outrageous buffoonery, Tom Nobis, Charlie Taylor, Donnie Anderson, Mike Ditka, Earl Gros, Bill Truax, Ralph Neely, Stan Hindman, etc.

("When it became apparent in 1964 that the club wasn't really serious about signing the truly outstanding rookies, I think a lot of the veterans kind of gave up, because they knew help wasn't on the way," George Blanda would say one day, looking back over the years. "A lot of us got this feeling of hopelessness, as if the core of Oiler veterans would have to carry the club until they dropped dead on the field.")

Just when several Oilers begin to wonder where the rings are, the club owner makes one of his typically grandiose gestures. As a reward for stomping the new league into the turf, the Houston club is going to train in Hawaii. And the year after that, there is a strong possibility that the Oilers will hold their sitting-up exercises in Spain. Exhibitions will be played in the Madrid bull ring, Adams explains without bothering to inquire if a fighting bull needs 100 yards, plus end zone space, to die in. The players clap their hands until their palms get raw and bloody. The coaching staff, led by Rymkus, falls into a catatonic state. How can you teach young men to go to war in paradise?

"What am I going to do?" Rymkus asks, troubling deaf heaven with his complaints. "When we go to training camp, a new year starts. We're just last year's champions. That will be tough enough. But when a tropical moon is out and the palm trees are swaying and you can hear the surf crashing against the beach and you know that the restaurants and bars are full of horny schoolteachers from Iowa and it's 10:30 P.M., how in the hell can I convince the players that they ought to go to bed?"

These are cruel times for Rymkus, too. Even though he is the American League's first coach of the year, nothing good happens to him. Willard Dewveall, a tight end of high quality, plays out his option with the Chicago Bears and joins the Oilers, thereby making up for the loss of Ditka to the Bears. In order to sign him, Adams takes out a big policy with the insurance firm Dewveall works for. This rubs the proletarian Rymkus six or seven different ways, every way but the right way.

"Why doesn't Adams buy a policy from me? I'm the coach of the year. I've proved what I can do," he tells writers. "Another thing, I don't like this Hawaii trip at all. It's a way for Mr. Adams to entertain his big-shot oil company friends. The only comfort I got is the fact that George Blanda is my quarterback. The old coach could be a whole lot worse off, eh?"

The words get into print and there is trouble between coach and owner before the elderly DC-7B ever lifts off from the airport, heading toward the islands. All of those lofty thoughts that rattle around in Rymkus's skull will not save him. He is hell-bent for suicide. He has flown too high, too fast.

A turning point—a genuine turning point—has been reached. There is a difference between the Rymkus of the first year and the Rymkus of the second. Blanda sees it immediately. It makes him fret.

"Understand, I liked this man," he recalls. "He and I came from the same origins. He wanted us to play hard. He wanted us to have an explosive offense like the Cleveland Browns always had when he was there. He developed hard-hitting players. That's the kind of player he'd been, and that's the kind of football team we had. Hell, I wanted to play for him forever.

"But he underwent some kind of personality change. I don't know how to describe it. Maybe it was something that was there all the time and success just brought it out in Lou. He still used the same coaching technique. Something in his personality was altered. I think that he began to believe that he was a great coach. He'd read all that stuff in the paper. Anyway, he changed from being a team-oriented coach into being a coach-oriented coach. He developed this big thing about Sid Gillman of the Chargers. He had to beat Sid.

"They'd been together in the National League and it kind of carried over into the AFL. We had that damned training camp in Honolulu in 1961 and it wasn't a training camp, it was a vacation. We had played the Chargers in San Diego before we went over. They beat us 28-14 and Lou fretted all the way because we'd lost this exhibition to Sid Gillman. It all but drove him crazy. I was worried about the way he reacted to the loss. Now we have to go out to the islands and play San Diego again and Lou is frantic.

"Well, we gotta play the Chargers again in Hawaii and by game time we aren't ready to play, because there is just too much to do over there—too many distractions. My roommate is a center named George Belotti and all the way over he's moaning because Al Jamison is hurt, can't play and I have to put up with some rookie over there at left tackle.

"Ernie Ladd has just joined the Chargers and he's 6-8 and 300 pounds and Belotti keeps saying how I'm going to get killed because no rookie tackle is going to stop this monster from Grambling College. Some of that stuff sunk in and I threw something like five interceptions. Oh, I was horsefur, but no worse than anyone else after a week in Hawaii. It was unbelievable. I must have thrown those interceptions the first quarter-and-a-half. Every time I felt that damned Ernie Ladd was near me, I just got rid of the ball. They had us 39-0 at the half and Hogan Wharton says, 'Let's sprint to the dressing room and lock the door, so Lou can't get us.' And Cannon says, 'Better yet, let's just cut under the stands and take off.' Rymkus hears us and shouts, 'Get in there, goddamn it.' "

So Rymkus closes his eyes to vulture slits and looks around the room.

"If you sons of bitches want to tell your children you were members of the first pro team ever to get beat 100-0, you go

out and play the second half just the same way you played the
first half," he says.

Unquestionably, the Oilers look better in the second half. If
they played any worse, the Honolulu sanitation department
would have to send a truck around to pick up the remains. The
final score is 46-28, favor of the Chargers, and Rymkus is
crushed.

"It really affected Lou to lose to Gillman as badly as he did.
He just wasn't the same after that. I felt terribly sorry for him.
Nobody wanted to win worse than Lou Rymkus. Nobody
wanted to succeed as a head coach more than he did. I could
sympathize with him. I was sorry as hell to see what was
happening."

The players are turned loose on a 72-hour pass. By now
Rymkus figures he might as well let them run as try to nail their
windows shut. Resistance is futile. When rape is inevitable . . .
try it, you'll like it.

"Where can you get the money changed?" asks Don Floyd,
the defensive end from TCU. "This here is the first time I ever
been outside the United States."

Armed with aloha shirts, porkpie hats and a lust that passeth
understanding, the Oilers hit the beach. Not since the Imperial
Japanese Air Force struck the place two decades earlier has
Honolulu seen such an assault group. One offensive lineman
hurts his ankles slightly jumping out of a second-story hotel
window one leap ahead of a particularly angry husband. Fortunately, the sand below is loosely packed. Three rookies go
splashing into a canal, car and all. One of them, halfback Claude
King, is convinced that he is dead. It is damned near impossible
to talk him out of it. After all, he knows he can't swim.

"At first, the wives wanted to hear all about the Hawaiian
trip," says Mrs. Laurie Hennigan. "The husbands wouldn't say a
thing. Then, after the years passed and some of the legends
began to get back, we decided that the wives didn't want to
hear, after all. Naturally, my Charles insists that he didn't do
anything except sightsee and go to the movies."

The troops reassemble. Rymkus takes one look at them and

goes, "Arrrrrgh!" With maximum effort, the Oilers pull their shattered bodies together and destroy the Oakland Raiders, the league's shabby step-children, by a 35-17 score. Now it is time to leave these enchanted islands to the natives and to the tourist trappers. The airplane is waiting at the terminal. Slowly, the survivors limp up toward the boarding platform.

"I don't mind the players looking so awful, but where in the hell is my trusty trainer, Bobby Brown?" Rymkus recalls. "We wait an hour and here comes the guy who is in charge of keeping our lads in condition. He looks worse than anyone. I don't even bother to chew him out. I just yell, 'Paint a red cross on this goddamned thing and let's find Houston.' "

Struck by the head coach's act of infinite mercy, Brown nods weakly. The door is screwed shut. The propellers turn with a perplexed whine. The airplane sags off toward Diamond Head. Lou Rymkus's brief but glorious hour is almost over. Hawaii kills him. His dream dies in paradise, of all places.

EPISODE 17

Quotes that history has almost, but not quite, forgotten:

"Let's have no more pinching of the hostesses. If there is any pinching to be done, from now on the coaches will do it."

—Lou Rymkus, over the intercom on the tragic flight home from Hawaii, 1961.

"Where will this club train next year? I don't know, but I was talking to Bud Adams the other night in Honolulu and he said that he likes either the Madrid bull ring or the one in Mexico City . . . 110,000 at 20 pesos a head . . . not bad . . . not bad."

—John Breen, speaking to a *Houston Chronicle* columnist on the same flight.

EPISODE 18

It is mid-October and already the winds have come screaming down off the arctic ice pack, stripping the trees of their flaming artistry and setting a chill on the land. The temperature drops rapidly in New England as if some frugal Yankee has discovered that the thermostat has been set too high. The players step down swiftly from the ramp at Logan Airport in Boston. The last man off is Lou Rymkus. He moves with vast effort. As they say in the business, he is carrying a piano on his back.

For days the newspapers have been saying that he is through as head coach of the Houston Oilers if he cannot convince his club that the proper thing to do is beat the Boston Patriots. The club owner is angry. Some people say that Bud Adams does not like the way Rymkus tells the truth in public. Others say that the head coach was at a party before the season began and that he said something unfriendly to Mrs. Nancy Adams, the owner's little flower of a wife. Others insist that Big Lou is suffering only because he has committed that most despicable sin—he has won only one of four ball games. Whatever the reason, the club owner is angry. Rymkus has to win.

"A new coach would at least focus attention away from the Oilers," writes Jack Gallagher—evil, nasty old Jack—in the *Houston Post.* "Adams thinks he sees a number of opportunities where his high-priced talent could be better used. He has an important date with Dallas coming up a week after the Boston game. Can he attract a big gate if Lou Rymkus brings in a team that has lost four in a row? A switch in coaches would serve to hypo the box office."

With that economic possibility quivering in his mind like a cherry in aspic, Bud Adams is getting ready to do something that he will repeat over and over again through the year—deal from panic, curious behavior for a millionaire. Obviously, Rymkus must smash the Patriots in order to survive. Isn't that what Jack Gallagher has decided?

The troops are muttering among themselves. In his agony, Rymkus has placed several delicate rumps on the bench. Some of the demoted accept what has happened. Others growl. The starting quarterback is Jacky Lee. And as the fog comes puffing off the nearby Charles River, he has the finest evening of an otherwise uneven career. He completes 27 of 41 passes for 457 yards. He hits Hennigan 13 times, a record. And when there are only five seconds left, Rymkus yells for George Blanda, who does not get edgy late in the game. Amazingly, the Patriots are ahead 31-28. All that throwing, all those tired muscles from shoulder blade to wrist, and Jacky Lee is still behind. A field goal from 14 yards out will still fetch a tie. Maybe Adams will turn his thumb up. Maybe?

Onto the field Blanda runs. As he reaches the huddle, one of the Oilers whom Rymkus has been putting down, whispers out of the side of his mouth, "Miss it, George. Teach the son of a bitch a lesson he'll never forget."

Blanda turns and tells the intriguer to forget his schemes.

"I grab this guy by the jersey and tell him never to say stuff like that to me again. If I can kick field goals for George Halas, I sure as hell can do it for Lou Rymkus, a guy I've always liked. And why the hell should I miss something on purpose? That's not what they pay me to do," George says.

So the ball goes floating through the proper hole in fog and the Oilers get ready to go home with a profitless tie. Rymkus knows he is through, but he talks bravely. "I have never been more relaxed," he tells Frank Godsoe of the *Houston Press*, a newspaper that won't survive Rymkus by much itself. "I never worry about my job, only my team."

The next morning, he has no team to worry about, only his job. He will spend years wandering, endlessly asking what happened to him. Wasn't he dedicated? Wasn't he hardnosed? Didn't he put victory above everything else? Didn't he believe in every platitude, didn't he worship every coaching cliché he ever heard from the mouths of those sweaty saints, Paul Brown and Frank Leahy?

Didn't he go to mass every morning and pray for success in his first head coaching job? Why, then, did he fail? The answer is that football is not mother and father and family. It is a 100-yard war, pure and simple. In any war, there are bound to be casualties in the ranks, some empty spaces in the general staff.

The object, as George Frederick Blanda has learned in Chicago, is to survive in order to fight another day. Lou Rymkus is a general without stars. The new Houston Oiler coach is Wally Lemm. And this will not be the first time he gets the job. He will quit once and, not satisfied, will return only to get fired. If Bud Adams doesn't nail you the first time around, he'll get you the second. And if the head coach calls the office, girls, get his name.

EPISODE 19

Requiem for a fired head coach:

"Lou's fault was that he wanted to emulate Paul Brown too closely. He copied a lot of Frank Leahy's mannerisms. He could have been a big success if he had just wanted to be Lou Rymkus. I liked the man and I played hard for him. But the second year, he became more aloof. If he had just been concerned with just doing his own job and not trying to outdo some other coach, he was the man for our ball club. He had the kind of personality that could genuinely inspire a team. When he was being just Lou Rymkus he could fire you up. If he had just been happy to have been himself, he never would have been fired. It was the continual turmoil in the coaching staff and in the front office that cost us a lot of bonus players who could have helped rebuild the Oilers when the original players started getting old.

"But when Lou left it started a landslide. They saw coaches come and go and they started getting the idea, 'Well, fellows, if we don't like this guy, we can get rid of him in a hurry. All we have to do is lose a few.' That's an unhealthy attitude, maybe the most unhealthy attitude a football club can have. The Oilers got off to a great head start. Maybe if Lou could have held onto his job and they had put a football man in charge of the front office operation, they might still be on top today."

—George Blanda, looking backward from the year 1972.

EPISODE 20

Here is the bible verse that all Sunday school children in Houston must learn by heart before they can become confirmed:

"And so it came to pass that Rymkus left the Garden of Adams and went to dwell in the land of Nod, which is only east of Texas. The players were sore afraid, for their defense was

faulty and their enemies were all about them. Before Rymkus
left, he begat Wally Lemm, whose face was like that of a
friendly bulldog and whose heart was warm and kind to all
those who were travailed and were heavy-laden. He was of the
house of Rymkus, having been an assistant a year earlier.

"Lemm came to live in the Garden of Adams and all was
good, because Lemm was the preacher of defense. It came to
pass that he tightened and strengthened the defense. And the
Oilers took heart and they went forth from their garden and
slew the enemy, though they be nine in number. This miracle,
called a 'winning streak' by the unwashed, gave them yet
another Eastern Division championship. And the great war
leader, Blanda, rejoiced and said unto his rebellious fellow,
'See? If I had heeded thy venomous advice in Boston and had
missed the field goal, we would have been 10-4 and tied for first
place in the division.

" 'But I was loyal unto my master and I kicked the field goal,
which gave us deadlock. Now we have the division outright.
Heed this lesson and learn. A loyal servant reapeth the reward,
even sometimes when his master is fired.'

"So it came to pass that the Oilers defeated the Chargers in
the playoff game again, this time in San Diego on the feast day
of Our Lord and they were called 'glorious' and 'exalted' and
'champions for the second straight year.' Again it was the
faithful warrior, Blanda, who proveth himself mighty. He
passeth for one touchdown and kicketh a field goal. The
Chargers smiteth the defense of Lemm for a solitary field goal
and it endeth, 10-3. Now Blanda standeth alone at the summit.
Who else could giveth away six interceptions and still prevail?

"And the Almighty rewardeth Blanda with a two-year contract calling for much more in material wealth. This is just.
Blanda has passed for 36 touchdowns and 3340 yards. No
matter how cheesy the evil Halas and the scurrilous Maule saith
American League defensive backs are, this is some kind of fancy
throwing.

"Now stirs a restlessness on the bosom of Lemm. Off he
goeth to seek a head coaching job with the St. Louis Cardinals,

for he is of the blood and the lineage of the Cardinals. The Almighty Adams is vexed. He saith, 'Lemm, ye have played me false. When ye were out of football, I did beckon to thee and give thee suck. But now ye covet another job and ye wish to give me hind tit. Verily, I say, go, take this job. It is yours.'

"And Lemm rose up and left the Garden of Adams and Lemm begat Pop Ivy, a smooth man, who had been cast out by the Cardinals. And Ivy did survive for two full seasons, winning the division, but blowing the league championship. Then Ivy was cast out by Adams and Ivy begat Sammy Baugh, who tended cattle. And Baugh begat Hugh Taylor, who begat Lemm again. And Lemm begat Ed Hughes and Hughes begat Bill Peterson.

"And, they are begatting head coaches in Houston until this very day and they shall continue to begat so long as the Oilers are owned by Adams, whom the scribes and wisemen call 'Quixotic' and 'picayune' and 'myopic' and other phrases not suitable to holy scripture."

Here endeth the reading of the gospel.

EPISODE 21

Memories, memories:

"When Lemm took over, he said he wasn't going to change a thing. So he started Jacky Lee the first game. Early in the second period we were behind 7-0 and Wally put me back in. That was the only time I ever heard so much cheering for me in Houston. They gave me a standing ovation. No booing, only cheers. It never happened that way again."

—Blanda, looking back from the year 1972.

EPISODE 22

The autumns are whirling past in a beautiful golden haze. Despite the Oilers' palace revolutions, with the garroted coaches and the dismembered general managers, George Blanda is finally living the life he was born to. He has established himself as the quarterback he insisted he was during the Babylonian captivity in Chicago. He has seen the American Football League survive

far into its third season. Now television is getting deeply involved. Now cities are coming around asking how soon the AFL
will expand—not die, but expand. Now the clods in the steam
rooms and the handball courts of Chicago have ceased to talk of
Mickey Mouse leagues.

Blanda's name litters the still modest AFL record book. He
throws touchdown passes. If some NFL partisans are suspicious
of their quality, he makes up for it by giving them quantity.
Because he struggles so impatiently to get the ball into the end
zone, he throws a lot of interceptions, too. This he accepts as an
occupational hazard. If the new league was going to live, it was
going to have to offer the public something sensational. So
George puts the ball into the air. He wishes others would
understand. They won't and he knows it. The dry rot of
executive neglect has now begun to chew away at the Oilers.
This is 1962 and Houston is Eastern Division champion for the
third straight year. Writers suggest that it will always be this
way, that the Oilers will drain the blood out of the AFL the
same way the Cleveland Browns opened the veins of the All-
America Conference. Competition will perish and with it, the
league. Still, it is beautiful to be a winner. George Blanda has
endured a thyroid operation, in which three small growths were
removed from his neck.

They rushed him from the summer practice field at Ellington
Air Force base for a quick operation. His recovery was quicker
than anyone dared hope. During the regular season he has
thrown for 2810 yards and 27 touchdowns. He has had a record
42 passes stolen away. Here is the only real blemish on an
otherwise perfect life-style. The money is good. Recognition is
coming—at age 34. Blanda is the acknowledged leader of the
pack, the ultimate Alpha Male. The others gather around him,
Billy Cannon, Charlie Hennigan, Charlie Tolar, Bob Talamini,
superb subordinates, all of them. They listen to his philosophi-
cal observations. They endure his sometimes shattering humor.
They respect him. Power flows from his peer group.

It would be perfect if Jack Gallagher did not pain him like a
carbuncle on the psyche. There are probably more vicious

reporters than this mildly bashful man. As a technician, Gallagher has numerous skills. He writes smoothly and generally knows what's going on.

As a newspaperman he has two small faults. One of them is curable. The other isn't. Having roomed in college with Hamilton P. B. (Tex) Maule and Steve Perkins, he tends to let strong opinions flavor his reporting. He is not enchanted by George Blanda and he undoubtedly wishes that the NFL had got to Houston first. That is Jack's curable fault. The other one takes some understanding. It is a natural thing. Try as hard as he can, Gallagher cannot be tactful in print. It is freakish, but true, that if you asked six columnists to sit down and rewrite "Mary Had A Little Lamb," the only version that would sound vicious would be the one Jack Gallagher wrote. Jack himself does not fully understand his own innate power to infuriate. When Blanda takes offense, Gallagher cannot understand what has gone wrong. The feud will reach classic proportions, until one man cannot think of the other without wincing.

"That Jack Gallagher hated the world and he took it out on me," Blanda will say one day when Houston is no more than a distant part of his past. "He tore me down. He tore down the league. He tore down the Oilers. I think some of the things he wrote about me may have been libelous. I don't know. I'd want to show them to a lawyer first."

"Like many aging athletes and losing coaches, Blanda likes to blame writers for his own shortcomings," Gallagher will write, years later.

At one point in the war between athlete and journalist, Mrs. Betty Blanda, the family's resident pixie, will conceive of the perfect birthday present for her husband. She will order 2000 bumper stickers. Printed on each of them will be this simple slogan: "Help Stamp Out Jack Gallagher!" She will dutifully paste the first batch on the cars of women attending a meeting of the Football Wives Club at the Tidelands Motel on Houston's neon-lit South Main Street. The blame will fall upon a *Houston Chronicle* columnist who has been the wives' guest speaker. It

will be at least four years before even George Blanda knows
where they came from.

Other than Penelope of Ithica, was there ever a more fanati-
cally loyal wife? Don't answer that, John Mitchell!

Regardless, the Oilers are entered in their third playoff game
and already the hairline cracks are starting to show around the
foundation of the AFL's first super team. Dirty Al Jamison is
playing with a back so bad that the city's chiropractors are
submitting bids. Billy Cannon has had one season to inspect Pop
Ivy's triple-wing offense with its multiple reverses and its odd
formations in which George Blanda sometimes stands alone in
the backfield. Everybody else is out on the flank.

"After this game I'm taking all my gear with me and I'll never
be back as long as Ivy is in charge," Cannon says.

Blanda isn't sure what to tell his faithful southern companion. Personally, George likes Ivy. He is willing to overlook two
things: (1) Pop is a man with a delicate voice that seems to
indicate weakness, but doesn't, and (2) this is the same man
who told him to get lost in 1959 when George was a Bear-
dangling-in-limbo and Ivy was head coach of the Cardinals.
Blanda wants Cannon to be equally forgiving. George thinks
that Pop is an offensive genius whose time is probably a dozen
years in the future. Until then he needs tolerance.

This match is not to be believed. It is by Hans Christian
Andersen out of J.R.R. Tolkien. It lasts well into the sixth
quarter and it represents two turning points, one up and one
down. Henceforth, the nation will take the American Football
League seriously. It will consider it inferior, but it will take it
seriously nevertheless. For the Oilers it is a long day's journey
into night. Never again will they dominate their universe. Inside
of two years they will become one of the joke teams of the
league. Only George Blanda won't be laughing. His glorious
summer is ending. The shadows are getting long again. Death
and Resurrection, right, Betty Blanda?

This is stark drama. It is also good entertainment, a fact the
networks will not fail to notice. It requires 77 minutes, 54

seconds of elapsed playing time to determine if the Dallas
Texans or the Houston Oilers are the best club in the AFL. A
crowd of 38,981 is watching. This is capacity, sports fans. Bud
Adams won't lose $710,000 this year. Maybe $389,451.71, but
that's progress.

Dallas gets off to a healthy start, running up 17 points in the
first half. The weather is dark and dangerous. Clouds are
pouring up from the gulf, clotting the skies to the east of the
stadium. Interceptions are murdering George again, killing
several scoring opportunities.

"As the second half started, I told myself, 'This is the biggest
game you've ever been in, you better get after it.' "

At the start of the third period, Blanda gets the Oilers within
range and throws 15 yards to Willard Dewveall for the score.
That's seven points. In the fourth he kicks a field goal and then
takes Houston down close enough for Tolar to score from the
one. It is now 17-17 and the overtime is starting. A blithe spirit
named Abner Haynes is about to make one of football's most
unforgettable blunders. In his whole life no one will ever let him
tuck the memory of the moment away. And no one will ever
bring up the point that it did not hurt the Texans one little bit.
That is incidental. The time has come for Abner to make an ass
of himself in public. Destiny is beckoning to him, with a bony
finger. Dallas head coach Hank Stram leans over and says: "Go
out there and call the coin flip. They'll never move the ball
against us. Let's kick to them.

"We're holding them well, so it makes sense. The way this
wind is blowing we'll only want to kick toward the clock. Got
that, Abner? We'll kick toward the clock."

Abner nods his head. Of course, he has it. Isn't he a North
Texas State man? The strategy is interesting and typical of
Hank Stram, who triple-thinks everything, much in the manner
of the Patriarch himself, George Halas. If the Texans receive,
Blanda kicks off and drives the ball out of the end zone and
that means that Dallas will have to move 80 yards in order to
win the sudden-death period. Stram doesn't figure the Texans
can go that far against the Houston defense. "If we have to

punt, that puts Blanda within field goal range," he tells Haynes. "They can't get that close that quick."

Unfortunately for Abner the coin comes up heads, the way he called it. The referee looks deep into his eyes and Haynes answers smartly, "We'll kick to the clock."

Fine, says the referee, but you can't have it all your way. You can either choose to kick or not to kick or you can choose which side of the field to defend. If Abner selected to kick off, Houston would get its choice of goal lines.

"We'll still kick," says Abner.

Blanda, standing across from him, blinks and says: "We'll run toward the clock," thereby taking away both the ball and the wind. It has no effect on the outcome, but Abner must sleep with the scene forever.

Several episodes from that game will remain etched on George Blanda's brain for a long time, too. Just before the regulation game ends, he has a field goal opportunity from the 42. If Houston can just hold Sherrill Headrick out for another second . . . But the Oilers don't. The kick is blocked.

Then, in the sixth period, it happens. Blanda throws his fifth interception of the day. The ball is supposed to go to Cannon, who has E. J. Holub clinging to his jowls. Later George will admit a mistake. It should have been a look-in pass. Instead it was a down-and-out and a rookie named Bill Hull from Wake Forest, who will never set the sweat business on fire again, picks it off and returns it to the 50-yard line.

"All I needed was one yard for the first down," says Cannon. "If I had just caught that ball, George, if I had just caught it."

The darkness is everywhere as Jack Spikes maneuvers to the Houston 18 on a run and a pass from Len Dawson. Up steps Tommy Brooker, who has irked people in these parts before, kicking a field goal in the 1960 Bluebonnet Bowl in Houston that gives Alabama a 3-3 tie with Texas. This time, he breaks the tie. The ball goes flipping through the air and George Blanda takes the whole blame. He slinks into the dressing room with a deep wound in his soul.

No one laughs. No one moves. Dirty Al is slumped over,

finished as an athlete because of his back. Tears drown his
eyeballs.

"Maybe we got too keyed up for this one," says Blanda,
plucking at the fibers of defeat. "That can happen and you can
get sluggish. I don't know. I didn't play my best, that's for sure.
I was horseshit."

A few lockers away, Cannon explodes. He cannot let George
take the blame, such is the emotional level everyone has
reached.

"If I catch that pass, George is a hero. Don't anybody
second-guess a man who has called as many good games as he
has. Maybe I'll do better next year in Oakland," says Cannon.

"What makes you think you'll be traded to Oakland?" a
writer wants to know.

"That's what the rumors say. I'm gone. I know that. I just
don't want to see everybody rip George up. I could have caught
that ball."

Whatever Cannon's sources are, they prove correct, just one
year off, that's all. He stays with the Oilers during the 1963 and
then goes to the Oakland Raiders, to make the way smooth for
the advent of Blanda no doubt. The blame does fall on George.
Worse than that, the ugly whispers start. The small gamblers
have gone home to mourn the loss of $50 bills. The natural
process has begun.

Within a few weeks, the word is leaping from private saloon
to private saloon. The gamblers have got to Blanda. That's right.
He's shaving points. No! No! Worse than that! He's dumping
games! No? I hear it's even worse than that. The way I get it, he
and Bud Adams are in league. George rigs the games and Bud
lays off the money and they split it on a percentage basis. No!
No! It's a whole ring of thieves. Why, even Lamar Hunt's in on
it. His father doesn't give him any money and he's going broke.
So that's why he organized the American Football League. It's a
great big thing for gamblers ... honest it is. I know for sure,
because somebody in Las Vegas told me ... no! no! ... everybody's involved. Right from Joe Foss on down to the ball

boys . . . they're all crooked . . . I've lost a bundle . . . well, I've lost $50 this week alone . . . my barber says . . .

The stories drag on for years, getting larger and more implausible every time George throws an interception. Finally, a Houston sportscaster comes snuggling up to Joe Foss at a league game. This sportscaster has evidence, which he will reveal as soon as the commissioner shows that he is earnest about the situation. When the investigation starts, this sportscaster will provide the coup-de-grace.

So the investigation starts. In his desert villa sits Joe Foss. It has been several seasons since he was commissioner of the American Football League. He is hunting and fishing and doing network shows on the great outdoors now. He lives in Phoenix and he occasionally speaks if you can afford him.

It is the winter of 1971 and this story has been slithering around too long. Certainly, he knows all about them.

"Criminy sakes, I've heard all that talk I want to hear," Foss says. "I brought in two agents, guys who had worked for the FBI and were now investigators for the league. I led the investigation myself. We poked around for weeks. We talked to everybody involved with football, with the newspapers and with gambling. You know what we discovered? Well, we found out that Old George was as straight up and down as six o'clock. He'd trim you for $100 in a poker game or he'd take you for whatever you'd hold still for on the golf course. He loved that $10 window at the race track. But that was it. Period. Nothing more.

"We found out that George was a businessman with a good income from that trucking company, who didn't need or seem to want more money. We found out he respected the game too much to take a chance on getting barred from it for life. He wasn't the kind of guy who'd do anything illegal. In other words we discovered that the rumors and the whispers weren't true. In the course of the investigation we did turn up the fact that another member of the same Oiler team was betting on games. I won't say who.

"I gave George a first-rate bill of health. But I had to call the other fellow in and say, 'Son, we know what you've been up to. Now neither one of us wants a big scandal. So why don't you just announce that you're giving up the grand old game?'

"You'll notice that George is still going strong. I called that Houston sportscaster and told him he'd better be careful talking about that 'evidence,' because if he didn't have any, George would have a mighty fine slander suit. And I don't believe for a moment he really had anything looking like evidence. He was just trying to make himself sound like a big-time reporter."

At about the same time Foss was conducting his investigation, John Breen was serving on the Harris County grand jury. The vice squad was making a report and Breen asked: "Have you ever investigated George Blanda on suspicion of gambling on football games or on suspicion of shaving points?"

"We have," said a spokesman for the vice squad.

"What did you find?" Breen continued.

"Absolutely nothing that would incriminate Blanda. There is no evidence at all that he isn't 100 percent honest."

"That's what I thought you'd find," said Breen, chewing furiously on a cigar.

So much for rumors, alleged evidence and barroom innuendos.

"I know who the sportscaster was," says Blanda. "What makes me mad as hell is the fact that this guy was an ex-athlete himself, a former major league baseball player. He knew exactly what that kind of talk could do to a player's reputation and he talked like that anyway.

"I honestly don't know what he thought he had or what he was trying to prove. He never walked into our dressing room in Houston because he knew that I knew who was spreading all those damn stories. It may sound corny, but I love football too much to ever risk damaging it. Hell, if it isn't for football, I'm a schoolteacher in Somerset, Kentucky, or I'm working for the Robertshaw thermostat company in Youngwood, Pennsylvania. Besides, I'm too honest to throw games or shave points."

Such stories plague all quarterbacks. It is an occupational hazard, not much different from talking to retarded children from the newspapers or throwing too many interceptions. The small bettor is a dangerous man when his $50 has been plucked from his grubby fingers. He never stops to think that George Blanda went to Kentucky with several basketball players who shaved points and lived to suffer. Only a fool fails to get the message. George Blanda is nobody's dummy. His natural sense of self-protection forbids it.

EPISODE 23

Several significant historical items, to be filed away in the Football Hall of Fame at Canton, Ohio:

(1) The great confrontation between Lamar Hunt and Tex Schramm has taken place. The coin has come up heads. And tails means that the Dallas Texans are now the Kansas City Chiefs. Both clubs get rich. For the first time there is rapport between the leagues, even if it comes between clenched teeth. The date is February 8, 1963.

(2) Harry Wismer's fabulous New York Titans are dead . . . dead as a doornail . . . dead as Jacob Marley. They pass into receivership on March 28, 1964. The new owner is more like it. He is small and a trifle owly. Despite his gray hair and horn-rimmed glasses, he looks bright and clever, a superannuated bar mitzvah boy. His name is David (Sonny) Werblin and . . . ooooh, boy . . . does he have class! He is a former president of Music Corporation of America and he knows all about the star system. He does two very clever things. He helps the AFL get a $36 million contract with NBC-TV. What's more, the network will help the new league outspend the National Football League, which is backed by CBS. Then Werblin turns around and trades to Houston the draft rights of Jerry Rhome, quarterback of Tulsa University, for the Oilers' first-round draft choice. The Oilers finish dead last and Werblin selects Joe Willie Namath of Alabama. And he pays him $442,000 just to play football. Imagine that! Just to play football.

Messiah has come!

(3) One morning Frank (Pop) Ivy, who has taken the Oilers to their first losing season in four years on this planet in 1963,

*comes whistling into the Adams Petroleum Company building
on Fannin Street in uptown Houston. He nods to the girl in the
lobby, presses a button and drops down to the basement where
the boss has his offices right next to the football club's suite. As
Ivy turns toward his own desk, the secretary, Mrs. Dania Fisher,
smiles apologetically. First the good news: Don't bother to
clean out your desk. It's already been done. Now the bad news:
Mr. Adams wants to see you.*

*There is a press conference scheduled in Bud's office, the
subterranean chamber with the cage full of singing birds, the
bubbling spring and the Indian symbols on the wall that depict
the life of K. S. Adams, Jr. (Watch out for the panel where the
kid is swinging the tomahawk!) Fortunately, Ivy has no hair to
lose, only his job. Adios, Pop! Hello, Sammy Baugh! While the
American League rises, the Oilers sink.*

EPISODE 24

Let us all sit down now and examine this schematic map of
K. S. (Bud) Adams's head. Interesting, isn't it? Ever see anything quite like it? Of course, you haven't. Over here in this tiny
chamber is where the ideas germinate. They wind through this
torturous maze, where guile is added. Now they climb this steep
stairway to the storehouse. The money is kept there. When the
ideas are properly financed they are speeded to this huge staging
area so that they may grow to grandiose proportions. Now the
mouth, which George Halas says is the biggest and most active
in the Western world, summons a publicity man. The ideas are
now ready for the public to hear and marvel at. Bud Adams is
going to strike again.

His fellow club owners and his employees may watch him
uneasily, but newspapermen never get enough of him. He is a
thing of beauty and a constant source of squawking headlines.
He seems emotionally unable to go more than a week or two
without seeing his name in print. There once was a man who
wrote a column for the *Houston Chronicle*. His telephone
would ring every other night, usually between 11 P.M. and
1:30 A.M. The owner of the Oilers would be calling, directly

from his bedchamber in River Oaks, which is the city's wealthy white ghetto.

"Hi, this is Bud," he would say in a low, almost hesitant voice. "I think you ought to know what we're up to."

He would then proceed to spill some highly classified information about the ball club.

"Now, don't tell anyone where you got this," he would caution.

Naturally, the information is translated into print. Adams sees it and feigns shock, pain, indignation. He starts hammering the call buttons on his desk until his publicity man, the pseudo-dapper Jack Scott, sticks two quivering lips inside the office, the one that has its own lily pond and barbecue pit.

"See, here, Jack," says Adams, making thunder and lightning. "There's a leak in this organization and it's up to you to see that it's plugged."

Good clean, sadistic fun, huh, boy? The players call it Crazy Horse's revenge. Scott then calls the columnist and begs him, pleads with him to reveal his source. Poor dear Jack has five children, a house in the suburbs and an image to support. The image, he hopes, will one day make him general manager of the Houston Oilers, a job he covets with a breathless passion.

"Please, please, tell me who's giving you this information," he whines.

"Bud Adams!" says the columnist matter-of-factly.

"Don't joke with me at a time like this. Bud's really hot. Tell me who the leak is. I'm in all kinds of trouble."

It does no good to tell Scott who the leak is. The next best thing to a lie is a true story nobody believes.

This is not to suggest that Adams does not have a generous or a playful side. He buys an obsolete fire engine for use on his ranch in Waller, Texas. It is so bright and shiny that he cannot resist tooling around River Oaks with its drooping Spanish moss and re-created antebellum mansions. His parties are the sort of affairs that Edna Ferber imagined all Texans—even poor ones— give. Meat is flown in from the Adams family ranch in Bartlesville, Oklahoma, and it includes buffalo, bear, venison, Osage

Indian Nation turkey and black fallow European deer. Two or three jug bands move from dining room to dining room. The booze gushes like oil from a well. Among the Adams legends is the one about the marathon cocktail party he threw in Chicago during the coaches' convention. It lasted two days and Bud poured 5381 shots at 85 cents a drink. Each night the coaches were asked to list the five best pro prospects on their teams. Then Bud drew ten questionnaires out of a box and awarded $1000 to each lucky coach. Is there a cheaper way of establishing a scouting system?

Because he was a reasonably good blocking back at Kansas, the owner of the Oilers considers himself the finest football man he has ever had the exquisite pleasure of knowing. The feeling is mutual. There is a war on between the two leagues and money flutters in the air like dried leaves in an autumn wind. The lower draft choices are left to flunkies, men who have spent their whole lives in the football rackets. The big names are a job for Super Owner. And he pursues them with a flare and an imagination that scares some of the toughest college seniors in the land, guys like Tommy Nobis and Donny Anderson, for instance.

He has Louisiana State University tackle Dave McCormick all sacked up. The two men shake hands after the Cotton Bowl in Dallas. When McCormick draws his hand back there are ten $100 bills in it—earnest money. The next morning, Adams opens the *Houston Post* and discovers that McCormick has signed with the San Francisco 49ers. Heartbroken, Adams calls the papers.

"It kind of makes you lose confidence in American youth," says Adams, who will probably never buy a candy bar from a Boy Scout again.

One night, very late, it strikes him that it would be clever to fly to Austin, pick up the University of Texas's all-universe linebacker, Tom Nobis, and sign him to a Houston Oiler contract while the Adams Petroleum Company plane flies low over Longhorn Stadium. It turns out that while Bud is not publicity shy, Nobis is. At least the kid has no stomach for such nonsense. Nobis has been deliberating over which team to sign with, mostly because he does not care for the Oilers' revolving-coaches program. But this is the dizzy stunt that helps him decide where he wants to play.

He does not want any part of the carnival in Houston. He calls Atlanta club owner Rankin Smith and begs him to come rescue poor Tommy. As their airliner passes over Houston on its way to Georgia, Smith turns to Nobis and says: "Want to sign your contract here?" And he does—right over Bud Adams's office, perhaps.

Determined never to be out-gunned again, Adams turns the full force of his finances on Donny Anderson, running back and left-footed punter from Texas Tech. This one he will not lose. Anderson is jetted in from Lubbock and given the same suite at the Warwick Hotel that the Duke of Windsor usually hires when he's having repair work done at the Houston Medical Center. Anderson brings along his best friend, another Tech player. No pleasures of the flesh are denied these two princes of the plains. Meanwhile Adams is working with an adding machine.

All the treasures of Texas will be piled next to Anderson's sweat socks. He will get an $887,000 package, all wrapped with green ribbon. Included are a string of 16 gasoline stations, a $200,000 house, $16,000 worth of furniture, a $36,000 swimming pool and a $7000 car. There will also be a lifetime job for Anderson's father with Phillips 66. And the old man can have a car, too. A less expensive one, naturally.

Anderson nods, and using his best Marlon Brando grunt, says he'll give it some thought. Now, he and his buddy would like to meet some of those wild, willing Houston women they've heard so much about. The buddy's tongue is getting a bad sunburn from excess drooling, so the ladies had better take a fast cab. Adams is staggered. He expected Anderson to break the old course record for sprinting to a pen. Instead, the kid acts like he gets $36,000 swimming pools thrown at him daily.

Several days later, Adams reads that Anderson is in Green Bay, talking seriously to the Packers, who are offering only $600,000. What's more the kid tells reporters he thinks he's going to sign with the National Football League. How does Adams meet this threat? Well, sports fans, he *lowers* his bid. That's right. Don't bother to read that line over. He calls Anderson, all full of righteous anger, and says the Houston bid is now $230,000 less than it was a week ago. This time Donny does break the record getting to a pen.

"My confidence in American youth is just about shattered," Adams says. The Girl Scouts can forget about those damned cookies, too.

In a desperate effort to turn up unclaimed talent, which Adams insists is everywhere, he pretends to fire a team scout named Red Dog Ettinger. No one doubts the veracity of the news since Red Dog is a spaniel-faced flake whose presence on the payroll unnerves a lot of people anyway. One of Ettinger's great talents is sneaking into the coaches' room and drawing mice with chalk on the blackboard. One day, an Oiler assistant notices that Red Dog has sketched a large piece of Gouda on the board.

"What's that for?" the assistant asks.

"Well, them little rascals gotta eat," says Ettinger, pointing to the mice.

The firing turns out to be a cover story. In reality, Red Dog is the master manipulator behind Operation Cross-Check, a sinister spy network that Adams himself has devised, undoubtedly after piloting his fire engine over a particularly bumpy road. There are 325 part-time agents in Cross-Check. None of them knows each other. And no legitimate Oiler scout is aware that Cross-Check exists. This Adams scheme costs roughly $250,000, the price of a second-round draft choice in the inflated mid-1960s.

Operation Cross-Check's center is a vacant storefront in Phoenix, Arizona. Allegedly, Ettinger is there trying to organize the Phoenix Fire Birds, whom Adams says he is going to enter in the Continental League as an Oiler satellite club.

Red Dog insists that Cross-Check is a howling success. He has even discovered which minor league team the Minnesota Vikings are using to hide tackle Mike Tillman on. Resolutely, Ettinger marches down to the bench and leads Tillman off by the hand. In all, Cross-Check signs 130 players, who are simply dumped on the Oiler training camp without warning. The head coach asks, timidly, who all these people are. Nine of them flunk the physical. Ettinger is proud. Adams cannot keep Cross-Check a secret any longer; he makes a midnight telephone call.

"Tell me, Red Dog, if somebody suspected who you were, what would you do with your Operation Cross-Check card?"

"Eat it," said Ettinger.

None of the Cross-Check players survive the squad cut. Most of them are gone after the third day of camp. Adams is not disturbed. This is an idea that is years ahead of its time, he says. Soon other teams will have underground scouting networks, too. In fact, he knows of three clubs that have already contacted Ettinger, asking advice on how to create Cross-Checks of their own. Maybe so. Red Dog soon fades. So does Cross-Check. But Bud Adams goes marching on.

Foiled in his schemes to find new talent through legitimate approaches, he turns poacher, going up to Ernie Ladd and Earl Faison, two San Diego linemen, in the Charger locker room after a game. They are playing out their options and Adams lets them know that he will give them the salaries they seek as soon as they are free agents. The word gets back to Sidney Gillman. Until a man's option is up, he cannot be contacted by other clubs.

Gillman is furious, but he waits for revenge. When the season ends, Adams calls and proposes a deal—tackle Scott Appleton, guard Gary Cutsinger, linebacker Johnny Baker and safety Pete Jaquess for Faison and Ladd. Fine, says Gillman, who makes the deal at the All-Star game. While reporters are assembled, he announces that he is bringing charges against Adams for tampering with his players. The commissioner admits that San Diego has a case. He upholds Gillman's complaint and nullifies the trade. Adams gets whacked with a fine and a censure.

"I've done it! I've done it!" Gillman tells Jerry Magee of the *San Diego Union.* "I've finally screwed the fat Indian."

The Astrodome is ready for occupancy, but on the advice of

the former oil pipe salesman who has become his general manager, Adams pulls out at the last minute. He does not like Judge Roy Hofheinz's rental proposal, which calls for the Astrodome management to receive all parking proceeds from Oiler games, all receipts from the sale of programs, plus the right to promote all exhibition matches. Carroll Martin, the salesman turned football genius, says he can get Rice University to rent its stadium now. Well, says Adams, there are 70,000 seats at Rice Stadium and only 50,000 at the Astrodome.

People do not fill those 70,000 seats. They are so angry because they expected to see the Oilers indoors that they stay home. Well, not all of them. Roughly 17,000 show up every Sunday. Attendance is low enough to encourage rumors that the National Football League will soon place a franchise in the Astrodome. Does Adams announce that he is reconsidering a move to the great plastic pimple on the plains, something he will eventually do anyway? No, indeed. He makes one of those late-night calls. If people don't start reporting for active duty as ticket buyers at Rice Stadium, he's going to take his damn club to Seattle. So there!

EPISODE 25

Frustration is rising up to throttle Jacky Lee. No matter what he does, no matter how hard he struggles, he cannot be George Blanda. He has come to the conclusion that destiny hates him. He has tried to take the first-string quarterbacking job away from George and he has failed. He has tried beating Blanda at gin rummy, golf, Ping-Pong, poker, shuffleboard, anything. Each time he has failed.

"He's a fine athlete," says Breen, "but he's developed this thing about George. Oh, he never criticizes Blanda, publicly or privately. That's not the issue. When Blanda beats him he loses his poise or his cool or whatever you call it. Because George is around, he's the most frustrated kid in the world."

They have roomed together, Blanda and Lee, and Jacky discovers that he and George have the same philosophy when it comes to calling pass patterns. But Lee says he needs to call audibles—changes in the play selected in the huddle—about 25 percent of the time because the defenses have changed since he came to the line of scrimmage. Blanda tells him that Old George doesn't have to audible, because his experience is so great that he can adjust to changes without altering the play. Oh, God, says Lee, his ego slumping.

"I went to management and told them I'd never beat George out and that I didn't like the salary they were paying, something like $15,000. I figured I could make $21,000 as the first-string man for another club. I suggested that they trade me and pick up some career second-stringer they could pay $15,000," Lee recalls.

Blanda tells him not to be a fool.

"You're making enough money Jacky. Wait a while. The club is going bad. Let me take the abuse for a few more years," Blanda tells him, not entirely in jest.

This is not bad advice. The Oilers are aging faster than Dorian Gray. There is no one being signed to take the place of the Originals, who are growing fewer with each passing season. The pass-protection blocking, excellent under Rymkus, is deteriorating rapidly. The other teams are blitzing hell out of George. The veterans dig in and try harder, because Blanda is their leader.

"When Lee comes in, we just can't make ourselves go for him. He's cocky and he has a great arm. But he couldn't get us in a group and lead us across the street," says one player. "He wants us to think he's a man when deep down inside he knows himself that he hasn't grown up yet. Maybe when George is gone, we'll try and make ourselves go for Lee—for our own good."

Now Lee is getting panicky and when the panic really gets him down deep, the Oilers compound it by signing Don Trull, who has set three national passing records for Baylor. Now Jacky knows how George felt the year Blanda thought he had a chance at the Bear job and Halas brought in Bratkowski and Brown. The frustration ends shortly.

The Oilers work a lend-lease deal. Through some obscure

passage in the league bylaws, a team may loan a player to another club for a period of two years. Lee goes to Denver for a first-round draft choice and tackle Bud McFadin. He departs, not in peace but in anger, quacking loudly at the management.

Now all the elements necessary for an all-out assault by the public on the quarterback are combined: (1) The Oilers have been turned from a champion into a chronic loser through the baggy-pants blundering of the owner, (2) they are playing in Rice Stadium when the people want them indoors at the Astrodome, (3) they are reminded constantly by Jack Gallagher that George Blanda throws interceptions and (4) they have a young second-string quarterback with a national reputation, who is a native Southwesterner and who has gone to college at a Texas school.

All together now—"Boooooo, Blanda, you bum! We want Trull! We WANT TRULL! We WANT TRUUUUUULLLLLL!" For added emphasis and gusto it is helpful to smuggle a shaker of screwdrivers (two parts orange juice to one part vodka) into the stadium and get half-crocked by kickoff. You can do it. You're entitled. It says so right on the back of your ticket. Where? Well, it's there someplace.

EPISODE 26

Words they ought to chisel in marble and hang in the Hall of Fame:

"If those people in the stands had any idea what an unfair pressure they put on the team they're supposed to be rooting for when they boo, they'd shut up!"

—George Frederick Blanda, spoken before a meeting of The Ruffneks, the Oiler booster club, one evening in 1965.

EPISODE 27

Now the Oilers are crash diving toward the bottom. Cannon is, indeed, traded to Oakland. The old order is changing fast. Some 14 rookies make the final squad cut.

"Sammy Baugh was the coach in 1964 and old Sammy, all he cared about was his chewing tobacco and his ranch out in

Rotan, Texas. He loved those cows a whole hell of a lot more than he loved us," Blanda recalls. "Sammy was a fine man. He was a genius at showing technique to young quarterbacks. But high-powered organizational methods just plain didn't interest him. I honestly don't think Sammy ever really wanted to coach. They just kind of pushed the job on him. We had no playbook under Baugh and no game plan. Sammy didn't believe in them.

"I'd had the thyroid operation the year before and I'd lost a lot of weight. I'd got into some bad habits . . . a hell of a lot of bad habits. I'd get rid of the ball too quick. Pop had you playing without any backs back there to block and that encourages you to really get rid of the ball too quick. There are a lot of reasons for interceptions, more than the public realizes. Sometimes it is simply the fact that the quarterback throws the ball bad. Sometimes it happens when the receiver runs the wrong route, which guys do a lot. Sometimes the defensive lineman tips up the ball and it's an interception. But interceptions didn't bother me. I didn't care, even if people condemned me for them.

"The kind of quarterback I've always been is the kind who wants to win. Maybe I've forced a lot of passes that were intercepted. I could have saved a lot of them, I suppose, by playing more conservatively. A lot of people look at my interception total and think of me as just an average quarterback. Well, I've always been the kind that hates a quarterback who, when he gets three or four touchdowns ahead, stops going for the end zone and throws cheap little passes that will fatten his percentage.

"Damn, in Houston we had some great games because we took a lot of chances. What frosts me is a quarterback who's down 34-7 and he starts throwing those little flare passes, wasting eight minutes to get in field goal range, so he can lose 34-10 and come away with a nice-looking passing statistic. That's pure bullshit. You're just trying to make a name for yourself by completing 55 percent of your passes. Most of my interceptions came when we were going in to score. I probably had more interceptions in the other team's end zone than I did anyplace else. You're on your own 20 and you can't run it in, so you try to force it in passing. That's when I lost a lot of passes. If I hadn't lost all those passes in the end zone, I probably would have kicked another 30 or 40 field goals.

"Most of the writers in Houston climbed on me about the interceptions. Well, those Houston writers didn't know a damn thing about professional football. They were oriented strictly toward Southwest Conference college football and that was it. Gallagher? I didn't like him right from the start. You'd talk to him and he'd quote you out of context. He was biting and cutting. He was always trying to make your words fit his theories. Oh, I got on him a lot. Billy [Cannon] and I rode him a lot—in the dressing room, on the practice field, all over. We pulled his leg a lot. Maybe he had a reason to be bitter, I don't know.

"Anyway, getting back to Sammy . . . it was a real change from Pop Ivy. You know I really liked Pop. He was one of the best coaches I played under. He was a good organizer, he knew talent, he knew football. His personality wasn't red hot. But he was a fine coach.

"I really wasn't surprised by Pop's firing. Nothing that happened in Houston really surprised me. Everything was getting pretty goofy there. We never thought a coach would last more than a year with the Oilers, not the way Bud Adams operated. It surprised me really that Pop lasted two years. A lot of people accused me of having a lot to do with those coaches getting fired. But that was an exaggeration. The coach has a lot to do with how much enthusiasm you play with. And it wasn't easy getting enthusiastic for some of those coaches.

"There was talk that I 'took the club over' when Sammy Baugh and Hugh Taylor coached the Oilers. Well, someone will assume leadership responsibility on a team. If there's a wishy-washy coach and a strong quarterback, it's going to look like the quarterback is taking over. In Oakland, the 'team' is everything. If you aren't a good team man, you're gone. In Houston it was a matter of survival. You had to survive somehow in order to play pro football because of the crazy circumstances.

There was really no 'team' after the Ivy years. Nobody cared about the team during the Baugh-Taylor years. Everyone was concerned about keeping their jobs.

"The coach was worried about keeping his job. There were people fighting to be general manager. The team was always secondary. Sammy gave us a complete turnover of personnel. His philosophy was 'if we play well, they won't get on us . . . nobody expects us to win because we have so many rookies . . . just go out there and keep it close.' We go out to play the first league game under Sammy and San Diego beats us 27-21. Baugh is elated. We kept it close. So that's all we did the rest of the year—we played to keep it close. Why kill yourself trying to win?

"Sammy didn't have a playbook of his own. He never had one. We used some old ones from the Lemm year that we happened to have around. Sammy figured they were as good as anything he could come up with. In Sammy's day, pro football was a grab-ass affair and that's how he coached. I'd been over-coached with the Bears. We even had a play for going to the toilet. But with the Oilers under Sammy we were under-coached. Now I agree with John Brodie when he says a game plan is overrated. All it is is a guide. But it is helpful in some respects. It tells you what you should do and what might work. That's all.

"During the week, Sammy would put in plays in practice before a game. He'd say, now we're going to do this this week. He'd explain some play and I'd ask what to call it and he'd say, 'Who gives a shit what we call it, just do it!' I used to get mad as hell at him. I'd have to make up signals to use.

"We didn't have audibles . . . we didn't have audible number one. Sam would say, 'Go out and do whatever you think is right.' We did and we were 4-10. It isn't true that I used to draw plays in the sand. We had two basic plays—cut-in and cut-out. On one, the tight end cut in. On the other he cut out. That was it.

"Personally, I had a lot of fun that year. I could innovate all I wanted to. And we moved the ball. We scored. Our defense was terrible, but we scored. I think we must have given up something like 35 points a game. I threw and threw that year. Hennigan caught 101 passes. It's still a record. Talamini was all screwed up by the lack of a system. He was a great guard but he didn't know where to block because we didn't have a playbook. There was nothing to do but block straight ahead and throw the ball. It was like a touch football team. I think I set a record with 505 pass attempts. At Buffalo, I threw 68 passes in one game. And that's a record. I had all the freedom and all the fun in the world for me. We were fun to watch. We didn't win many games. But we were fun.

"Sammy's real ability as a coach was his skill at hitting a bucket ten feet away with a chaw of tobacco."

And when the season ends and the rest of the league stops laughing, Baugh exchanges jobs with one of his assistants, a friend and former teammate from the Redskins, Hugh S. (Bones) Taylor. It beats getting fired. This way Sammy can spend more time kissing his horse back in Rotan.

Taylor is all arms and legs and sweet talk. He wears a tiny hat on top of a long head. He looks as if central casting sent him over to play the part of the 1928 drummer from St. Louis who shows up at the mountain cabin and woos the innocent Arkansas maiden with his exotic talk about the big city. His quaint stories about his Ozark home town have the Houston press loving him. Mr. Bones is what one writer calls him because he seems to have stepped down out of a minstrel show. If you're going to lose, you might as well be entertained.

Taylor has a couple of minor flaws, easily overlooked. He doesn't believe in game plans or playbooks either.

EPISODE 28

Interesting quotations, continued:

"There were always these stories that I was up to something sinister in Houston. I don't know what the hell it was supposed to be. But there was always that kind of talk. I'll say this: I exerted a lot of influence on the guys that we had around from the five years I'd been with the club. I had my opinions and

*they listened to them. And I guess they valued them. We hung
tight together. We started getting a different breed of kids in,
so-called super stars who were getting paid all kinds of money.
They're coming in and sitting around and we're doing all the
playing. Well, those kind of kids were pampered and spoiled.
They didn't want to pay the price. And the older players kind
of looked down on them.*

*"A lot of those stories started with Jack Scott. He was a guy
who thought that the public relations man made the players. He
thought he was more important than any player on the roster.
He used to put us down and call us 'jocks' behind our backs.
There isn't any PR man in professional football who can make a
player all-pro if the guy doesn't have all-pro ability. Well, Jack
was above everybody. I really distrusted Jack and I tried to stay
away from him because I disliked his attitude. I think he did
everything he could do to put me down. Some of the stories
started with him. He wanted to get rid of me. Why? I don't
know.*

*"I believe this: If the coaches and the organization are
wishy-washy, then somebody has to do something to make you
win."*
                                                    —George Blanda

EPISODE 29

Now the public has taken a firm stand. The Houston Oilers
are flopping and gagging on the turf. They have all the signs of
terminal illness. After winning all five of their exhibitions and
their first two league games, they have stopped winning. The
public wants fresh meat. It wants Don Trull. There are all sorts
of silly stories going around. George Blanda is an evil man who
has driven poor Dobie Craig out of football by complaining to
the front office about him. Dobie who? Well, he's a wide
receiver. George throws to him ten times. And ten times Dobie
drops the ball. The front office draws its own conclusions.

"Craig had bad eyes and couldn't see the ball," Blanda
recalls. "But everything that went wrong that year was my
fault. The stories got around and they expanded."

Rymkus has now returned as a line coach. So Adams has a

new head coach who has two former head coaches as assistants.
So fragmented is the coaching staff that Bones and Sammy
dress in the regular coaches' dressing room. Walt Schlinkman, a
neutral, grabs his street clothes and rushes home to shower and
change. And Rymkus and Joe Spencer change in the equipment
room.

During a game in Denver, there are several violations of good
sense. On a fourth-and-fifteenth situation deep in his own
territory, punter Jim Norton breaks and runs. Soon afterwards,
linebacker Johnny Baker refuses to leave the field when
ordered. On the following Tuesday, general manager Carroll
Martin calls a meeting and slaps fines on everyone involved.

"You cannot violate the game plan," he says, suggesting that
Moses got the game plan on Mt. Sinai.

Immediately, George Blanda rises and brings up an interesting
point. "How can these guys violate something that doesn't
exist? We don't have a game plan or a playbook and we haven't
had them since Pop Ivy was coach."

Indignant, the players take up a collection to pay the fines.
One of them calls the newspapers to make sure that the story
gets in circulation. Martin asks Blanda and defensive captain Ed
Hussman to stay after the meeting and explain themselves.

"There's no game plan or playbook," Hussman confirms.

Martin shakes his head and orders Taylor to compose both a
playbook and a game plan for the next match on the schedule.

"I think that irritated Taylor. He was basically lazy and he
got mad at me because I did something that forced him to go to
work," Blanda believes.

Now it is October 26, 1965 and George Frederick Blanda is
mad enough to make miracles again. It always happens this way.
Put the man down hard enough and he rises with equal force.
For weeks, Blanda has been talking with Betty. When matters
get rough, George always seeks his wife's advice. She is one of
the few people he is certain he can trust. She tells him if he
wants to quit, that's fine. He has been slapped down on the
bench. Trull is starting against Kansas City. To lighten the
situation, Betty suggests that they ought to find an old-

fashioned leather helmet and let George wear it on the sidelines.
Perhaps he ought to be rocking back and forth in a rocking
chair, too.

Trull is awful. The Chiefs put on a kamikaze rush and he
retreats. At the half it is 17-0. Taylor asks Baugh to go over and
tell George he will start the third period. Bones has not talked
to Blanda since the infamous revelation about the game plan
and playbook. In fact, Taylor has tried very hard to tell a
Houston columnist that Adams will have to choose between
coach and quarterback when the season is over. Because the
columnist loathes dissension stories, he doesn't print a word.

"Sammy came over and said, 'Taylor says you're going to
start the second half.' I just walked away from Baugh, I was so
damned angry. Finally, I went over and said, 'If he wants me to
play after all the crap he's put me through in the papers the last
few weeks, he'll have to ask me himself.' I'd thought about
quitting after the game. Now I want to quit at halftime. But
Bones comes trotting over and tells me he'd like to have me
start the third period. I said 'okay.' I don't even remember what
happened at the half. I was that hot."

The management, ever fretful of what it thinks the public
wants, has dictated Trull's start. Blanda knows it. He realizes
that he is being phased out.

Watching Blanda in the second half is one of the great thrills
of a sporting lifetime. Superb is a poor way of describing him.
He's everywhere. It is almost as if he is the only man on the
field. The furies are driving him. His soul is crackling with heat.
He is a living flame.

"The management may ruin Trull," he says afterwards.
"They pushed him into the starting line-up just to sell some
tickets. That's why I was benched. I have a no-cut, no-release
contract. Unless they send me to Miami in the expansion draft,
I'm going to be the quarterback through next year."

Blanda shows them. Oh, lordy, how he shows them. He
scores five of the first six times he gets the ball. The Chiefs punt
or kick off and George just prods the offensive unit downfield.
He throws a 64-yard pass to Charlie Frazier for one touchdown

and a 49-yard pass to halfback Ode Burrell for another. The
third score is more modest. It travels only 17 yards to tight end
Willie Frazier. And Willie gets the fourth one, too, a mere nine
yarder. Kansas City is trampling Houston's feeble defensive
unit. So Blanda gets a fifth scoring pass into the air. This one
goes to Bob McLeod. It flies nine yards.

With 1:50 left—are you paying attention, Bill King?—George
begins to move the Houston offense 56 yards. It is almost like a
dream sequence, with the sweatiest of action dropped down to
slow motion. Now the Oilers are on the Chiefs' eight-yard line.
Houston is behind 36-35. George's knee is sore and Jack Spikes
is kicking. He gets the field goal from 15 yards and Houston
wins, 38-36. It is incredible, amazing, fantastic—words they'll
use all over again to describe Blanda five years later.

"That is the greatest thing I've ever seen a quarterback do,"
says Baugh. "I don't know of anything I ever did that topped
that."

Now they are hugging and kissing George. He is going to be
American League player of the week, according to both wire
services. In the dressing room, he tells all the writers to go
commit an act which he knows is not only obscene, but
physically impossible. Then he goes back to his apartment and
calls the guy from the *Houston Chronicle*. Take that, Jack
Gallagher, for all your years of horseshit! Take that and that
and that and that!

"You know I heard I wasn't going to start in mid-week," he
tells the *Chronicle*. "I had to read it in the newspapers. After 17
years in the game, no one had the guts to tell me personally.
Can you imagine that?"

George's sense of justice has been challenged again. In the
hated *Houston Post*, columnist Mickey Herskowitz has these
kind and understanding words: (See, George, those *Post* writers
aren't all bad.)

"There comes a day when the proudest of men must look in
the mirror and say, my friend, you've had it. George Blanda
hasn't had this little chat with himself or, if he has, the above
answer isn't the one he got. George was trying to tell us
something Sunday. It was as plain as the nose on the football

that he flung with such skill and purpose. No one has ever faulted Blanda for his leadership. He is the sort you see shouting orders into the teeth of a typhoon or above the roar of guns.

"Right or wrong a lot of us public-spirited citizens felt that George had overstayed his time. It was said that he was 37 years old and a drop-back passer. George didn't deny it. There is a curious trend in sports. When a hero overstays his time, the fans turn on him and judge him severely until his old deeds of glory are dimmed and all but forgotten.

"George feels that the press and Oiler management made him a scapegoat for the team's recent slump and turned the fans toward him. Maybe he has a point."

It is not the sort of treatment Blanda expects from the *Post*. He decides to renew his subscription.

EPISODE 30

Two more great quotes of the century:

(1) *"There is no way I can be right in this quarterback crisis. No matter what I say, I can't be right with the fans, the press and my team. I'd like to be that. But I care only about doing what is right for the Houston Oilers. The decision lies with me, not with management."*—Bones Taylor, speaking at the weekly Oiler press luncheon at the Sheraton-Lincoln Hotel.

(2) *"Listen, you've been pretty harsh in some of the things you've written about us lately. I'd like to make you an offer. I know you do a column and a regular daily story on the Oilers in the* Chronicle. *What I'd like to propose is that you do a 'special story,' say, once or twice a week for us. We'd be willing to pay as much as $100 a week. That's a lot of money, isn't it? We'd want something favorable to us, of course. Can you arrange it?"*—Words spoken by a certain Oiler executive over lunch at George Dentler's Pier 21, just across from the team's practice field, to *Houston Chronicle* writer Wells Twombly on October 28, 1965. (Editor's note: The offer is declined, without thanks.)

EPISODE 31

The traditional donuts and coffee, which are present at all Oiler hirings and firings, are being wheeled in by Miss Bette

Young, secretary to Bud Adams. It is January, 1966, and the
New Era is about to happen. And that is exactly what it is—a
happening. There have been rumors, ever since the Oilers completed their second 4-10 year in a row, that Carroll Martin will
be replaced as general manager by Don Klosterman, a whiz-bang
boy wonder from the Kansas City Chiefs, and that Wally Lemm
has already been signed to replace Taylor, despite the fact that
Adams announced at a game between San Diego and Houston at
Rice Stadium that Bones had been given a new three-year
contract.

The press conference is blessedly brief. Klosterman appears
through the rear door in Adams's office, where all new Oiler
general managers and coaches make their dramatic entrances.
When it is all over, a writer for the *Chronicle* phones in the
story and then goes drifting off in search of Taylor. Is he really
the head coach? Did he actually sign that contract? Have he and
Klosterman had a chance to talk? Why wasn't he at the press
conference? Is it true that Lemm is going to replace him?

The reporter wants to ask all those questions. He finds Taylor
in the hallway inspecting a large book filled with clippings from
the past year. Near him is Christy Chandler, a talk show performer and a sportscaster for Channel 2 in Houston. The three
of them go into Taylor's office. The *Chronicle* man starts to ask
him questions, but Taylor interrupts. He wants to talk about
George Blanda.

Chandler, who admits later that he is hard of hearing, sits on
one chair, near Bones's desk. The *Chronicle* writer sits somewhat further away.

"Oh, yes, Klosterman and I know each other. He was with
San Diego when I was there. I'll tell you this, if I come back
next year, George Blanda won't. He's an evil man. He's a bad
influence on some of the older players, guys like Charlie Tolar
and Charlie Hennigan. It is either him or me. And I've told Mr.
Adams that."

The newsman wants to change the subject back to Taylor's
contract. But Bones prattles on and on about Blanda. Finally,
Chandler, the television personality, stands up in a high snit.

"If you aren't going to let me talk," Chandler says, "I'm

leaving. I had an appointment with coach Taylor and you've horned in."

The writer stands and thanks Taylor for the interview.

"Don't print that bit about George being a poor influence on Tolar and Hennigan," Taylor tells the man from the *Chronicle.* "Whatever you want from the rest of what I said is all right."

Later on, Chandler will deny that Taylor ever said what he said in that room. So will Taylor. The *Chronicle* will hold the story out of its first edition, in order to contact Blanda, who says he knows nothing about any bad blood between him and Taylor. The story will appear on the wires and make nearly every major paper in the nation. The Oilers will use it as an excuse to fire Taylor, when in reality they have already signed Lemm to a contract. And Taylor will go from a $14,500 job as Oiler head coach to an $18,500 position as receiver coach for the Pittsburgh Steelers, swearing that he has been damaged by the *Chronicle* story.

"He must have been mad at me for making him get out a playbook and a game plan," Blanda will conclude. "What else could it have been?"

And Lemm does get the job, within days after Taylor's leavetaking. Another opening, another show. Do you count Grover Cleveland as one president or two? Do you count Wally Lemm as one Oiler coach or as two? Interesting question.

EPISODE 32

Yet another catchy quote posterity might otherwise have missed:

"I've been in Houston for just two months and I have come to the conclusion that the only three people anyone ever talks about are Judge Roy Hofheinz, Percy Foreman, the lawyer who defended Candy Mossler, and George Blanda. Am I wrong?"
                              —Don Klosterman, March 3, 1966.

EPISODE 33

The technique is flawless, studied and spectacular. It is carefully calculated to surround you, overwhelm you and conquer you. It is possible to resist the onslaught for a few fitful minutes, but ultimately you will surrender. There is no hope. There never was. Lights flash on—yellow, green, orange, purple. A hand reaches out and slaps you on the back. The latest, freshest jokes explode around you like flak during the blitz. You are the victim of the world's hardest soft sell and you are growing weaker . . . weaker . . . weaker. You can no longer resist. You are now in Don Klosterman's power. Who is Don Klosterman? Oh, c'mon now! You must have been rooming with the Abominable Snowman the last 15 years.

Everybody knows Don Klosterman. Governors know him. Millionaires know him. Kings-in-exile know him. Even Howard Cosell knows him. He's everybody's friend. Why he was Dick Nixon's favorite football player when he was playing quarterback for Loyola of Los Angeles. Everybody knows Don Klosterman. Little people, big people, funny people, beautiful people know him. He planned it that way. Join the psychedelic parade.

Professional football is the switched-on, kandy-koated, tangerine-flacked game for swingers. It's deep. It's heroic. It's complicated. It's the *in* sport. It's today. It's now. It's Don Klosterman, baby. And he is in Houston to straighten the Oilers out. He's the swinging, sideburned prophet of something nebulous that he calls The New Era. Everything old must go.

He spends $11,000 taking the Houston press corps to Las Vegas for a four-day binge, which winds up in an hilariously drunken seminar on what's wrong with the Oilers. ("They just plain fucking stink, Don," says one writer. "They plain fucking stink.") He passes out electronic ashtrays with "The New Era" stamped on their sides. He holds so many parties that people forget why they're there.

He changes the uniforms, deemphasizing Bud Adams's precious Columbia blue, and splashing around a lot of modish silver and red. Ever wonder what happened to the kid who used to let the air out of your tires on Halloween? He grew up and became Don Klosterman. Becoming his friend requires absolutely no effort. Just wait your turn. Don't shove. Take a number and he'll get around to you. There's plenty of that sunburst personality to go around. Understanding what makes Donald Clement Klosterman run requires a little study.

Lots of guys dress sharp. Few of them affect the clothes that Klosterman does, a striking combination of Early 1950 California Modern and Pop-Culture-Edwardian. Lots of guys drive big cars. Few of them drive massive limousines painted to match their eyes. Lots of guys throw away their crutches and get up and walk as well as they can. Some of them were even as close to being a total cripple as Klosterman was . . . but not many. Once upon a time he was a quarterback. Once upon a time he was skiing in Banff National Forest and he hit a tree. Once upon a time they said he'd be in a wheelchair the rest of his life, just like Roy Campanella.

But Donald Clement Klosterman fooled them all. He's been doing it all his life. Now he is attempting to turn the Oilers from buffoons into swingers. With an advertising slogan like "The New Era" flashing in lights from every signpost in Houston, how long can a 38-year-old quarterback expect to last? The answer: Approximately 14 months, 28 days, 17 hours and six minutes—give or take a second or two.

EPISODE 34

There's a war on, don't you know, and the heavy thinkers who own American Football League franchises are meeting in solemn conclave at the Shamrock Hotel in uptown Houston. There is talk that both they and their feudal master, the network, have grown weary of spending $400,000 for corner-backs. They have decided to force a peace settlement with one last major offensive.

Clearly, Joe Foss is not the man to lead them. Despite his reputation as a fearless, ruthless destroyer of Japanese aircraft, he turns out to be too nice a man to perform the dastardly deeds a football commissioner must when two leagues are battling each other, cheek to jowl. The trouble seems to be that the National Football League doesn't use Zero fighters when it attacks. There is a snide joke slithering around the lobby. It concerns the league's indefatigable vice-president, Milt Woodward.

"You know all those Japanese planes? Well, Milt really shot them down."

Arf! Arf! Arf! Joe Foss is on his way out. Criminy, don't let the door bump you in the ass.

For weeks, Wayne Valley has been on the telephone, growling like Victor McLaughlin. Through an enormous blunder, the commissioner of the American League has succeeded in losing the city of Atlanta to the enemy. The AFL has been forced to fall back firing through the swamps, not stopping until they reached Miami. Everyone knows Atlanta is prime territory. An expansion team is bound to get sodden with profit there. Miami is dubious. It is regarded as a tourist trap and a college football town. Foss has made the mistake of awarding a franchise to one Atlanta group, while Pete Rozelle has given an NFL team to another. As you might suspect, Pete's bunch turns up with a lease on the only stadium in town.

It is time for a commissioner who will go straight for the jugular and hold on until every drop of blood flows in the street. Where can such a man be found? Valley has Honest Al Davis and he will donate Al to the war effort. The change is made. And what is Davis's first duty as the warrior chieftain sworn to burn, loot and pillage? He makes peace.

There Davis is presiding over his initial meeting of the league's executive council when in walks Jack Gallagher, ever tactful Jack Gallagher. He is there to set up a picture for *Post* photographer Dan Hardy.

From his seat at the conference table, Bud Adams looks up and says to Gallagher, who does not have any hair, "Hello, skinhead!" Adams is very tactful, too. Everyone is dressed in shirts, ties and jackets, except for the owner of the Oilers, who has just come in from the ranch and is wearing cowboy clothes. So Gallagher suggests that, for picture purposes, they shoot one with Bud in it and one with him absent.

"Go ahead, sonny boy, get your picture," says Adams, departing the group in a galloping snit.

"What did you say?" asks Sonny Werblin of the Jets, thinking Adams meant him when he said "sonny boy."

"No, I wasn't talking to you, Sonny, I meant this Irish son of a bitch over there," says Adams. "I might do something if I got in his damn picture."

"If you're going to do something, go ahead and do it," says Gallagher, stepping forward, fists clenched, chin out, skull glowing a delicious flavor somewhere between strawberry and cherry. Now Adams meets the challenge and then two of them exchange punches. Well, Adams threw a left, a right and a left and Gallagher, outweighed by 50 pounds, tries to get off what looks like a jab.

It suddenly occurs to Davis that one of his wealthiest owners is trying to murder a sports writer who would not be adverse to seeing the National Football League run the Oilers straight out of Houston. Oh, my God!

With the help of Buffalo's sensible Ralph Wilson, the two are pulled apart, but not until Hardy gets several disastrous pictures which are spread over seven columns on the front page of the next morning's *Houston Post*. On the break, with Wilson and Davis holding him under the arms, Adams tries hard to kick Gallagher's face in. At the emergency hospital, they take x-rays. As bloody and as swollen as it is, Gallagher's nose isn't really broken.

The next day, Foss is talking to Davis on the telephone, discussing a few items of old business that Al ought to know about.

"That's about it," says Foss. "Have a thick hide, wear a soft smile and, for criminy sakes, carry a sense of humor."

Criminy sakes, what else is there to do?

EPISODE 35

Two different views of roughly the same thing:

(1) "I'll say this for George, he was rough on young quarterbacks. It was the system he was brought up with on the Bears. The idea was to see whether a young quarterback could take it or not. He might have ran a couple off while he was here, but they were players who wouldn't have made it anyway. But don't ever forget this about him: George was willing to work for

250   BLANDA

hours with a kid. He figured it was part of his duty to the game
of football."   —John Breen

(2) *"The thing I objected to in 1966 was that the whole*
point behind the season was to give a third-year quarterback a
year of experience. Nobody talked about winning, only getting
experience. I tried to impart everything I knew about football,
offense, defense, the way you handle yourself, leadership,
everything. Don Trull and I had a good working relationship.
We played a lot of golf together and I liked him. He was a good,
friendly kid. Don listened to me and he never gave me any
bullcrap. He had a lot of knowledge of the game. He had
everything but the physical ability to play professional football.
He wasn't a good strong thrower. He didn't know how to set up
deep. If I had been the coach I wouldn't have played Don
except in certain situations. And Jacky Lee ... I tried every-
thing in the world to make him a major league quarterback. But
he wanted to throw the bomb ... bomb ... bomb."

                                                        —George Blanda

EPISODE 36

The days are growing short and the customers are howling
senselessly. This is George Blanda's final year in the heat, the
humidity, the glittering towers of the Texas Land of Oz. The
crowd is wild with power. It can actually get the quarterback.
The front office is nervous. All this New Era talk is simply
pointless sloganeering. Don Klosterman hasn't even had a
chance to draft college seniors yet.

He has made a couple of personnel moves, one of which
brings in running back John Henry Johnson, who claims he is
34, but is probably older than Blanda. Everything has gone
wrong. In the off-season Lemm calls George in and tells him
he's the number one man, the Alpha Male. Perfect, says Blanda
who knows that a quarterback doesn't have to say he's old just
because he's 38, going on 39.

George makes no concession to age. He feels it is mentally
defeating. In the off-season he works hard, playing handball
daily, running five or six miles. The nonsense is over. Taylor and

Baugh are both gone. And good old Wally Lemm is back,
sensible Wally with his deep command of the English language,
with his tough but friendly attitude. Life is going to get good
again. Then Blanda comes down with the first sore arm of his
entire career.

The manufacturers have been experimenting with this water
repellent coating for the official American League football. In
theory it works just dandy. In practice, it is a disaster. The
Oilers are training in Houston where even scorpions drop dead
of the heat in summertime. Blanda's hands sweat. Instead of
defeating moisture, the new substance has the reverse effect.
George spends the whole training camp throwing a slippery ball.
He cannot grip the ball, he has to palm it, like a shot putter.
Trull and Lee, back from exile in Denver, are younger. They
have thrown less passes in their lifetimes. They have some
stiffness. Blanda gets tendonitis. So does Jack Kemp at Buffalo.

"It hurt so bad I could hardly stand it," George recalls. "I
think John Brodie said that if a quarterback plays long enough
he will eventually have a sore arm some season. Well, 1966 was
my year."

The Oilers get off to a good start. They win their first two
games. Then everything starts to bump down toward the
bottom of the hill. Their third match of the season is against the
Jets in New York's Shea Stadium. On the grassy plain next to
Braes Bayou, where the Houston club trains, there is no protec-
tion. The ball club is simply out there in the open, naked to its
enemies. There is an espionage agent from the Jets in town. He
spends his afternoons in a nearby office building with a pair of
field glasses and a note pad. Evenings he spends with a certain
secretary who happens to be a devout Oiler fan.

One night, in the midst of a passion-induced euphoria, he
tells the lady what his mission is. Too late, the Oiler charter has
departed. Actually, it has departed twice. The first time it takes
off without George Blanda, who has overslept. The carnage at
Shea Stadium is unbelievable. It makes Little Big Horn look like
a Sunday school outing. The final score is 52-13 and Jet
defensive backs keep stopping Oiler receivers on their way back

to the huddle and telling them, "Dummy, can't you get the plays right? That last one was supposed to be "Z-right-90-straight."

The next weekend almost destroys George Blanda. There are only 55 seconds left and he stands in the huddle at War Memorial Stadium, that erector set of a park on the shores of Lake Erie. There are dark clouds to the north. God is about to be merciful and cover Buffalo with a layer of snow, so that no one can see the mouldering neighborhoods, the corroded downtown. The score is tied 20-20 and George is pondering two possibilities: (1) either trying a 47-yard field goal or (2) throwing a short, flat pass to move a little closer to the uprights.

His arm is screaming. Back he goes to throw his 53rd pass of the day, to tight end Bob McLeod, who runs a five-yard curl pattern to Blanda's right. The clock is ticking. There are 34 seconds remaining when Hagood Clarke, whose instincts are greater than his speed, flashes between the scrimmage line and McLeod. The pass is thrown softly. It settles in Clark's hands and he turns downfield toward the Houston end zone. A defensive end, Roland McDole, whom the Oilers once decided to get rid of, throws the Buffalo block that gets Clarke moving on a 66-yard touchdown run.

"I don't know who I blocked, but I went for the legs and I think I hit him clean," says McDole afterwards.

"You certainly hit him a good shot," says Tommy Day, the other end. "That Blanda took a long time getting up after you hit him."

After McDole delivers the coup, Blanda just slumps there on the turf as snowflakes fall on his helmet and his shoulder pads. Now George takes the helmet off and just kneels there. This is the first snowfall of the season. And this may have been the last pass of his career. Finally, Ode Burrell taps him on the shoulder and he stands up.

Steve Weller, columnist for the *Buffalo News*, writes George's obituary. Reports of Blanda's death are, of course, greatly exaggerated.

"Blanda was a class quarterback when the AFL had no other class quarterbacks. He had the knack for irritating hostile crowds that is possessed only by athletes with talent. Yapping at defensive players who brushed his usually spotless uniform, barking at teammates who didn't perform as expected, nagging officials who overlooked what he considered flagrant breaches of the rules by enemy cornerbacks, Blanda made sure that nobody went to sleep. Sunday afternoon the busy tongue and vast vocabulary still were there, but the arm that had backed them so many times was not."

Indeed, the arm is not there. It is weak, sore and afraid. Its owner, though, insists that the trainer, Bobby Brown, keep his mouth shut. Pride is only part of the motivation.

"I don't want anyone to know because they'll say George is whining and making excuses for a lousy year. To hell with that. I'll just wait for the soreness to pass."

The screaming at Rice Stadium is louder and more vicious than ever. As the players are introduced, there is polite applause for nearly every other villain involved in these Oiler defeats. Then comes George Blanda—No. 16 in your program and dead last in your hearts. The kill is closer and the customers are almost giddy with blood lust. In the upper deck somebody pastes up a bed-sheet banner that says: "Blanda is still the greatest."

There is a brief, angry scuffle and the banner comes down. Respect and admiration—never love—for George Blanda have turned to senseless hatred. For reasons of his own, Johnny Temple, the former major league infielder who does the sports on Houston's Channel 11, leads the booing, goading the crowd nightly on his show.

"Sure, I can hear the booing," George tells John Hollis, a warm, understanding, tail-wagging sort of guy who has replaced Gallagher on the Oiler beat for the *Post*. "I'm only human, John. I don't like it. But I can't let it ruin my mind. We've been losing for two seasons and I'm having a bad year. This is probably my last season. I say 'probably' because I don't want to shut the door entirely for next year. I'd like to keep playing. Football has been damn good to me. Where else can you work the kind of hours we do for the kind of pay we get?"

This cheerful, swaggering talk is strictly for the press. In his soul, George Blanda is a mass of pain. His arm may be dead and he is being pushed bodily out of professional football, un-loved, un-appreciated and un-recognized. He laughs and acts tough, because that is what young Slavic boys from western Pennsylvania are taught to do. But the booing hurts. How could it be otherwise?

It is October 30, 1966 and George Blanda is only hours away from being finished as a Houston Oiler. The club has flown to Kansas City to play the Chiefs, who are crunching along on their way toward history's first Super Bowl. The war between the leagues is over and peace is descending like a velvet curtain. Minutes before the teams go out onto the field, Lemm calls everyone together and tries to do something nice for George Frederick Blanda. He is bucking an overwhelming trend.

"Men, the papers are climbing all over us," he says in the classic rhetorical style of the football locker room. "The people in the stands are down on George in particular. Here's a guy who has done some fantastic things for this team over the past seven years. Someday look at our club record book. George's name is all over it. You can't let this man down. You've got to get out there and win this one *with* George and *for* George. Everyone will be watching on television back in Houston. Let's silence those boos."

The words are graceful and heroic, but Blanda's arm is not up to it. He cannot do a thing and Kansas City knows it.

There the Chiefs go, back in their zone defense. If a quarterback is a millimeter off against the zone, he is a dead man. George is, for the moment, a dead man professionally.

"This is the 'Win One for George' game," says Blanda, looking back. "And there's Old George out there throwing interceptions. I think I gave away two of them. At the half, Wally is upset. He yanks me out of there. I didn't blame him. He says, 'You and those damned interceptions!' This was a different situation. In the earlier years, I'd thrown interceptions because I was gambling for touchdowns. The league needed something exciting to attract customers. So I took my chances. This time it was because I was just plain playing poorly. I couldn't throw. I took cortisone shots. I had x-ray lights focused into my elbow at the Houston Medical Center two or three minutes every day. I didn't throw during the week.

"I didn't see any reason to tell anyone outside of Bobby Brown and Wally Lemm about my sore elbow. Who cared about it anyway? Nobody cared when I played with broken ribs in 1962. It didn't make big news when I had a knee so sore I couldn't kick field goals a couple of games in 1965. That thyroid operation weakened me severely. But that's bull talk. I didn't want to have any excuses. I didn't want people to say I was a crybaby. I don't think a football player should have crutches and use injuries as an excuse. He knows he's going to get hurt. That's part of the business.

"If I go around saying I have a bad arm that is a signal for a defensive end to take more shots at me. All the time I was in Houston, nobody ever took up for my side of why things went wrong. If the team was bad it was always because I played bad quarterback. No other reason. People couldn't look and see that our defense was giving up 430 points a season and we were scoring a lot of points and we were still losing. It was the quarterback's fault. Well, that's nonsense. There are 40 people out there. A bad quarterback can look great with a great club and a great quarterback can look bad with a bad club.

"No reporter ever asked me, in 1966, whether my arm was sore. Everyone was too busy waiting for the fall. They couldn't wait for Old George to leave. The crowds are always for the underdog. The second quarterback is always the darling. It was that way with me in Chicago. When you're number two, there's no way you can get in and show how bad you really are. People want the number one man to fall. They like to see the big boys fall."

And George falls. The final score is 48-23 and the *Houston Chronicle* writes the epitaph in 72-point type: "Kansas City

Catastrophe Ends King George's Reign." It also ends the heir
apparency of Jacky Lee. He comes on near the end of the first
half, injures a knee and is never a contender for the job again.
The next summer he goes to Kansas City in a trade for yet
another quarterback, Pete Beathard, who doesn't survive long in
Houston, either.

Ready or not, the new Oiler quarterback is Don Trull, with
his tangled teeth and his wonderfully rural face. He starts the
last five games of the season and Houston ends up 3-11. The
great champion of the new league's early years is a moldering
corpse. The final loss comes in Miami. Afterwards, the Oilers are
bused out to the airport. They lumber on board their wheezing
old DC-7B. The pilot asks everyone to disembark for a few
minutes. There is a strange sound in engine No. 3.

"We're going to take her up and try her out," the captain
says.

Each faction on the club holds a caucus in the lobby. The
Southwest Conference delegation, all white and led by Trull,
votes to stay over in Miami. The southern black group, headed
by the impressive Ernie Ladd, votes to catch a later flight. So it
goes. The DC-7B takes off with roughly 15 athletes on board. It
is forced to land in Oklahoma. On the morning after the first
year of The New Era ends, Oilers are scattered from Miami
Beach to Tulsa. Somehow, it seems altogether fitting.

EPISODE 37

A significant quotation:

*"By the time the 1966 season was over, I was fed up with all
the changes in the Oiler organization. I was fed up with the
organization. I was fed up with the fans booing my fanny. I was
fed up with being unappreciated after all the success we'd had
in the early years. Hell, those first few Oiler clubs had the best
offense they'll ever have in Houston. It fell apart because we
always had a bad front office in Houston. They were always
more concerned with the power structure and saving their own
jobs than they were with improving the club."*

—George Blanda, 1971

EPISODE 38

On April Fool's Day, 1967, whatever season's ticket holders the Oilers have left wake up to discover in their morning newspaper that they no longer have George Blanda to kick around. In a remarkably un-stylish fashion, the style-conscious new general manager of the Houston club has announced the release of the most dominant figure in the franchise's history.

It has been done in a simple mimeographed form letter to the newspapers and the radio and television stations. It is as warm and nostalgic as the changing of a Russian premier. The public has simply been informed that George is now, officially, an un-person as far as the Houston Oilers are concerned. The club is dropping some over-age athletes, Blanda among them.

There is no teary press conference, no grand gesture on the part of management, only this sterile notification of some routine club business. Why get all fussed up? In his seven years on Bud Adams's payroll, Blanda has passed for 165 touchdowns and 19,149 yards. He has kicked 304 extra points and 91 field goals, including nine from 50 yards or more. He has scored 596 points for the Oilers. The league record book is littered with his name. But he also threw 189 interceptions, so it is best to get him out of town in a hurry.

"Is there any possibility that you might retire George's jersey?" asks a writer from the *Houston Chronicle*, who also thinks it wouldn't be a bad idea to take Hennigan's and Tolar's numbers out of circulation as well.

"There's no reason to do that," says Klosterman, who is probably in a hurry to have lunch with Queen Elizabeth.

It turns out there has been some plotting in the palace. The coach wants one thing. The general manager wants another. And the club owner wants to save money. With the Houston Oilers it is difficult to tell the schemers without a scorecard. Let George Blanda try to explain. Be merciful. It isn't easy.

"When the 1966 season ends, Wally calls me and tells me he has a proposition for me," he recalls. "He tells me he wants me to be an assistant coach. I'm going to coach the quarterbacks and still be a player. I'm going to be the kicker and I'm going to back up whoever the number one quarterback is going to be. I told Wally that I'd be interested. So I go home to Chicago thinking that's what is going to happen. Now I'm a player-coach. Lemm says it appears that my arm is at the point where I can't be a starting quarterback anymore. I'm damned interested in the job.

"Several weeks later, Don Klosterman calls me and tells me that they want me back just as a kicker. He tells me that he's going to have to cut my salary, from $38,500 to $20,000. I told him what Wally told me. Don told me that couldn't be done. Bud wants me just as a kicker. They can't cut me more than ten percent and all they were trying to do was scare me into retiring. I had a non-release, no-trade contract. If I wanted to come back the next year, they had to take me and at my regular salary. I called Wally and asked him what was going on. He said, 'There's nothing I can do about it. That's the way they want it.' I know he wanted me, but either Bud or Don didn't. Who can tell?

"So I called Klosterman and said, 'I don't want to take a cut in salary. I don't want to just kick for you. Give me my release.' One day I picked up the paper and I read where I was no longer an Oiler. They really did it in style. They released me and a couple of other veterans, along with 19 other insignificant guys. If that was the way they wanted it, that was fine. I figured that I'd quit. I was a free agent. I didn't want to retire feeling that the Houston Oilers still owned me. If you're still on a team's negotiating list, they own you.

"If you feel like going into coaching you have to ask their permission. I've seen Halas trade a guy who wants to be a coach to another team for players and draft choices. You're nothing but cattle when they start dealing with you like that. The person just becomes insignificant. They're moving you around like a piece of beef. I was pleased to get my release. It probably never would have worked out, my hanging around Houston another year. They were so conditioned to booing me, it would have hurt the ball club the first time I missed a field goal."

And so George Blanda and Houston are granted a legal separation. It was never much of a marriage anyway. For seven long years, the man and the city cursed each other, kissed each other and missed each other. Never did they ever really come to understand each other. They were strangers when they met and strangers when they parted.

"I had my off-season job in Chicago, because that was my future. But I had no offers from anyone in Houston to work for them. I didn't make too many friends in Houston. In the later years, after those stupid gambling stories started, I didn't associate with too many people. It was by choice, then. Betty and I didn't eat out much, because if you go to a restaurant, somebody is going to stop you and ask questions about the team. You never know where gamblers hang out. You don't know when one is going to pop up and start pumping you for information. So I just avoided any possible contact with the public.

"Nobody ever seemed to be too interested in me, except for the image that Jack Gallagher created of me. I was never approached by groups as a speaker. Once the *Houston Chronicle* asked me to talk at their banquet for their All-State high school football team. But that was the only time I ever made a public appearance in seven years. Nobody on the local papers spent much time interviewing me directly. I never met anyone of any importance, any business contacts. Nobody ever wanted me to endorse anything. Betty and I had a little apartment near the University of Houston campus and, with the exception of my teammates, we never met anyone."

Once, when a friend from Chicago stopped in Houston to visit the Blandas, he had a question. "How well do you know your neighbors?" he asked.

"Well enough, I guess," said George.

"Don't be too sure," said the visitor. "As I walked up the drive one of them yelled over, 'Hello, George! How's the ball club gonna do Sunday?'"

The news of Blanda's release is in both papers. All there is surrounding it is silence. One day, George is one of the three most controversial people in Houston. The next day he's gone and it doesn't even cause a twitch in the seismograph. Those zealots who swore they would never purchase another ticket as long as he was an Oiler do not swamp the club's business office with requests for seats. Neither is there a tidal wave of cancellations.

It is an eerie situation. And two weeks after the release is announced, George is on the telephone from La Grange Park, Illinois, talking to a writer from the *Chronicle.* He has purposely waited two weeks before saying anything about his leavetaking. He doesn't want to go out in a thrashing patch of controversy. So he has taken time to prepare himself. It is a needless precaution.

"You know how I am. I might have said something I wouldn't have liked to see in print, if I had responded right away," he says. "Tell me what was the reaction? I didn't see the Houston papers. Surprisingly, I didn't hear from any of the players—you know, Bob Talamini, Jim Norton, Charlie Hennigan, Charlie Tolar. You know, the gang."

There is no reaction. None at all. The glittering towers of the oily Oz slip out of George Blanda's life forever. The American Football League will live. It is heading for complete equality and ultimate merger with its old business rival. Nobody, not even George Halas, considers it a Mickey Mouse League any longer. One by one, the pioneers who made it possible, people like George Blanda, are being dropped for younger, taller, swifter athletes.

So George sits in retirement at his La Grange Park home, a full-time trucking executive, figuring out how to avoid the sloppy beltline that is a hazard of middle age. Damned if the telephone doesn't ring. It's Al Davis calling from Oakland. What unconditional release? The Raiders have just claimed George Blanda off the waiver list.

Good God!

— End of Period —

Historical footnote:

At the end of the 1970 football season, while George Blanda is receiving the Bert Bell Award, the Sporting News *Player of the Year Award, the Associated Press Male Athlete of the Year Award, the Miami Touchdown Club's Player of the Year Award and the Vincent T. Lombardi Trophy for "dedication to professional football," two other news events take place. (1) Jacky Lee, age 31, informs the Kansas City Chiefs that he no longer cares to be a member of their taxi squad. He prefers to go home to Houston and work at his insurance business full time. (2) The Edmonton Eskimos of the Canadian Football League give Don Trull, age 29, his outright release.*

Now, what was all that booing about? Does anybody remember? Does anybody really care?

FOURTH PERIOD

Superman is alive and well and kicking for Oakland.

(Or how to be worshiped simultaneously by small children, pot-puffing hippies and middle-aged men in support hose.)

EPISODE 1

Home is the general, home from the awful war. He looks less youthful, less vigorous, less fearsome. Worry lines clutch at his eyes. He does not glide as smoothly when he walks. Something rude has happened to him. He has done exactly what the club owners paid him to do. He has dragged the arrogant lords of the National Football League to the bargaining table, scaring hell out of them in the process. This complicated Brooklyn boy has succeeded where the great aviator-turned-duck-hunter, Joe Foss, failed.

Now the conflict has ended and Al Davis, the second and last commissioner the American Football League will ever have, is not especially pleased with the peace settlement. He feels badly betrayed. They told him to whip the enemy to its knees and he did just that, employing the most diabolically direct of strategies. Davis reasoned correctly that no football league, no matter how smug it feels, can function properly without quarterbacks. Davis started pilfering all the NFL quarterbacks who wanted to get rich rapidly. A surprising number indicated they were interested, San Francisco's John Brodie and Los Angeles's Roman Gabriel among them.

Davis had the National League on its spine, a sword point grazing its jugular, and the AFL owners gave away the advantage. Now he has returned to Oakland, wearing black and silver clothes, driving a black and silver Cadillac and mailing off $125,000 war-reparation checks to the NFL every year. He will do so for 20 years. The taste is sour and he is starting to get an insight into how Jefferson Davis felt in the summer of 1865.

In the final analysis, club owners like Lamar Hunt and Bud Adams were so anxious to bring their franchises into the NFL that they were willing to give their old opponents just about anything they asked for. Now there is one high commissioner, Pete Rozelle. Until the merger is complete in 1970, the AFL will be ruled by a puppet government. Its propaganda facilities have been taken over by the National League. And the Oakland Raiders will spend two decades renting their side of San Francisco Bay from the 49ers, regardless of whether both teams sell out their stadiums every Sunday.

"It was some peace settlement," Davis is fond of telling friends, in his silkiest Citadel accent.

"Why, we were on our way to becoming the dominant league. We whipped them three-to-one signing quality players in the last two competitive drafts. Then we started taking their quarterbacks away and they were frightened. They came looking for an armistice. But when the negotiations were over, I thought the AFL had lost the war.

"At least they let us keep our horses for the spring planting. When I got back to Oakland, my house was still standing. My wife and son were still alive, so I felt blessed. They took away my medals and broke my sword. But, shoot, I don't mind. I'll probably get rich writing a book about my experiences."

He will do no such thing. Direct publicity curls Davis's toes. Never has he even held a press conference. He prefers to work in a dark fog of mystery. Right this minute he is working with an intensity rare even for him. Someone is going to pay for his frustrations. He is strictly a front-office man now, a part-owner.

He has a deputy doing the actual coaching, John Rauch, a former quarterback who may have quit playing too soon.

For recreation, Al Davis reads the waiver lists. This morning in late May he has found an interesting name lurking there. Not long ago he read that the Houston Oilers had given George Blanda his unconditional release. So why are waivers being asked on him? He immediately files a claim with the league and dials the offices of a certain Chicago trucking firm.

The conversation is memorable:

DAVIS *(coyly):* "I see where you got your release."

BLANDA *(matter-of-factly):* "That's right. I got my release."

DAVIS: "You going to play next year?"

BLANDA: "I don't think so. I don't think I can."

DAVIS *(growing warmer):* "Well, would you play next year?"

BLANDA *(growing coy):* "For the right team I might. I don't know what I want to do. For the first time in my life I'm free to go where I want. I can play for the club of my choice."

DAVIS *(voice very soft and very low):* "I have news you might be interested in. You aren't free. Houston neglected to waive you out of the league. In the off-season a team has two weeks to ask waivers on someone. They can't just let you go without doing that. I know that you want to go play with Sid Gillman. You're not fooling me. I know you're on your way to San Diego."

BLANDA *(filled with shock and indignation):* "I wouldn't play for Sid Gillman if he was coach of the last football team on earth. I didn't want to play for him in 1960 and I don't want to play for him in 1967. You don't want me, you just want to make sure I don't play for anybody else."

DAVIS *(feigning pain):* "Well, you're now property of the Oakland Raiders. We've picked you up off the waiver list. If you want to play, that's fine. If you don't want to, that's fine, too. At least you're not going to play for Sid Gillman at San Diego."

BLANDA: "You mean to say you won't let me have my unconditional release so I can dicker with whomever I want to? I don't believe that."

DAVIS: "We don't care about you as an individual. Either you play for Oakland or you don't play. We're not going to let you run around the country with an unconditional release and then come back someday and beat the Raiders."

End of conversation. End of mini-dream. Curtain.

EPISODE 2

On such a theme of friendship, trust and brotherly love do the warm vintage years of George Frederick Blanda begin. Suddenly, it hits him. There is no way out of the mines. There are just better, brighter, more profitable mines to be trapped in. If it isn't the Allegheny Bituminous Coal Company or the railroad or the thermostat factory that wants your body and your soul, then it is the University of Kentucky or the University of Pennsylvania or the Chicago Bears or the Houston Oilers or the Oakland Raiders. It is inescapable.

"I can't fight city hall any longer," Blanda recalls. "Actually, I'm madder at Houston than I am at Davis. He's super smart and he's protecting himself. But those bastards with the Oilers! They come out with this big deal about giving you what you ask for—an unconditional release. What heroes they are. They release you and next thing you know you're just property of someone else. I feel about *that* big. The Houston front office can't do anything right.

"So Davis calls me back and I tell him yes, I'll play for his ball club. He tells me he's going to have to cut my salary by $11,000. I'm just going to kick and be the second-string quarterback, so he can't afford to pay me what I was getting in Houston. According to my contract, he can only cut me ten percent. Well, I keep telling him that and he keeps telling me he can cut me more than that. Finally, I dropped it on him.

"I told him, 'Look, you picked up my option from Houston. It was a non-release, no-cut contract. My last year of contract is in force whether I sign with you or not. If I don't sign all you can cut me is ten percent for not signing. That is a league law and I'm coming out there and you'll have to pay me. Isn't that what the option clause is all about?'

"I told him I'd take the mandatory ten percent cut and play out my position. If I reported, he'd have to pay me. He knew I had him. He thought he was messing with some young kid. He thought he was getting a virgin.

"I stood up to George Halas and Bert Bell and Bud Adams. And Al Davis didn't scare me that much. I had a lawyer who said, 'You're right, George. By law he has to pay you and he can't cut you by more than ten percent.' The lawyer sends Al a letter and he calls and says, 'You can't do that.' I tell Al Davis, 'Read the standard player contract sometime. You didn't want me to be a free agent. You said you didn't care about me. Why should I get sentimental over you?'"

The rules are irrefutable. A player signs a contract for one year, two years, three years, whatever. Tacked on the end is an "option year." The team has one year to renew its option on the athlete's body. If the player chooses, he can refuse to sign and play a year with no contract. There is a ten percent pay decrease as a penalty. At the end of his option, he is technically a free agent. By picking up Blanda's non-release contract, the Oakland club is bound to pay him his full Houston salary, less the ten percent penalty. Even if Blanda does not make the club, the Raiders are hooked. George has them by the pubic hair and now he is starting to yank.

In his desire to build up his ball club as quickly as possible after the war, Al Davis has done something untypical. He has made a mistake. Fortunately, it is not fatal for either party. A few days later, Davis calls Blanda and tells him to forget the business with the lawyer. If he'll report and sign a new contract, the Raiders will give him a salary representing only a 12 or 13 percent decrease in his Houston pay. Well?

"I let ten days of training camp go past before I made a decision. I do some thinking. Oakland has a real good football team, better than the Oilers by a whole lot. Maybe I can be a help to them. They need a kicker. They might even need a first-string quarterback. They have Cotton Davidson and he's been hurt a lot and they've just got Lamonica in a trade with Buffalo. Nobody knew how good he was going to be then. I

knew Al ran a hell of a fine organization and I thought that
after seventeen years in the game, it might be stimulating to
play for a real good organization. The change might do me
good.

"So I decided to stop irritating Al. I really wouldn't have
sued him or anything. This way he'd save some face and so
would I. That's important to both of us. So I reported ten days
late and signed. I still come every year ten days late. The
reporters all think it's because I'm older and the club doesn't
want me to get too tired."

Both faces are saved. The beautiful years have started.

EPISODE 3

A quotation that will live as long as men play professional
football for a living:

*"Our association may have got off to a poor start, but I made
the right move reporting to the Raiders. For the first time I was
playing for a club that wasn't going to screw you just because
they didn't like you personally. And unlike the Oilers you knew
there wasn't going to be a new general manager or a new coach
every five minutes. They act like men in the Oakland front
office and they treat the players like men."*   —George Blanda

EPISODE 4

It is the Christmas season and all through the house at Rice
Stadium, everyone is booing, including the mice. Suddenly
Houston recalls an old blood craving. Forget all that treacle
about peace on earth, goodwill to men. The silence that began
with George Blanda's outright release six months earlier has
been broken.

By some charming fluke of scheduling, the Oakland Raiders
are in Texas, with an opportunity to clinch the Western Division
championship of the American Football League. And who is
with them, wearing a strange-looking black and silver worksuit?
Why, George Blanda. He is no longer a number one quarterback.
He is that rarest of woodland creatures, an Alpha Male who has
refused to leave the pack and die. He is a Beta Male again,

playing behind Daryle Lamonica who has won his position by
the simple yet effective device of leading the league in passing.

One by one, the visiting players are being introduced. The
customers aren't booing Jim Otto or Hewritt Dixon or innocent
lambs like them. They are screaming their guts out at Blanda.
There are 36,375 citizens present and the only human beings on
the lot who aren't booing are the officials and George is watching their lips very carefully.

Early in the first period, Blanda misses on a 45-yard field goal
attempt and the laughing is loud enough to be heard inside
those pretty plastic hats the athletes all wear.

"My God, what did you ever do to these people?" Lamonica
asks, shuddering. He has just become a number one quarterback
and Blanda sees no point in explaining the obvious. It is far too
terrifying.

Few minutes later, the Raiders line up for another field goal,
somewhat shorter. The booing has now reached storm force. It
is wet and rainy and cold. This is a dandy way to relieve the
misery.

"Don't they ever stop?" says Lamonica. "What a bunch of
jerks!"

Now George starts kicking down the middle. His third goal,
with 11:46 left in the game, puts Oakland ahead for good, 9-7.
His fourth, with 3:06 left, assures a Raider victory.

It is now so still in the stands, you can hear a Texas Baptist
drop a hidden hip flask. The final score is 19-7 and some old
admirers with long memories lean over the railing and cheer
George. Albeit there aren't many of them. It has been a long
time since 1961. They have had to wait a while, because Blanda
has been the postgame guest on national television, so they
must be at least semi-sincere.

The Raiders wait around, listen for another score from
another town and then pitch Honest Al Davis into the shower,
expensive overcoat and all, when they discover that San Diego
has lost, giving Oakland a victory in the west.

"Who ever said you were washed up?" shouts a Houston
writer.

"You did," shouts George Blanda.

They both laugh. It is an excellent joke. Very accurate, too.

"I felt right at home out there," Blanda says. "The first time I went out there, the boos kind of shocked me. I thought maybe ... just maybe ... the fans would respect me a little more than they did. This was fantastic, the best day of my career ... to come back here and show all these rube fans that the booing really doesn't bother the old man."

If you listened real close, Mickey Herskowitz writes in the next day's *Post*, you could have heard George Blanda smile.

"How does one describe that smile?" Herskowitz asks. "Well, start with this: If you put them side by side, the Mona Lisa would appear to be crying. A canary feather seemed to be fluttering from his lips."

Blanda tells another writer that if Oakland wins the Super Bowl, he will probably retire. After all, he's no child. He's boring in on 40. Somebody throws him the game ball and the champagne party begins. Death and Resurrection! Death and Resurrection! How many times can one football player professionally die and still come back to life?

A few weeks later, there is an anticlimax. Don Klosterman's New Era Marching Band and Electronic Kazoo Khorus has been surprisingly successful. The Oilers win the Eastern Division and go forth to Oakland to play for the league title and the chance to—gasp!—play Green Bay in the second Super Bowl. Again Blanda kicks four field goals. The Oilers are excused by a 40-7 score. Not having to play Green Bay in front of the whole nation at Miami is one of the finest things that has ever happened to the Houston franchise.

"Blanda Has the Last Laugh—Again!" says a *Houston Post* headline.

All together now ... hah-hah-hah!

"God, George," says Tom Keating. "I hope the hell we never decide to get rid of you."

Damned if George Blanda, who started out wearing leather helmets, isn't going to play in the Super Bowl, the first major sporting event created entirely through the power of television.

EPISODE 5

Every Sunday morning when the Oakland Raiders are scheduled to appear on national television, Mrs. Mary Blanda of Youngwood, Pa., rises very early and goes to mass at Holy Cross Roman Catholic Church and lights a candle for the safety of her seventh child, George, who long ago became converted to Lutheranism. Then she lights another candle for the entire team, because it is not proper nor very Christian to think only of your own son.

In the afternoon, she watches the game. She knows exactly what is happening on the screen. She knows end zone from fair catch, and slant pass from blocked punt. Why shouldn't she be an expert? The Blanda boys all played football, even though Peter Paul, the oldest, had to lie to his father in order to get away with it. In fact, old Mike Blanda the miner didn't even know he had a son who was an outstanding athlete at faraway Texas Tech until his friends and companions down at the neighborhood saloon began to compliment him about it.

Then he decided it wasn't such a bad thing, football. Someone was always willing to pay your way through college if you were good enough at the sport. And Mike Blanda made sure his children finished high school, even if he had to rattle their dentures to get them through. So Pete played and all the rest did, too. If not football, then basketball. And they were good at sports. When George was with the Bears, the ninth child, Paul, who had gone to Pitt, was doing very well with the New York Giants when he hurt his knee. And the glittering jewel of the family, the youngest and most admired by everyone else, Tom Blanda, was a brilliant quarterback for Army. But he never played professionally. He was, and is, a career military man, a major and a mathematics instructor at West Point.

In theory, Mary Blanda isn't supposed to watch football. The games might excite her too much. But that is doctor talk, she says. Several years earlier she had driven to Buffalo with her daughter, Mrs. Margaret Blanda Yakubison, who lives across the street and watches out for the older woman. The steps at War Memorial Stadium are steep enough to discourage Tiger

Tenzing. But the Houston Oilers and her son George were in town to play the Bills and nothing was going to keep her from watching. So Mary Blanda hiked up, found her seat and suffered a mild heart attack.

Some people use the fact that they are past 70 to get frail and feeble. Not Mary Blanda. Age is nothing so fearsome as life itself. Her husband worked in the wretched mines and drank a lot to forget what destiny had done to him. But he was a good man, a hard man, and he never missed work. And he died only 13 days after he escaped into retirement.

They had met in Prague, where she was born. He had been born in Pennsylvania, wherever that was, and had returned to the old country. They were married there and they booked passage to America on the Lusitania, on the very voyage where German torpedos ripped the ship's keel and sent her to the bottom. But the Blandas had been delayed and had been forced to take a later boat. They did not know until they reached New York that the Lusitania had been destroyed.

Mary Blanda raised eleven children in the small frame house with the aluminum siding on South Third Street—Mary, Peter, Helen, Mike, Margaret, Joseph, George, Irene, Paul, John and Thomas, names that reoccur over and over in Slavic families all through western Pennsylvania and central Ohio and southern Illinois. The boys slept in a dormitory set up in the attic. Everyone ate and lived and argued in her kitchen, which opened onto a garden she planted in order to keep everyone in *kapusta* to go with their *keilbasas*. She didn't exactly feed an army, but she fed a platoon. She did the platoon's laundry, too, and picked up after it. And she chased the platoon out the door to school.

Was one small heart attack going to slow her down? Was she stopped or even slowed down the winter the house burned and everyone had to be farmed out to relatives and neighbors while a new one was being built? Did small paychecks and large food bills halt her? Of course not! She watched George play, went back to the hotel where the family was meeting after the game and ordered a double shot of whiskey. ("For the cold weather," she explained.) That soothed the pain. Calmly, Mary Blanda got into her daughter's car and rode home to Youngwood without telling anyone about her condition, which may prove a theory some scientists hold that certain athletic qualities are inherited from the maternal side of a man's bloodline.

"I light a candle for everyone. I want George's team to win," she says. "I wonder if somebody else isn't lighting a candle for the other team, too. Five of my sons played football. I know the game. The violence is part of the game and people who play it know it is violent. Once I jumped up and down like a teenager when George kicked a field goal on television. My doctor told me the excitement wasn't good for me. I told him it would be worse for me not to see George than to watch him. I'd always be wondering what was happening."

When the Raiders clinch the American League championship in 1967 and get a chance to go to the Super Bowl, George receives a telegram from home. "The candle was lit," it says. Friends and relatives in Youngwood tell Blanda that it was more than one candle. Holy Cross Church has an altar that is better lit than any stadium in either league.

As children, the Blandas never really realized they were poor. Oh, times were tough, but Mike Blanda insisted on plenty of food and plenty of coal for the furnace. Nobody went to school in rags.

It wasn't easy. Mike Blanda would work all week in the mines and come home and do odd jobs on weekends. The kids would help, cutting grass, painting garages and mending broken furniture. They trapped muskrats and sold the pelts. They picked up odd bits of coal from the railroad yards. They worked in the town's only bowling alley, setting pins for three cents a line. Mike Blanda cut the kids' hair and fixed their shoes. Mary Blanda made their clothes. They handed them down until there was nothing left but rags and then Mary Blanda made rugs out of the rags.

"My father had a right to drink," says George Blanda.

All of western Pennsylvania is like this. These are those warm, wonderful, opinionated people who gave you so many

Polish outfielders, Lithuanian tackles, Hungarian guards and Slovak quarterbacks, etc. Stan Musial is from Donora, 20 miles away; John Unitas is from Pittsburgh, 30 or 35 miles to the west; Joe Namath is from Beaver Falls, about 40 miles over there; Lou Kusserow from Glassport, just over the hill, and Johnny Lujack from Connellsville where the train stops next.

Trying to understand George Blanda can give a man a frightful headache, unless his origins are considered. He is as much a product of his environment as any ghetto black. His people were part of the great Slavic immigration wave. They worked the mines. They coaled the railroad engines. They stoked the steel mill fires. If they had any intellectual skill it was pounded out of their skulls by the monotony of the assembly line. They were exploited for their physical strength and scorned for their ardent Catholicism. They were supposed to be white niggers forever. They suffered under the same sort of ruthless stereotyping. They were drunk, stupid and inane, fit only for service in the mines and the mills.

A sample piece of ethnic humor:

First Polack: "Hey, Stosh, my oldest boy is going to college. I guess they can't call us stupid Polacks anymore."

Second Polack: "That's great, Chester. What college is he going to?"

First Polack: "Marquette!"

Second Polack: Oh, great! What Marquette is that? The A & P Marquette over on Main Street or the First National Marquette on Grove Street?"

So they worked the mines, listened to the garbage and waited. They begat dozens of children. They drank too much and depended upon their wives to raise their families. Nobody ever held a civil rights movement for them. They didn't need one. They never tried to beat the Establishment head-on. Instead, they infiltrated. They assimilated in their own curious way, becoming more WASPish than any Des Moines WASP. They made Notre Dame more Yalie than Yale.

They protected their flanks, those Poles, those Slovaks, those Bohemians, those Hungarians, those Lithuanians. They let all the other people laugh at the funny Polacks. They got the hell away from the coal dust and they planned to stay away. No power on earth could drag their children or their grandchildren back. Who's funny now? Was it selfishness? No, merely self-protection. They adopted the Puritan ethic and made it fit Central European Catholicism. They took the American Dream and, instead of complaining that it was an empty promise, they made it work. In a sense, they were the last—and, perhaps, the only—really rugged individualists the country ever produced.

EPISODE 6

Quotation to be placed on the base of the Statue of Liberty, in case tourists get tired of reading Emma Lazarus:

"My childhood was miserable, right? You're wrong. If we were miserable, we never knew it. We thought we were happy. A kid in Youngwood with a rock to kick or a tire to roll or a pair of tin cans on his shoes could clatter around town and annoy the other nationalities—why, he was a lucky kid. We swam bare, we arm-wrestled, we kicked the can, we raced and played cards and pitched pennies and shot pool and threw rocks and played hockey with sawed-off tree branches. We competed till we were ready to fall down. We didn't get into trouble because we were too exhausted. Besides, during the Depression there was nothing to steal."—George Blanda, speaking to *Sports Illustrated* staff writer Jack Olsen, July 10, 1971.

EPISODE 7

The sunshine, which tourists from New York purchase at prices starting at $60 a day and up, is pouring down free on George Blanda's grizzled scalp. He stands in the tunnel under the northern stands at Miami's steel-plated Orange Bowl. His body is in the shadows. His head is poked out into the daylight. Professional football has become the national sport. Baseball can still call itself the national pastime. But professional football is the national sport.

Out on the field, two gigantic balloon figures are standing toe-to-toe for the benefit of television. One is dressed like a

Green Bay Packer, the other like an Oakland Raider. Bands are wailing and thumping. The field is filled with toothsome ladies. Floats keep pouring out of hidden exits. This is wretched excess at its grand old American best. Television cameras are devouring the entire gaudy spectacle. Thousands of dollars are being squandered for a few minutes of visual splendor. The world has seen nothing to match it since the most beautiful female slaves from around the empire were thrown to crocodiles in Colosseum aquatic shows.

There is no beating the Green Bay Packers and the Raiders know it. Vince Lombardi is in his heaven, all's right with the world. Afterwards, Daryle Lamonica admits that he was so nervous at the start that he does not even remember the first series of downs. Nobody blames him. Nobody makes mistakes against Green Bay and lives. And the Raiders are not without sin.

There are 75,546 customers on board the Orange Bowl and they know that this is to be a ritualistic slaughter. It is only a matter of time. No one knows that the Packers' empire is having one last brilliant epoch. Within four years, Lombardi will be dead, gone to the Washington Redskins before cancer eats at the iron of his innards. And the Packers will be dullards, mere also-rans. But this is the height of empire and they cannot lose.

It is still 13-7, favor of Green Bay, when Oakland defensive back Roger Bird glances up into the glistening sky and fails to find a Packer punt. There is a whisper of impending equality between the leagues when one Dick Capp, cut by the American League Boston Patriots and picked up by the imperious Packers of the Old Established League, falls on the fumble. Don Chandler kicks a field goal, with seconds to go before the half. The ball strikes the crossbar and flops over into the end zone for a three-point play that puts Green Bay ahead, 16-7, and takes Oakland out of competition.

So the Raiders lose to the Packers, 33-14, which doesn't make them any different from any club in the National Football League. In the press box, Hamilton P.B. (Tex) Maule draws conclusion No. 54,189 of his gossamer career.

"They can play for ten years, but the American League will never whip the NFL in a Super Bowl," he says, with that Charlton Heston rumble in his throat. "The really big game of the year is the National Football League playoff. This is just anticlimax and it will be years before the Super Bowl is real competition."

Poor, dear Tex! This is his zenith, too. Only one year hence, Joe Willie Namath will drive him to the punchbowl sobbing like a woman scorned. For the moment, he is the high priest of fact and nobody will dispute him.

"This was no execution," says George Blanda. "That's bull. Green Bay is a big, strong, well-trained team that works well together. They didn't try anything we didn't anticipate. They didn't try to fool us. They just went about their business. You can't beat perfect plays."

Later on, there is a gathering of the clan back at the hotel. George looks fatigued. He sighs. Mother is watching. She snorts.

"What are you so tired about?" Mary Blanda demands. "You went out there and moved your leg twice for extra points. Your mother had to walk all over that stadium. I'm the one who ought to be tired, not you."

EPISODE 8

A couple of quick quotes to cut out of this book and pin in your wallet, which you may carry next to your heart:

(1) "In 1964, I took my son Rick out of school and told the principal that I wanted to take him to see his father play his last professional football game. In 1965, I took Rick out of school and told the principal I wanted him to see his father play in his last professional game. By 1968, the principal told me, 'Look, Mrs. Blanda, take the boy out of school, but for God's sake don't give me that excuse one more time, because I don't believe it.' "   —Mrs. Betty Blanda, after the 1971 season.

(2) "During the 1968 season, they only gave me one start, against Denver. I hadn't started a game since that Kansas City thing in 196, when the Oilers decided I was through. I threw four touchdown passes, including one to Warren Wells that went

*94 yards, the longest in Raider club history. When I left, the
score was 40-7. I pointed to Cotton Davidson, age 36, and said
to Rauch, 'Why don't you give the kid a little experience?' I was
41 and some dummy from the* Oakland Tribune *was saying I
should quit. What for?"*
                                                        —George Blanda

EPISODE 9

The course of empire in professional football seems to be
flowing westward, from Green Bay, that sullen, sleepy city on
Lake Michigan, to Oakland, the most exotic town on the
eastern shore of San Francisco Bay. Excellence means the
Oakland Raiders and there are not enough fantastic adjectives
to apply to Daryle Lamonica. People openly suggest that he is
Bart Starr and John Unitas all over again. Maybe he is both of
them, combined. There has been a change of coaches. Rauch
has gone shuffling off to Buffalo, muttering evil things about Al
Davis. Lightning will strike Rauch, so everyone stands back.

In charge of The Organization, on the field, at least, is John
Madden, a public relations man's enigma. Here is a friendly,
witty pumpkin of a person who has no particular image. His
clever remarks vanish almost as soon as they leave his lips. If he
is as fine a coach as some of his athletes insist he is, no one will
ever know because the press suspects that he is just Davis's
surrogate. When things go well, the writers bow down and praise
Honest Al. When matters get rotten, no one is to blame but
Madden.

This first season, no one can say much. Lamonica has been
stuffed to his gullet with pride and poise, just like a holiday
bird. Oakland has a 13-1 season's record. It has whipped Kansas
City twice during the regular schedule. But Pete Rozelle is now
Czar of All the Rushers. And he has this thing. He wants more
teams in the AFL playoffs. So clubs that finish second get a
chance to compete. It isn't strictly fair, is it, Al?

Naturally, it comes down to Oakland and Kansas City. That's
the way God wants it. It makes no difference that the Chiefs
finished second in the West to the Raiders. This is the way it's
going to be. In the cross-matching, Oakland has obliterated

Houston and Kansas City has eliminated last year's Super Bowl champions, the New York Jets, the club that made an honest man out of Hamilton Prieleaux Bee Maule. This whole thing seems anticlimactic. The first half is something best discarded by historians. Going into the third period, it is 7-6, favor of the guys in the silver and black hats. Everyone at the Oakland Coliseum assumes that Lamonica will discover a way to keep the Chiefs from gaining. In the Year of Our Lord, 1969, he has completed an amazing streak. He has taken the Raiders to 36 victories in 40 league games. Who can guess that the stars are now moving against him? In the third period, he throws the ball deep just as defensive end Aaron Brown comes careening through. As Lamonica completes his follow-through, fingers on his right hand gracefully extended, there is a collision. Brown's helmet strikes Daryle's fingers and something gruesome happens. He comes running off the field, holding his passing hand under his left armpit.

"Oh, my God, how do you feel?" asks Blanda.

"Terrible," says Lamonica truthfully. "I can't play anymore. Get ready. I can't go back in. Something feels broken in there."

So Blanda goes over and takes a few warmup passes. Madden crooks a finger. He wants that angry old warrior from western Pennsylvania. Blanda goes in and moves the ball on a couple of plays. Then Warren Wells, whose skills George deeply admires, goes cutting over the middle and slips just as Blanda lets the ball go. Kansas City intercepts. The Chiefs move 95 yards to score. As George is figuring what to do on the next series, Lamonica runs back into the game and throws an interception, too. Suddenly, Kansas City has a 17-7 victory.

"I go walking up the stairs and I'm disgusted. Everybody is disgusted. So is Daryle. He's hurt his hand. He's made up his mind to go back in and try it anyway. Maybe he's right, maybe he's wrong. But you can't argue with his guts. Well, he's in the training room getting a cast put on the hand, and I'm angry because I'm 41 and how many chances am I going to get to play on a 13-1 team? And how many chances am I going to get to go to another Super Bowl?

"If we could have won this one," Blanda concludes, "I could have retired. Of course, there never would have been all that publicity over the miracle season of 1970. I mean I must have got $10 million worth of publicity that next season. But this game is 1969 and how do I know what's going to happen next year? And besides, I like the Super Bowl. I want to play in another one. I want to win one.

"I'm really upset. So I'm trying to get dressed and George Ross, the sports editor of the mighty *Oakland Tribune*, comes over and tells me he's been talking to Lamonica. Okay, fine! He says that Daryle told him the offensive line wasn't blocking too well for him, so he had problems. He asks me what I think. So what am I going to say? Am I going to say the line blocked bad? Then I've got the whole line against me. And I'm 41 years old. If I don't say that, I have to say Daryle is wrong. Now it sounds like we hate each other, which we don't. We have a lot of mutual respect. We have differences, like any two men, but we have respect.

"If I say that the line was blocking well then Daryle is mad at me and I don't want that. So I try to take the middle road. I said, 'Let me tell you something. We got in a position where we had to pass, where we were down 14-7 and 17-7 in a championship game. We had to pass and we threw the ball 18 straight times. Now Kansas City is a pretty smart football team and their forte is rushing the passer, and you just can't expect any offensive line to hold them out 18 straight times.' I figured that would suffice. Next day, the *Tribune* says that I criticized Daryle for throwing 18 straight times. And I didn't. That's his business. He's the number one quarterback. I know how he feels. I know why he did what he had to.

"That's when I decided I didn't need the *Oakland Tribune* or George Ross. He also asked me if I thought I could have moved the team. Now, I know that is just another 'Are you still beating your wife?' question. But I answer anyway. I must be a real horseshit quarterback if I don't think I can't move a football team, so I say, 'Of course I thought I could have moved the team.' That makes big reading. It sounds like I think I can do it and I think Daryle can't. I didn't say any of that."

There are more dangers lurking outside the dressing room. Blanda has given a few minutes of his time to Rick Talley, a happy wanderer who serves as sports editor and columnist of *Chicago Today*. The thing about Talley is that he does not take notes. He has fallen upon evil ways. The electronic dingbats have seduced him. He packs a midget tape recorder and he uses it like a Colt .45.

"I gave him a good interview inside the dressing room and I figured that would be enough for him. I leave with Tom Kole, my boss from REA and my best friend. With me are a couple of close Raider pals, Pete Banaszak and Harry Schuh. And we get out in the hall, waiting for the elevator to take us up to the parking lot. There's a party or something afterwards, not that any of us felt like a party.

"There's Rick waiting for the elevator, too. Kole tells me it's a shame to lose like that and I agree. And Tom says he wonders what went wrong in the final quarter when Oakland couldn't seem to do anything right."

One of the other Raider players asks an opinion. Didn't George think the game plan was too long? It is just shop talk. Like any other workmen, the athletes are second-guessing management, but not necessarily in a vicious manner. Why even newspapermen have been known to congregate down at Jerry and Johnny's Saloon and suggest how the publisher can grow in grace.

"Of course the game plan was too long," says Blanda, shrugging. "It's always too long. You have to go through the game plan and pick out what you want to do. You have to give enough stuff in there to give a quarterback some latitude."

"Why did we go to that spread formation, with guys all over the field?" asks one of the players, still talking shop.

"That's the quarterback's job. It was up to Daryle and he did it. That's what he decided. And it didn't work out. Happens all the time," says Blanda.

Now George notices Talley's tape recorder.

"Is that running?" he asks.

"Oh, no," says Talley, whose eyes sometimes get swamped with innocence.

"Look, I'm talking to my friends. This is a private conversation. If that thing is running, this is an invasion of privacy and I'll knock you right on your behind if you're taping a private conversation," says Blanda.

"*Was* the game plan too long?" asks Talley, who has stood up to Leo Durocher and now is not afraid of Lucifer, Hitler, Stalin and Attila the Hun combined.

"This is strictly off the record, but it was too long. It always is. It doesn't vary from team to team. The game plan's a guide for a quarterback, nothing more."

"Do you think you could have moved the club?" Talley asks.

"I'd be an idiot to say I couldn't."

Upstairs, Talley plays his tape for Paul Zimmerman, a thinking man's football writer, who uses some of the quotes for the *New York Post*. Now the whole world seems to think that George Blanda is in revolt. But against whom?

The headlines say that he is critical of Daryle Lamonica, of John Madden, of Al Davis, of God and several assorted prophets. The storm clouds are getting thick and ugly over the Raider office. The coaches call Blanda in and demand to know if he really said what Talley and Ross and Zimmerman have quoted him as saying.

"I said some of it," he explains. "But not in the context they used it in. I can tell you exactly how I meant it, if you'll listen."

The wreckage is fairly awesome. *Life* magazine simply picks out some words from the Talley-Zimmerman-Ross articles and rearranges them. Now they sound even worse: "Daryle was hurt. He should never have come back in there. I might have moved the club to a victory."

Later on, Talley tells a writer doing research for a biography on Blanda that George really hauled off and let Lamonica have it between the eyes. It was all there on tape.

"I'd love to hear it," says the biographer. "I'd like to present your side of it. Where are the tapes now?"

"I haven't played them in some time," says Talley. "They aren't made available."

So much for evidence that will last down the polished corridors of time. How much was actually said? How much was yanked out of context? For three days, Blanda's phone rings. Reporters want to know what he really said. So does Al Davis. Oh-oh! Blanda feels that he's finished with the Oakland Raiders, the only Organization tough enough to make him happy.

"Why don't you just forget about football, George?" says Betty Blanda. "Everything is going wrong. There's no reason not to retire. You're 42. You've set all kinds of records. What else do you have to prove?"

There is an interesting quality about Betty Harris Blanda. She is a marvel at reverse psychology. She understands her man. He has been brooding around the house because he wants to play one more year. What can one more year hurt? The last time Betty Harris Blanda really thought George might retire was 1959 when the Patriarch went for his innards.

So George Blanda rises from the grave once again. By now the record for resurrections must be well past. Oddly, the only man in America who isn't angry at Blanda is Lamonica. He understands, one Alpha Male to another. Tom Kole calls Daryle and tells him what really happened.

"We just blew the ball game, George," Lamonica says over the long-distance wire between Fresno and La Grange Park.

Now Kole is on the line again. If Blanda wants to become a full-time trucking executive with REA, that's dandy. But Kole is enough of a competitor not to want a man around who's sulking over something he can't help.

"Damn, George, you didn't do anything wrong. You know it. Daryle Lamonica knows it. And I suppose Rick Talley knows it. Don't let something as damn dumb as this let you quit football if you don't want to leave," he says.

Out in Oakland, the issue will not perish. It lives on and on

and on. The Athletics go to spring training. Baseball is the
seasonal sport and what is George Ross writing about?

"George Blanda, Freddy Biletnikoff and Juan Marichal are up
for the bigmouth-of-the-year award! That's all he, Ross, could
say. He wouldn't let the subject die. What I had said had been
off the record to a friend and he'd blown it into an artificial
story by himself."

Just when it appears that the only way the situation can be
settled is to have Blanda announce his retirement, peace
abruptly descends upon the black and silver blockhouse where
The Organization does its heavy thinking. Madden has a
Pentagon-style statement for inquiring reporters. The head
coach has said nothing on the subject since the moment of the
Great Fall.

"It was Daryle's decision to put himself back in," says
Madden. "When it comes to playing with injuries, Lamonica is
one of the most outstanding athletes I've ever known. The
x-rays the next day showed no fracture, only a bad bruise. So
Lamonica was correct in that respect.

"Daryle was the quarterback who took us as far as we went.
If you can't give one man credit when you win, you can't place
the blame on one man when you lose. The Raiders do not stress
individuality. We win or lose as a team. Here is a quarterback
who has played in only four losing games in three years and he's
getting blasted for something that happened in one-half of one
quarter of one game.

"As for George Blanda, I don't believe he said all those
things. And if he did say some of them, it is excusable because a
guy is going to blow off steam after a big loss. Reporters say
they have tapes of George saying those things. But when you
ask to hear the tapes, the reporters can't find them."

The Organization has decided that George is guilty of only
the mildest of crimes, being angry at the world after a particularly stunning defeat. It has also decided that his remarks were
yanked out of context and exploited. And it has further
decided to grant amnesty. Having come close to extinction once

again, naturally, Blanda is ready for the most dramatic resurrection yet—the many miracles of 1970, the damndest, giddiest,
most incredible star-spangled season any professional football
player ever had.

EPISODE 10

"It always seemed that fate was going against me until the
1970 season. I say 'fate,' but maybe a lot of it was things I did
or decisions I made," George Blanda decides one chilblained
morning as an airliner carries him westward to his first and,
maybe, his last big-time recording date.

Destiny has finally caught up to him. He is an authentic folk
hero, admired by small children, pot-puffing hippies and
middle-aged men in support hose. There isn't any writer anywhere, not even Jack Gallagher, who isn't willing to admit that
he belongs in the Hall of Fame. Acceptance and recognition,
things he honestly thought he'd never get, now belong to him in
vast quantities. Now he is trying very hard to analyze how it
happened. All those years, people were ripping at him, screaming at him, struggling to tear him down. Suddenly, he is a
warmly loved national idol. What the hell's going on here?

"It's all a matter of being in the right place at the right time,
isn't it? I made a lot of decisions affecting my own career.
Suppose I hadn't taken Halas's $6000 offer to sit out the 1959
season. Suppose he didn't even make the offer. Suppose I
played that season with the Bears. I probably would have quit
right after that year. I never would have played again. I would
have been so damned sick of football, I would have quit.

"Suppose Baltimore had been able to make that trade for me
in 1959. I still might have been there with the Colts, playing
behind Johnny Unitas. I could have spent 13 years there and no
one would have known my name. I made a choice to go to
Houston, too. I could have gone to Los Angeles and then to San
Diego with the Chargers. Chances are if I had been with them, I
never would have wound up with the Raiders. After all, the
Chargers remained a better organization. The team wouldn't

have fallen apart and the fans wouldn't have booed me. You know damned well Sidney Gillman wouldn't have let Al Davis have me on waivers under any circumstances.

"I could have quit the way I wanted to in 1965 when they benched me and started Don Trull. If I hadn't had that five-touchdown second half against Kansas City at Rice Stadium I surely would have quit after that season. And if somebody other than Al Davis had claimed me off the Oilers' waiver list, I might not have played again.

"I was thinking of retiring after that hassle with Rick Talley after the 1969 season. When the Raiders put me on waivers before the miracle year began and I cleared, I was tempted to quit, too. But something kept me from doing it. Don't know. Maybe it was pride. Don't know. Maybe I just didn't want to go home to Chicago and have people say, 'Well, I see you got fired.'

"It's a good thing I stayed. I finally made the people in Youngwood happy. They even gave me a testimonial dinner. Once when I was with the Bears, playing linebacker, the folks at the thermostat factory came up to Wrigley Field and gave me a watch. Yessir! In between they didn't have much use for me. I guess I never made it big enough with the Bears to suit them. Then I went off to the American League and they figured, 'What the hell is that?' But with the Raiders in 1970, I beat the Pittsburgh Steelers and the Cleveland Browns. That's what you have to do to impress the folks in Youngwood. Those are the only two teams they think exist. They even named a football field after me now.

"I don't know why it's always been such a struggle. You see guys come whipping out of college and they make it without a twitch or a quiver. Me? I'm always struggling. It was a struggle to get my dad to let us play football in high school. He wouldn't let my brother Pete play. But Pete went off to a CCC camp during the Depression and he grew up into a 6-1, 200-pounder and he got a football scholarship to Texas Tech where he was a hell of a passer and a punter.

"Everybody started telling my old man what a great thing it was that his son was a college football player. Well, my dad goes from being a nothing to being a hell of a big deal around town. He's the father of all those Blanda boys—Pete, Mike, Joe, George, Paul, John and Tom. Suddenly, he's the biggest booster of high school athletics that Youngwood has ever seen. But if my brother Pete didn't sneak off to play football at Texas Tech, I never would have been given the chance to play the game by my old man. I'd be working for the railroad right now."

Somehow that seems unlikely . . . general manager of the thermostat company, perhaps, but never the railroad.

EPISODE 11

Quotations from other books, continued:

"After Daryle had the bad game in 1969, it seemed that Blanda was louder and more boisterous than usual as he dominated his card games. It was as if he was signaling that he was ready to take over. The way to get George to accept you was to be like him, old and serious about the game. It frustrated him when he found someone quick enough to dance away from his sarcasm. He was a ringleader surrounded by guys who found something of value in his sadistic dialect. People would line up to see George's dummy bend over so he could get a better kick at his ass. I was the object of his attentions more than once. It seemed to me that he was out to get Lamonica's job and be Mr. America at age 43."

—Chip Oliver in his book *High for the Game.*

EPISODE 12

This is the era of the antihero and the social agitator in professional football. The game has grown so large, so quickly, that there must be something wrong with it. Linebackers who carry notepads into the shower have shot Burt L. Standish and laid Frank Merriwell in his grave. Football does not build character; rather, it is dehumanizing, they insist. Coaches are merciless savages with no regard for the individual. Athletes who love the game and play it with a passion are sadists. Racism is rampant. Drugs are everywhere. You can hardly show game films for all the marijuana smoke.

It seems that the new reason for missing bedcheck is not to meet some woman for a little hanky-panky, but to sneak out and type another chapter of your exposé. And is there a fatter, wider, juicier target in the entire game than George Frederick Blanda, the defiant old curmudgeon who has Middle America so thoroughly turned on? Of course there isn't. Trouble is the muckrakers fail to see that they are really assaulting a soul brother.

Blanda has been playing devil's advocate to professional football's Establishment for over two decades. It was he who threatened to bring suit against George Halas when the simple use of the word "sue" was considered grounds for a lifetime suspension from the game. Even though he has made a practice of abiding by the rules, George Blanda has never been slow to point out bad ones. He has challenged authority with conviction, but only when he felt that authority was either being abused or avoided. Clearly, he is the wrong man to shoot at. The strength of his individualism, plus his steadfast refusal to be cowed by the press, has made him a minor saint in the coffee houses of Berkeley and in the hippie pads of the Haight. He's no Mao or Che or Huey Newton, but he is admired, nevertheless.

He has been asked to appear on Irv Kupcinet's talk show in Chicago. He is being matched against Dave Meggyesy, the Lincoln Steffens of the locker room. The former Cardinal linebacker has written a book entitled *Out of Their League.* Meggyesy is an avowed Marxist and George is a devout capitalist, with stocks and bonds and real estate and everything else that is ugly in the world. The confrontation is less than electric. Their mutual contempt for each other's life-style creates an enormous amount of distance. Blanda believes in changing things within the system. Meggyesy believes that society will change to the point where football will no longer be necessary.

There is one witless attempt at riling Blanda.

Meggyesy: "Don't you find it galling, George, to have to go

through bedcheck at age 43? Aren't you old enough and responsible enough to go to bed early before a game and not have to
have somebody come by and rap on your door?

Blanda: "No, I don't find it galling at all. It's one of the rules.
If you want to do something, such as play football, you have to
abide by the rules that are set down for you. If a rule is bad it
will be changed. Let me tell you this, Dave, if there was no
bedcheck 99 percent of the guys would still be in the sack at
11 P.M. The guys who are going to stay out all night are going to
do it whether there's bedcheck or not. They'll find a way."

Later on, Blanda cannot help telling a friend exactly what he
thinks of Meggyesy and of Chip Oliver, his former teammate at
Oakland who quit the game to live on sunflower seeds in a
commune in Larkspur, California. He does not have a high
opinion of them.

"They say they're 'dropouts' from professional football. I
think they're 'copouts'—phonies. Meggyesy says football is dehumanizing. Well, what job isn't just a little dehumanizing? The
more I hear of his politics, the more I think they're dehumanizing. Football is just the opposite. If you want real brotherhood go out and sweat and strain and play with 39 other guys
all season long. Oliver and Meggyesy were always outcasts who
couldn't adjust.

"It took Meggyesy a hell of a long time to learn that he was
dehumanized. I suppose when he discovered what had happened
to him, he gave Syracuse his scholarship money back and told
the Cardinals that he owed them all that back salary. As for
Chip Oliver, he knew me from playing cards. The main objective
when you're playing something is to win. And you do anything
within the limits of the rules to win. There's always a lot of
gamesmanship. I don't think that some of the newer players
coming up understand what it takes to win.

"They aren't interested in winning. They don't have any idea
what it means to come up the hard way. They never knew a
depression. I learned from being hard-up as a kid that I had to
do whatever I had to do in order to win. There's a little
politician in me and I use gamesmanship and master salesman-

ship. It's what I've been taught to do in order to survive and be successful. A quarterback has got to be that way. Anyone who's a leader has to be that way.

"When Chip came in trying to sell his ideas, I didn't buy them. I told him so. Fellow who uses drugs isn't somebody I particularly want to associate with. There was no arguing with him. That's the trouble with these radical thinkers on the left and on the right. They talk about wanting to 'have a dialogue' with you. What they really mean is they want you to shut up and do exactly as they do. I don't buy that. That's why my politics are straight down the middle.

"Not all the kids coming up are like Chip. But a minority of them have obviously had their heads pumped full of something on the college level. I'm no right-wing fanatic who goes around shouting 'Communists' all the time. I can't stand those people, either. They're just as emptyheaded as the ones on the other side of the scale. But I think some of these kids are being motivated by people who have Marxist leanings. I don't think there's any question. They all want to revolt against authority. And on a football team who represents authority? Why, the coaches and the quarterback. You read Chip's book and Meggyesy's book and they're just telling kids to revolt against authority, that's all.

"The majority of the younger players aren't like that. There is a difference between them and me. They don't get their kicks out of a lot of things that I get a kick out of. Their life-styles are different than mine. They're just as dedicated to the game as I am. They just don't eat, breathe and sleep football 24 hours a day like we used to when I was a rookie with the Bears. Most of them don't like the discipline that I was always used to. Then again, most of them didn't grow up under my old man. They try to get away with more things. Some of them don't put out the full effort all the time.

"My feeling about football is that it enabled me to make something of my life. I got through high school. I graduated from college. I got a good job with a trucking firm. I owe everything to professional football. I can't complain. And I wouldn't.

"No one ever forced me to play football on any level. I never felt dehumanized. It's a good goddamned thing Dave Meggyesy didn't play for Bear Bryant at Kentucky in the late 1940s. He wouldn't have lasted six seconds with his attitude. Football is a humanizing experience. You meet people of different social backgrounds of different nationalities and different races and you go out there on Sunday and play to win.

"There's no discrimination within the group. When I first came to Oakland, Sam Skinner comes up to me and talks about racism. Now I know Sam and he's a hell of a good fellow. But he's black and he gets all wrapped up in this race business. He says to me, 'George, when you were in Houston I thought you were a racist because you wouldn't throw the ball to Charlie Frazier. But now you're in Oakland, I know you aren't a racist because you throw the ball to Warren Wells.'

"I tell Sam it's time he woke up to the facts of life. I can't tell whether a guy is black or white when he's in a football uniform and furthermore I don't give a damn. All you can see of a guy's skin is from his elbow pads down to his finger tips. If you want to be a bigot on the football field you have to look real fast. In a way I identify with a lot of the younger black kids more than I do with the younger white kids. They don't have to tell me what life is like in a ghetto. I've heard 'dumb Polack' as often as they've heard the words 'nigger' or 'rughead.'

"So I told Sam, 'Look, the reason I didn't throw to Charlie Frazier was he had bad hands. The reason I throw to Warren Wells is he's got great hands.' That ends the racial problem for me. I discriminate against receivers with bad hands. Actually, Charlie got so he could catch the ball well after a while in Houston.

"But getting back to Meggyesy and Oliver. Neither one of them made it big in professional football. One of the Cardinals told me that Meggyesy was 'the picture of frustration and confusion' when he was a player. He wasn't quite good enough to make it big. And nobody forced him to go to school on a scholarship and I don't think the Cardinals came to get him with a gun. If you sign a contract, you have to abide by the rules. If you don't sign it, you don't have to give the rules another thought.

"Chip wasn't a very big kid, but he gave you 100 percent when he played. I wouldn't discredit his playing ability. It's hard for me to say why he'd write a book tearing up his teammates, his coaches, Al Davis, everybody around him. If he just tore me up personally and tore nobody else up it might give credence to some of his social ideas. But he's just ripping everybody. He doesn't have a nice word for anything except drugs. If he wants to live in a commune, that doesn't make him a nut. It's probably a very lovely life.

"So why should he put me down for the way I want to live? I'm not against anybody doing whatever they want to. If he wants to mess with drugs, let him. That's his business and nobody should stop him, as long as he isn't hurting anybody else. I don't believe that drugs have helped his thinking any. And he isn't staying within the rules by using them.

"He claims in his book that he once kicked a 75-yard field goal while high on mescaline. Hell, once when I was at the University of Kentucky, I punted a ball 86 yards against Tennessee. At the time I was high on Polish sausage.

"Chip says that nearly everybody on the Raiders smokes grass. If that's true, they're hiding it from Old George for fear of what he'll say. I've never been around when it was smoked and I've never seen it. Come to think of it, maybe that field goal only went seven yards and Chip was so high he thought it went 75 yards.

"Hell, football is a game of life. It's survival of the fittest. It's a great teacher. To participate in a team sport is to discover very early in life that the world isn't a rose garden. People like Meggyesy and Oliver are trying to escape from life. That's why I call them copouts. Their books are designed to tear down the heroes of the Establishment. I can't imagine the books being popular. A guy who spends $7 for a ticket isn't going to turn around and spend $7.95 for a book that tells him the players he's watching are really nothing but a bunch of racist, drug-taking, broad-chasing bums.

"I guess to Chip Oliver I was a leader, and therefore I was somebody to rebel against because I symbolized authority. Maybe I'm like he says I am, but I don't think so. Football is a survival game. I've survived 22 years and Chip lasted only two seasons. Of course, I love the game. It's rough and it's tough and I love it.

"Meggyesy makes such a big deal out of players taking pep pills. It's not that widespread. I don't use them. I never would. The day George Blanda needs a pep pill to give him a sense of false security so he can go out on the football field is the day that George Blanda takes off his uniform, hangs up his helmet and heads home for good. Hell, I think I'm a classic example of why they aren't necessary. I've played 22 years without ever taking any of that stuff. Nobody needs the things. I don't need a thing to stimulate me. I've worked hard enough, I've disciplined myself enough and I want to play football bad enough, so that all I need to get me high for a game is to have somebody play the national anthem."

EPISODE 13

"Only God is two years older than George Blanda!"
—Betty Blanda

Not since the *Saturday Evening Post* went into disrepute and disappeared from breakfast tables all over the land, has the American public wondered so openly: What is our newest hero *really* like? There are legends now about George and all sorts of witty stories. He is the subject of a whole line of parlor jokes, based either upon age or imperishable youth, depending on how you happen to view a 44-year-old althlete. Several inspiring samples:

(1) "George Blanda has been invited to thousands of banquets in his career so he's probably forgotten the first one. It was called The Last Supper."

(2) "When George was in the service, he kicked a 67-yard field goal, but it didn't get much coverage in the newspaper. He did it the day Lee surrendered to Grant at Appomattox."

(3) "George has been around so long he remembers when God played the part of Charlton Heston in the movies."

On the men's room wall at a topless-bottomless dive along San Francisco's super-vulgar North Beach, there are the following graffiti:

Superman is alive and well and kicking field goals for Oakland!

And, scrawled right beneath that one—

George Blanda changes his clothes in a telephone booth.

Enough of that 1948-style, late-Sunday-night-radio humor. What is George Blanda really like? C'mon, c'mon, don't hold back a thing.

Miss Margaret Zera, women's editor of San Francisco's widely read *Slavic World*, is sitting in a restaurant in Chinatown, just off Grant Avenue, discussing the subject with Betty Harris Blanda. Who knows better than Betty? Who gets all those long-distance telephone calls whenever there is a crisis? Who has been advising George to retire since 1959? Who gave George all those wonderful "Help Stamp Out Jack Gallagher" bumper stickers for a birthday present once?

Question: What is George really like?

Betty: "I always love those headlines that say, 'Let George Do It' and 'George Does It.' We once had a trunk sitting in the front hall of our home in La Grange Park. It sat there for three months, while George stepped around it. He is not the handiest man around the house."

Question: Does he have any ... er ... cultural interests?

Betty: "I'm very much interested in art and George is very good about taking me to museums and galleries. It takes a little guile to get him there. But once he sees an art exhibit, he immediately becomes an expert on the subject. He'd even argue with the artist. George genuinely likes music and he willingly goes to concerts. I wouldn't say that grand opera is his favorite form of music, but he'll sit through it."

Question: What changes have come into your life since the

miracle year of 1970? I mean, since George became a national folk hero?

Betty: "The butcher! For all the years we've lived in La Grange Park, George has been going down and buying meat in this same store. As far as the butcher was concerned, George was just another customer. Now, suddenly, he treats George like he'd never seen him before. Every time we go into the store, the butcher acts like a real fan."

Question: What is your family life like?

Betty: "Utter confusion . . . twenty-two years of utter confusion. George is insistent about keeping some kind of stability. That's why we've always kept the house in La Grange Park. Despite all the moving around, that's the nest. It's a place to fly in to and out from. George's family didn't have a whole awful lot, but they always had the house on South Third Street with all the pictures of the boys in football uniforms framed on the kitchen walls."

Question: What was it like when the whole family was present in Youngwood?

Betty: "Like nothing you've ever seen. I've never seen so much food disappear. Slovak families really love family gatherings. They call George's mother 'The Easter Bunny,' because she's always hopping around, pouring drinks for everyone. After one family weekend in Youngwood, I remember a truck coming by to pick up the empty soda bottles. There were 20 cases of them. George likes a Polish cookie called 'kolachies.' When we were first married, I asked his mother for the recipe. The one she used called for 11 cups of flour. I had dough strung all over the apartment. I think George had enough kolachies. Her recipe made 130 dozen of them. Fabulous!"

Question: Did they always live in that house?

Betty: "No! The first house burned and they built another down the street. It's number 226½. The reason for the half is that they built it on the wrong side of the lot. That's the truth."

Question: Considering that George Blanda is so dedicated to the game of football, was there any tension in the family when his only son didn't take to the sport?

Betty: "Well, it was a matter of conversation around our

house for quite a while. Football comes first around our house. After Rick let him know he wasn't going to play the game, George took it fairly well. Oh, there was a lot of talk about 'you and your swimming and your musical group,' but Rick met him with, 'you and your football.' George gives ground slowly. But he's reasonable. If he has a failing, it's the same one Archie Bunker of 'All In The Family' has. George has strong opinions. People either love him or hate him."

Question: What's it like for a son who doesn't play football to have a famous football player for a father?

Betty: "Rick thinks of his father as a successful man, like most kids would think of their father if he were a successful banker or a successful writer. He isn't overawed by athletics. He's proud and pleased. The other day a woman called from a Chicago newspaper and wanted to do a piece on how Rick felt to be the son of a famous football player. He told her he didn't think he'd be very interesting. George is his father and that's how Rick thinks of him. Leslie is more of a hero worshiper. She likes the idea of being George's daughter. She's just starting to date. George is old-fashioned about daughters. He's quite protective. He told her she couldn't date until she was 16 and he meant it."

Question: How do you feel when you're sitting in a stadium and the whole stadium is booing your husband?

Betty: "I sometimes wonder, at those times, if the people doing the booing are very good judges of football or of character. I don't like it. But it's something you have to get used to. You steel your nerves, you look around and study the people who are booing. Why are they doing it? What are they getting out of it? They're working off their frustrations. I'm not as defensive about George as I am of other players. I don't have to defend George Blanda. He does a fine job of defending himself. His records speak for themselves. Every now and then, while you're sitting there, somebody says something that you absolutely know is wrong and you want to strangle them.

"They've been sitting there for hours, passing on information and you know that they don't know what they're talking about.

There are times when you just can't keep your mouth shut. You
have to turn and say something. Like those stupid stories about
George shaving points in Houston. If you really knew George
Blanda you'd know how stupid they really were. This man
would play for nothing. He really would. And you'd hear those
people whispering and saying dumb things. I'd get angry. But
the booing isn't all that bad. Those people pay their $2 and . . .
oh, what am I saying? . . . I'm dating myself . . . they pay their
$7.50 and they . . . have a right. What makes me sick is someone
who cheers when a player is hurt. That's disgusting."

Question: Can you take booing better than a sports writer
who constantly writes things that are unfair?

Betty: "There's no rebuttal to a writer who's down on your
husband. What could I say to Jack Gallagher in Houston? He
didn't like George. He didn't like the American League and he
didn't like the way George played. What could I do? I even
called the *Houston Post* to find out what the cost of a full-page
ad would be. I wanted to call it, 'Betty Blanda Answers Back.'
Those bumper stickers were good for my soul."

Question: You've had a lot of ups and downs, haven't you?

Betty: "We've been up and we've been down. Believe me,
'up' is better."

Question: What's the worst crisis you've ever been through?

Betty: "Once when Rick was in the fourth grade in Houston
and things were going bad, he came home crying. I asked him
what went wrong. He said, 'Somebody asked me if George
Blanda was my father. I said yes and he kicked me. Next time
I'll say I'm John Unitas's son.' "

Question: Do you ever get that kind of treatment?

Betty: "I've been snubbed at the supermarket after a bad
game. The one in the family who is really defensive of her
father is Leslie. She's not alone in that. One time Lennie
Dawson's daughter wrote a nasty letter to Johnny Baker of the
Oilers after Johnny had broken her father's nose. Baker was
studying to be a minister or something and he wrote back and
said he really hadn't intended to break her father's nose.
Children are affected. It's a good lesson in living for them. Do

your best. You can't please everyone. The ones who love you, will love you. The ones who won't, won't."

Question: What is George Blanda really like?

Betty: "When Leslie was little and her friends came over and wanted to jump rope, they knew better than to ask George to join them. Why? Well, if you ask him to compete, he'll figure out a way to beat you. Even if it's jumping rope."

Now you know what George Blanda is really like. Now you know what Betty Blanda is really like. Help stamp out Jack Gallagher? Well, the very idea!

EPISODE 14

It is time to think of George Blanda, not as a human being who makes miracles, not as an athlete who has endured well past the normal physical limitations placed on him by age, but as a super hero out of mythology. Surely he does not practice football during the week. More than likely he rests between battles in some mystical sanctuary behind the clouds. Surely, somebody made him up around a campfire on a cold night. He couldn't possibly be real.

In a quarter of a century he's gone through an incredible evolution, from coaltown boy to high school letterman to bewildered college boy to unwilling victim of the Patriarch's hoary wrath in Chicago to flesh and blood hero-turned-villain in Houston to national folk hero in Oakland. Now he is larger than life. And in an issue of *Dave Campbell's Texas Football*, even Jack Gallagher must grudgingly admit that George belongs with his jutting jaw and lobo eyes cast in bronze in Canton, Ohio.

In his athletic dotage, in his 22nd year in professional football, George Blanda has transcended mortality. When he comes into an Oakland Raider football game it is like Zorro buckling on his black cape, Clark Kent ducking into a telephone booth to change his clothes or the Lone Ranger placing another silver bullet in the chamber. Children clap their hands enthusiastically, ladies weep and strong men get jealous. Sports writers start racking their intellects, searching for newer, more impressive adjectives. If the Raiders had any theatrical sensitivity,

they would play the William Tell Overture as soon as George
starts warming up on the sidelines. Well, why not? Dah-de-
dump-ditty-dump-ditty-dump-dump-dump! George Blanda rides
again! Return with us now to those thrilling days of yesteryear.
Off the bench with a cloud of dust and a hearty "Hi! Ho!
Silver!" Yes, indeed, George Blanda rides again! And what a
fantastic act it is, too, sports fans.

It is Halloween in Oakland and spirits are flying. It's October
31, 1971, and it appears the miracles are starting all over again.
In this latest episode, the masked quarterback has come to the
aid of his faithful Italian companion, Lamonica, in the fourth
period of an exceedingly important match against Kansas City.
This is one that Oakland either has to win or tie. They are not
disposed to doing either. In fact, the Raiders are down by ten
points and getting ready to belly up. So head coach John
Madden decides that this is a job for Blanda, the folk hero. Up
in the stands, the customers know that George will not fail
them. He has the strength of ten, because his heart is pure—well,
almost pure. It can't be too pure after playing all those years for
George Halas and Bud Adams.

So, who's going to quibble? There is 8:38 left in the game.
Usually, George likes to work it a little finer than that, say
about three seconds. The ball is residing on the Oakland 34-yard
line. So Blanda reaches back and pitches it 36 yards to tight end
Raymond Chester, who isn't exactly having the greatest day of
his career up to the point where George arrives. Now the
Raiders are whirling along nicely and everyone is aware that
there is no way Kansas City can hold its 20-10 lead.

All it takes for Blanda to get a touchdown is 37 seconds. At
8:01 he puts the ball into Fred Biletnikoff's hands in the Chiefs'
end zone for a touchdown. After the kickoff, the ball goes back
to Oakland on a wretchedly short punt by Jerrel Wilson, who
normally kicks brilliantly. This time Blanda has the ball on
Kansas City's 45. Instead of passing, Blanda hands off to Don
Highsmith, who was smearing Pablum on his cheeks when
George was driving Sid Luckman around and loving it. The run
is good for 26 yards.

They get all the way to the three. George pumps it to Highsmith again. According to testimony given after the game, one of the following things has happened:

(1) Highsmith may have advanced the ball across the goal line or (2) he may have advanced his body, but not the ball, into the end zone. Highsmith is sure he has scored. Blanda isn't. The officials tell Highsmith to forget it. That makes it fourth down and about a silly millimeter left to go. George wants to go for it. He looks over toward the bench, longingly at first, then angrily. He gestures toward the bench. The bench refuses. In such circumstances the gamble simply isn't worth it. Madden shakes his head. The Raiders need either a win or a tie. And tying a game you thought you would lose is nearly as good as winning, but not quite. Got that?

"Going for the field goal to tie the game is automatic," Madden says afterwards. "You can't let emotion rule you. We came into the game tied with Kansas City for the division lead. If we tied this game, we'd still be tied for the lead with half the schedule to go. We had to kick a goal."

Blanda accepts the fact that recklessness is a mistake. Once, when Pop Ivy was coach of the Houston Oilers, George, in a moment of towering passion, waved Jacky Lee, his holder, off the field and went for the touchdown. The press in Houston, Gallagher in particular, never let him forget the incident. It is still considered a blatant act of defiance in Texas, something like getting drunk on the steps of a Baptist church right in downtown Waco.

So George backs up and from an extremely poor angle kicks the field goal that ties the game, 20-20, and makes George professional football's greatest scorer with 1609 points. Lou Groza disappears from the record book. The crowd gives him a standing ovation.

"I made some effort to convince Madden to go for the touchdown," he says afterwards. "The players always want to go for it. The move to make was to kick the field goal."

Somebody with a tape recorder asks Blanda if he wouldn't have rather set the new scoring record under less trying circumstances, say in a 54-6 rout of Buffalo or something. George, who has just been thinking that he has heard every asinine question a newsman could invent, sucks in his gut. This could be the all-time winning ignorant question. Instead of ripping the poor slob's head off, George considers the guy's age, which is fairly young.

"Gee, what better place to get the points I needed than in a game where we had to come from ten points to tie when we needed to tie?" he says. "This is a pretty important game. We knew we couldn't risk losing it."

The investigative reporter smiles cheerily. There is evidence that George is getting a trifle lazy. Only a year earlier, he waited until there were only three seconds left to tie Kansas City. This time there was 2:31 left on the clock at the Coliseum. Hopefully, George isn't slipping.

Outside, in the hallway, Blanda asks a newspaperman he respects: "Why don't you ask stupid questions like that one?" He is starting to admit that all reporters are not the same.

Now everyone starts to wonder if a new run of wonders has started. At KNEW, producer Ron Fell starts plotting new promotional spots featuring Blanda. This time he'll have Beethoven thundering angrily in the background ... "DAH-DAH-DAH— Duuuuuuumb!" and an Edward R. Murrow-broadcasting-from-London-during-the-blitz-voice ... and ...

Trouble is it doesn't work out that way. George does not get the opportunities this time around. He knows why. Football is a game of cycles. Football is a game of opportunities. Football is a game of mistakes. The name of the game is ... (fill in the blank.) Late in the schedule, the Raiders lose three games in a row. They go off to Kansas City, needing to beat the Chiefs on their own chilly turf.

"Our team loves pressure, so we let the pressure build," Blanda is fond of saying. And so, for the umpteenth time, it has come down to Kansas City and Oakland. The President of the United States, Richard Nixon, may love the Washington Redskins. But God wants to see Kansas City play Oakland under pressure.

Midway through the second quarter, with Kansas City leading 10-0, Lamonica looks over and sees Blanda warming up. Without a word, he gives way to George. And damned if George doesn't almost bring it off.

"We had to get something going at that stage," says Madden afterwards. "I know George can get something going, even at age 44."

Blanda moves Oakland for two touchdowns. But he misses a field goal from the 47 and has another blocked from closer in. Later in the fourth quarter, tackle Buck Buchanan, who hurts people, comes flying through and grabs Blanda in his loving arms and slams Old George to the ground with what appears to be unnecessary force. Blanda simply lies there like an old wolf who has wandered out onto the freeway and lost a quick decision to a Greyhound bus.

"I certainly hope he's all right," says broadcaster Curt Gowdy. "What thrills this 44-year-old man has given the nation."

Now George stirs. He lifts his head off the turf. Maybe he knows it's December 12, 1971 and he's in Kansas City. Maybe he thinks he's in Lexington and Bear Bryant is screaming at him. Now he stands up and shakes his head. A colleague helps him off.

"There goes a real man," says Gowdy, not meaning to be corny or vainglorious at all. Is this the end of George Blanda as an active player?

Several minutes later, when Oakland gets the ball back, Blanda comes swaggering back out onto the field. He finishes the game and Oakland loses, 16-14, on a field goal by Jan Stenerud from ten yards out. The miracles are over.

"They took me out of there and I can't second-guess them," says Lamonica. "They didn't tell me why. It's their decision and they'll have to live with it."

Somebody calls Blanda in the Oakland dressing room to inquire if he is all right. After all, Buchanan is not exactly a 97-pound weakling.

"You can't hurt a Polack," George says.

Now the Raiders are eliminated for the first time since George Blanda escaped from Houston. It is a strange feeling for The Organization to come down to the final season's game and not be pushing for some place in the playoffs. All week long there are stories that Blanda will announce his retirement after the Raiders play the Broncos in the Coliseum on December 19, 1971. No one knows where the stories come from, but they are not true. After the game, George has no announcement. Nothing.

At 44, he still showers with everyone, still dresses with everyone, still thinks like an active player. But he has been talking with Al Davis. At an age when most men are fretting about their rapidly retreating hairlines or their sudden inability to make a secretary smile, George wants to know if he's going to still have a chance to play some quarterback should he return for a 23rd season. A man who just kicks isn't a real athlete. George has been saying that since Truman was playing his damn piano.

EPISODE 15

The streets of New Orleans are narrow and cramped and, if you hold your hand up close to your ear, you think you can hear the click of horse-drawn carriages on the pavement. The houses of the French Quarter, which are covered with ancient filigree brought over from the old country, run on and on until it seems the whole world looks like this. Everywhere you look, tradition leaps out and grabs you by the eyeballs. This is a European city. It belongs to yesterday. It has no relationship to America and now. It hasn't changed since the Spanish had a governor in Louisiana or since Napoleon sold the whole thing to that incomparable bumpkin, Tom Jefferson.

They will play Super Bowl VI in New Orleans, the same place where the American Football League died two years earlier with the completion of the merger, only to be reincarnated as the American Football Conference of the National Football League. In his heart, George Blanda is still a member of the rebel league.

The entire clan has gathered, from Pete Rozelle right on

down to the owners. The Super Bowl is as large as, if not larger than, the World Series. In the Old Absinthe House, owned by a former defensive tackle, several athletes have gathered. A blonde lady with weary eyes is standing two bar stools away, admiring the physique of Doug Atkins, who used to play for the Bears and finished his athletic life with the New Orleans Saints. He is younger than George and he is retired.

Beyond the Old Absinthe House, people are laughing and joking and drinking and having fun. And beyond them is the Mississippi River, ancient and determined. It starts small and afraid in the headwaters of Minnesota. It twists and it turns down through the middle of the land. When it cannot flow free, it finds its own channels, slamming around mud flats and creating new islands. And when it reaches New Orleans it surges unvexed to the sea.

"Hell, I don't want to quit," says George Blanda. "I love this life. It means something to me, something I can't express. I've always had to struggle to stay in football. It has never been easy. I've never been pampered."

"I think I can still play quarterback," says George Blanda. "I don't give a damn about age. I can still do the job."

In the entire universe there is no more sorely misunderstood creature than the fluorescent-eyed, gray-muzzled quarterback. He is the victim, not altogether innocent, of an exceedingly imaginative press. He does not attack for the sheer pleasure of splattering blood on the landscape. He always has a plan. He is part of a highly disciplined unit which follows a single leader, an animal which naturalists call a quarterback. There is no challenging his authority. The pack follows the quarterback with a singular obedience, because the quarterback is the only sensible alternative to starvation. The quarterback is an Alpha Male, taller, tougher, stronger, more determined than the other members of the species. He will survive. He will find a way.

A small epilogue:

(1) *"Someone at the Bears' office has something against me. Somebody has an underlying hate for me. I won't say it's George Halas, because I don't know for sure. As far as I'm concerned, the Chicago Bears are a badly antiquated organization."*
>   —Bear receiver Dick Gordon, quoted by United
>   Press International on December 23, 1971.

(2) *"The Houston Oilers will never be a stable organization as long as Bud Adams is the owner. He fired coach Ed Hughes without giving him a chance. I really think it's a rotten deal. It's going to be the same damn confused thing next year. It just makes me sick."*
>   —Rookie Oiler quarterback Dan Pastorini, quoted by
>   United Press International on December 23, 1971.

Some things never change.

— The End —

Acknowledgments

Thanks go to: Ron Fell of KNEW; Tommy Grimes, Ken Bishop and Pat E. Montini of the Oakland Raiders' staff; Margaret Zera of the *Slavic World;* Lowell Reidenbaugh of the *Sporting News;* Rick Talley, sports editor of *Chicago Today;* Bucky Walter of the *San Francisco Examiner;* Glenn Dickey of the *San Francisco Chronicle.* And to the Swarthmore backfield; to Unknown Winston; to Bill Libby, to Pat Gallagher, owner of San Francisco's Prosperity Saloon, who pours them straight and strong.

—Wells Twombly

GEORGE FREDERICK BLANDA

Born September 17, 1927, at Youngwood, Pa.

Height, 6.02. Weight, 215.

Hobby—Golf.

High School—Youngwood, Pa.

Received bachelor of science degree in education from University of Kentucky in 1949.

Established following AFL career records: Intercepted passes, 194; extra points, 456; games, 140; consecutive games, 140; most seasons leading league in extra points kicked, five; most points after touchdown attempted, 462.

Established AFL record for most consecutive games scoring, 40, from December 11, 1960, to November 10, 1963.

Established following AFL season records: Passes attempted, 505, and passes completed, 262, in 1964; touchdown passes, 36 in 1961; intercepted passes, 42 in 1962; extra points, 64 in 1961 and extra points attempted, 65 in 1961.

Established following AFL game records: Passes attempted, 68, and passes completed, 37, on November 1, 1964; yards gained passing, 464 on October 29, 1961; touchdown passes, seven on November 19, 1961; extra points, eight on October 14, 1962; and longest field goal, 55 yards on December 3, 1961. Tied record for intercepted passes, six on September 9, 1962, and November 14, 1965.

First player ever to score over 500 points for three separate teams—541 for Chicago Bears, 598 for Houston Oilers and 508 for Oakland Raiders.

Established following AFL Championship Game career records: Most points, 42; most points after touchdown, 10; most field goals attempted, 12; most field goals, 7; most touchdown passes, 5; most passes had intercepted, 10; most games on winning team, 3.

Tied AFL Championship Game career record for most games on winning team, 3, 1967.

Established following AFL Championship Game records: Passes attempted, 46 on December 23, 1962; passes completed, 23 on December 23, 1962; yards gained passing, 301 on January 1, 1961; intercepted passes, five on December 24, 1961, and December 23, 1962; touchdown passes, three on January 1, 1961; and longest pass completion, 88 yards on January 1, 1961; longest field goal, 46 yards, December 24, 1961; most points, 18, December 31, 1967; most field goals, 4, and field goal attempts, 6, December 31, 1967.

Led AFL in passing in 1961.

Named by The Sporting News as AFL Player of the Year in 1961.

Named to The Sporting News AFL All-Star Teams, 1961 and 1967.

Named by The Sporting News AFL AFC Player of the Year in 1970.

Selected by Chicago Bears in 12th round of 1949 NFL draft.

Traded by Chicago Bears NFL to Baltimore NFL for guard Dick Barwegan, 1950.

Released by Baltimore NFL; signed by Chicago Bears NFL, 1950.

Signed as free agent by Houston AFL, 1960.

Traded by Houston AFL to Oakland AFL for unnamed player, 1967.

		PASSING								RUSHING					TOTAL		
	G.	Att.	Comp.	Pct.	Gain	T.P.	P.I.	L.P.	Avg.	Att.	Yds.	Avg.	TD.	L.R.	TD.	Pts.	F.
1949—Chi. Bears NFL.	12	21	9	42.9	197	0	5	44	9.38	2	9	4.5	1	5	1	27	0
1950—Chi. Bears NFL.	12	1	0	00.0	0	0	0	0	0.00	None					0	18	0
1951—Chi. Bears NFL.	11				None					None					0	44	0
1952—Chi. Bears NFL.	12	131	47	35.9	664	8	11	59	5.07	20	104	5.2	1	16	1	54	0
1953—Chi. Bears NFL.	12	*362	*169	46.7	2164	14	23	72	5.97	24	62	2.6	0	16	0	48	3

Year — Team	G	Att	Comp	Pct	Yds	TD	Int	Long	Avg	Att	Yds	Avg	TD	Long		Pts	
1954—Chi. Bears NFL	8	281	131	46.6	1929	15	17	76	6.86	19	41	2.2	0	19	0	47	3
1955—Chi. Bears NFL	12	97	42	43.3	459	4	7	51	4.73	15	54	3.6	2	10	2	82	0
1956—Chi. Bears NFL	12	69	37	53.6	439	7	4	69	6.36	6	47	7.8	0	17	0	81	2
1957—Chi. Bears NFL	12	19	8	42.1	65	0	3	13	3.42	5	−5	−1.0	1	1	1	71	0
1958—Chi. Bears NFL	12	7	2	28.6	19	0	0	12	2.71	None					0	69	0
1959					Did not play.												
1960—Houston AFL	14	363	169	46.6	2413	24	22	75	6.65	16	16	1.0	0	3	4	115	—
1961—Houston AFL	14	362	187	51.7	3330*	36*	22	80	9.20*	7	12	1.7	0	7	0	112	—
1962—Houston AFL	14	418	197	47.1	2810	27	42*	78	6.72	3	6	2.0	0	10	0	81	—
1963—Houston AFL	14	423*	224*	53.0	3003*	24	26*	80	7.10	4	1	0.3	0	7	0	66	7
1964—Houston AFL	14	505*	262*	51.9	3287	17	27*	80	6.51	4	−2	−0.5	0	6	0	76	7
1965—Houston AFL	14	442	186*	42.1	2542	20	30*	95	5.75	4	−6	−1.5	0	0	0	61	2
1966—Houston AFL	14	271	122	45.0	1764	17	21	79	6.51	3	1	0.3	0	1	0	87	3
1967—Oakland AFL	14	38	15	39.5	285	3	3	50	7.50	None					0	*116	0
1968—Oakland AFL	14	49	30	61.2	522	6	2	94	10.65	None					0	117	1
1969—Oakland AFL	14	13	6	46.2	73	2	1	20	5.62	1	0	0.0	0	0	0	105	1
1970—Oakland NFL	14	55	29	52.7	461	6	5	44	8.38	2	4	2.0	0	4	0	84	1
1971—Oakland NFL	14	58	32	55.2	378	4	6	37	6.64	None					0	86	0
NFL Totals—12 Yrs.	143	1101	506	45.4	6775	58	81		6.13	93	316	3.3	5		5	627	9
AFL Totals—10 Yrs.	140	2932	1398	48.5	20029	176	196		6.94	42	28	0.6	4		4	936	14
Pro Totals—22 Yrs.	283	4033	1904	47.7	26804	234	277		6.72	135	344	2.5	9		9	1647	23

PLACE KICKING

Year — Team	G.	XP.	XPM.	FG.	FGA.
1949—Chi. Bears NFL	12	0	0	7	15
1950—Chi. Bears NFL	12	0	0	6	15
1951—Chi. Bears NFL	11	26	0	6	17
1952—Chi. Bears NFL	12	30	0	6	25
1953—Chi. Bears NFL	12	27	0	8	20
1954—Chi. Bears NFL	8	23	0	8	16
1955—Chi. Bears NFL	12	37	0	11	16
1956—Chi. Bears NFL	12	*45	2	12	*28
1957—Chi. Bears NFL	12	23	0	14	*26
1958—Chi. Bears NFL	12	36	1	11	23
1959			Did not play.		
1960—Houston AFL	14	46	1	*15	*34
1961—Houston AFL	14	*64	1	16	26
1962—Houston AFL	14	*48	1	11	26
1963—Houston AFL	14	39	0	9	22
1964—Houston AFL	14	37	1	13	29
1965—Houston AFL	14	28	0	11	21
1966—Houston AFL	14	39	1	16	30
1967—Oakland AFL	14	*56	1	20	30
1968—Oakland AFL	14	54	0	21	34
1969—Oakland AFL	14	*45	0	20	37
1970—Oakland NFL	14	36	0	16	29
1971—Oakland NFL	14	41	1	15	22
NFL Totals—12 Years	143	324	4	119	252
AFL Totals—10 Years	140	456	6	152	289
Pro Totals—22 Years	283	780	10	271	541

Additional pro statistics: Gained seven yards on pass reception lateral in 1953; caught one pass for a 16-yard loss in 1961 and lost seven yards on pass reception lateral in 1964; punted 19 times for 39.3 yard average in 1949 and once for 33-yard average in 1956.

*Led league.

Played in AFL All-Star Game following 1961-62-63-67 seasons.
Played in NFL Championship Game, 1956.

Played in AFL Championship Game, 1960-61-62-68-69.
Played in AFL-NFL Championship Game following 1967 season.

PHOTO CREDITS

1. Blanda family album.
2. Blanda album.
3. Blanda album.
4. Youngwood (Pennsylvania) High School
   Maroon and White yearbook, Class of 1945.
5. Blanda album.
6. Blanda album.
7. Blanda album.
8. Blanda album.
9. Blanda album.
10. Harry's Studio, Jacksonville, Florida.
11. Russ Reed photo, *Oakland Tribune.*
12. Art Kunkel photo, Summerfield, Florida.
13. Blanda album.
14. Courtesy of the Oakland Raiders.
15. Russ Reed photo, courtesy of the Oakland Raiders.
16. Courtesy of the Oakland Raiders.
17. Andy Galvan photo, San Leandro, California.
18. Courtesy of the Oakland Raiders.
19. Russ Reed photo, courtesy of the Oakland Raiders.
20. Blanda album.
21. Blanda album.